the OPTIMIST'S GUIDE to DIVORCE

HOW TO GET THROUGH YOUR BREAKUP AND CREATE A NEW LIFE YOU LOVE

SUZANNE RISS & JILL SOCKWELL

Workman Publishing · New York

Library of Congress Cataloging-in-Publication Data is available.

ISBN 978-0-7611-8742-4

Design by Becky Terhune
Author photo by Lisa Rayman Goldfarb

Workman books are available at special discounts when purchased in bulk for premiums and sales promotions as well as for fund-raising or educational use. Special editions or book excerpts can also be created to specification. For details, contact the Special Sales Director at the address below, or send an email to specialmarkets@workman.com.

Workman Publishing Co., Inc.
225 Varick Street
New York, NY 10014-4381
workman.com

WORKMAN is a registered trademark of Workman Publishing Co., Inc.

Printed in the United States of America
First printing December 2016

10 9 8 7 6 5 4 3 2 1

For Jack

You inspire me every day with your sense of humor,
your expressiveness, and the way you see the best in everyone.
—Suzanne

For Brooke and Natalie

I hope you follow your heart and learn to love
the journey through every bump in the road.
—Jill

CONTENTS

Introduction A FRIEND IN NEED   vii

PART ONE: DEAL

Chapter 1 "I DON'T"   2

Having the "it's over" talk • When you leave him • When he leaves
you • Telling family and friends • Things to do now • Riding the
emotional roller coaster

Chapter 2 THE KIDS: HANDLE WITH CARE   24

Explaining the separation to your kids • Helping them express their
feelings • Easing the transition to two homes • Finding support •
Take the Parenting Pledge to avoid putting down their dad

Chapter 3 LAW & DISORDER   43

What you can expect financially • Understanding your divorce
options • Dos and don'ts of hiring the right professional help •
Popular misconceptions • Custody and child support basics

Chapter 4 TEMPORARY CHAO$ 61

Making a new budget • Safeguarding your job during the divorce
• Careers you can launch in six months or less • Single mom money-
savings tips • Leaving room for small miracles

Chapter 5 A PLACE TO CALL HOME   78

Moving out: Understanding your options • Can you afford to stay in
the marital home? • Handling credit problems • Selling your home •
The difference between alone and lonely

Chapter 6 THE EX FILES: COMMUNICATING 101   93

Lessons from the trenches • Strategies to keep your cool no matter what • Setting healthy boundaries • Why nobody truly wins a fight • What role does your ex play in your divorce drama?

Chapter 7 YOUR EX AND THE WARM BODY REPLACEMENT   108

When your ex moves on before your side of the bed is cold • Coping with jealousy—even if *you* left *him* • Feeling replaced or rejected • Focusing on your new life, not his

PART TWO: HEAL

Chapter 8 THE GOLDEN KEY: ACCEPTANCE   118

Letting go of how you thought things would turn out • Embracing uncertainty • Forgiving yourself—and him • Finding that after acceptance come energy and light

Chapter 9 IT'S AN INSIDE JOB   129

Learning from your relationship patterns • Being gentle with yourself • What to do differently next time • Why a romantic relationship can't fix everything • Simple steps to healthier relationships

Chapter 10 FINDING PEACE OF MIND   145

Meditating to find calm anytime, anywhere • Dealing with depression • When you need professional help • 20 things that will make you feel good • Cultivating self-reliance

Chapter 11 YOUR TLC ACTION PLAN   162

Embrace our 3-week plan for a healthier you • Sleep your way to the top • What to eat to improve your mood • Sweat the stress out with exercise • The power of gratitude

Chapter 12 WRITE YOUR OWN HAPPY ENDING 179

Reframing your divorce story to accentuate the positive • Avoiding the shoulda-coulda-woulda trap • Accepting things as they are • Learning from the past • Exploring new possibilities

PART THREE: REVEAL

Chapter 13 GUIDE TO GORGEOUS 192

Updating your wardrobe from married to single • Fake it till you make it—with makeup • Rebound hair beyond compare • Recognizing that true beauty comes from within

Chapter 14 HAPPILY EVER AFTER . . . WITH YOURSELF 210

Knowing your best qualities • You're complete just as you are • Dating yourself • Reasons not to put your life on hold • Goals vs. dreams • Creating a vision board for your future

Chapter 15 SOCIALIZING AGAIN: THE SCARLET *D* 220

Strategies for stepping out solo • Easy conversation starters • Getting out of your comfort zone—in heels • Confidence boosters • Navigating the holidays • Creating new traditions

Chapter 16 DRINKS @ 8—TIME TO DATE 240

Ready-to-date quiz • Prepping your dating profile • Online dating: fakers, felons . . . and fun prospects • Meeting people IRL (in real life) • Dating dos and don'ts • Your next relationship

Chapter 17 CREATE YOUR OWN COMMUNITY 262

Launching the Maplewood Divorce Club • Easy steps to start your own club • Guiding principles • Tips for running successful meetings • Paying it forward: friendship and support

Afterword IT GOT BETTER 277

Introduction

A FRIEND IN NEED . . .

When Jill separated from her husband back in 2010, she planned to binge-read her way through the pain and learn from the experiences of divorced women who had preceded her. She searched for answers in the self-help section of the bookstore. She found clinical tomes written by marriage counselors and divorce lawyers. She also found memoirs written by women who were able to travel the world to find themselves and, eventually, happiness with a new man.

Jill was looking for something different: uplifting advice from women who had survived their divorces and could inspire her by sharing their lessons, admitting their mistakes, and showing her realistic paths to a new and better place. This book didn't exist.

What Jill did find that helped her through her separation and divorce was Suzanne.

When a mutual friend introduced us a few summers ago, we were determined to make the best of what felt like one of the worst times of our lives. We felt isolated, overwhelmed, and anxious about all the uncertainty we faced. But the moment we connected, we realized that we were no longer going through our divorces alone.

Though we had friends and family supporting us, we were acutely aware of how meaningful it was to know someone who reflected our divorce experience. We had the same set of worries over our children, the custody schedule, work, and our finances. We had similar stressors: We were both single moms; we were navigating disagreements with our exes; and we had both moved out of the marital home to set up house elsewhere. We also realized, most importantly, that we shared the same attitude and intention.

We wanted the pain of our separations to serve a purpose—to be a catalyst for something better. As optimists, we wanted to challenge the notion that divorce is necessarily one of the worst things that will ever happen to you. Of course, there are feelings of sorrow and loss that can't be sidestepped. There is also a chance to rally the village and carry one another during this difficult time. We were determined to find a way to make the best of it and grow through the experience.

"Having someone to talk to who truly understood what I was going through made all the difference in the world."   —Suzanne

We started meeting for weekly "walk and talks," powering through our neighborhood, sweating out our stress as we discussed everything from our exes, our kids, and living on our own to our hopes for the future. We were sounding boards for each other and shared what we were learning about the divorce process. We always managed to have a few laughs along the way. It was during one of our walk and talks that we realized how powerful and inspirational the support of a girlfriend who is going through the same challenges can be.

What if—we wondered—we added more divorcing girlfriends to the mix? Would we exponentially increase our power, our hope, and our support? We decided to launch a divorce club. We invited other women to join our circle, share experiences, learn from one another, find humor in our collective heartaches, and boldly chart new courses for our lives, knowing we had one another's backs.

When we thought about how to structure the Maplewood Divorce Club, named after our town, we were inspired by the way twelve-step programs, such as Al-Anon, function. They keep the focus on the individual attending the meeting rather than on anyone else. The Al-Anon fellowship is a place where people impacted by alcohol come to share their experience, strength, and hope. Similarly, we wanted to provide a safe place for women to come to talk about themselves, not their exes, and share their stories, lessons, and optimism.

We spread the word about our first meeting in March of 2013 and were curious to see how many women would attend. To our amazement and delight, more than fifty women showed up. We were off and running. Our club continues to grow, and we all reap the benefits of the love, friendship, and support it offers. (In chapter 17 we'll show you how to form your own divorce club in your community.)

Inspired by the impact our club was having, we decided to write a book that would recreate the feeling of community and sisterhood that we value, capture the many voices of our diverse circle of friends, and share our best advice for starting over on your own. We hope that as you read our stories, you feel as if you're surrounded by friends who have been there, divorced that, and are by your side to encourage you as you heal. You will meet ten of our friends and get to know them, including Carlotta, who discovered her husband's affair by hacking into his iPhone; Denise, who left her husband in search of passion; and Amali, whose husband up and left her with a note scrawled on a scrap of paper.

A FEW THINGS TO KEEP IN MIND

- For simplicity's sake, we address the reader as "she" and her ex as "he." We also refer to potential dates as male. We recognize and support same-sex relationships, and our words are intended for same-sex couples as well as heterosexual couples going through a divorce. Please adjust the pronouns as needed.

- The ten members of the Maplewood Divorce Club who appear in the book are composite characters, each one based on two or more real-life women. We also changed many of the details of their lives to protect their privacy. We hope the lessons they learned shine through so that women everywhere may benefit from our collective experiences.

- We are grateful to our ex-husbands for their support, and acknowledge that only our point of view is represented in these pages.

- There are many wonderful books on helping children cope with divorce and the changing dynamic within a family. Though we mention our children, the focus of this book is separated and divorced women themselves.

We believe that the end of a significant relationship is one of the best times to take a look at yourself to see what's working, what's not, and where you have opportunities to introduce some positive changes in your own life. We went to therapy, enjoyed the support of our club, and studied our behavior so that we would not keep repeating old patterns that didn't serve us. We also chose not to delay our happiness waiting for a new man but to boldly pursue it, whether it meant buying a house on our own, switching careers, or even taking our kids to Disney World without the help of a spouse.

The book is divided into three sections—Deal, Heal, and Reveal—and will take you through the entire divorce process from start to finish. It's different from many of the divorce books out there in that it doesn't end with everyone getting remarried. This book is not about finding a man; it's about finding yourself. After all, the most important relationship of your life is with yourself.

We were able to find happiness, fulfillment, and moments of serenity even in the middle of our divorces. What made the difference was having a supportive circle of friends, an open mind, and an optimistic attitude.

You get to choose, as we did, whether to embrace change and grow with it or use your energy to swim against the current. We will help you try on the attitude of being an optimist, if this doesn't come naturally to you. This means you listen for the good, focus on what is going well, and decide to make your own sunshine, even while you weather personal storms. We found that nurturing an optimistic outlook helped us not only as we went through our divorces but as we continue to navigate our lives.

—Suzanne and Jill

Part One
DEAL

Meet our circle of friends who will show you ways to make each day a little better as you begin this new phase of your life. We help you make some big decisions, like hiring the right lawyer and choosing where to live. We offer our best advice as you talk with your kids about the split, negotiate a settlement with your ex, and get your finances in order. Most important, we share our stories and welcome you into our sisterhood. We've been there and we've got your back.

"I DON'T"

"The world is round and the place which may seem like the end may also be only the beginning."
—Ivy Baker Priest

W hen we say, "I do," with our heart full of love and hope, we never imagine our happily ever after will one day end with "I don't." "I don't think I can keep doing this." "I don't want to keep arguing." And most difficult of all, "I don't love you anymore."

For many of us, having the "I don't" conversation is the kickoff to our separation and divorce. Even if deep down you thought your relationship had insurmountable problems, actually uttering the words changes everything. If he's the one to say, "I don't," you may feel like a rug was just pulled out from under you. Whether he feels misunderstood, bored, hurt, or simply "doesn't want this anymore," as Iris's husband announced, he's gone, baby, gone. Your world and everything you have come to call home have been thrown off-balance. You find yourself holding the pieces of your crumbled life as a couple, wondering how you didn't see this coming and whether there was anything you could have done to prevent it. The impact of being blindsided when someone else decides the relationship is over can shake your sense of self-worth to its core.

If you were the first one to say, "I don't," as we were, you likely weighed the pros and cons of separating for months or even years before you took action. For us, the tipping point was realizing our marriages were bringing out the worst in us and in our spouses, the bad times were outweighing the good ones, and nothing we tried was making things better.

It was during the tumultuous time after we separated from our husbands that we created the Maplewood Divorce Club to find familylike support and friendship. Talking about our breakups and sharing our experience, strength, and hope with other women helped us feel less alone.

Listening to each other in our meetings allowed us to see ourselves more clearly. We were all flawed and had more questions than answers. As we shared our pain, mistakes, and recovery, we amassed a lot of wisdom. Among our most important discoveries is that optimism is contagious. The energy and attitude we bring into the world impact everyone we meet and are reflected back to us.

We learned that blaming and trash-talking our exes hurts us more than it hurts them. Keeping the focus on our own actions is the secret to real growth. We were reminded that nobody else can make us happy. No man is going to make us feel whole—that's work we need to do on our own.

We now know that when we find ourselves trying to control others, we're usually acting out of fear. These days we choose to let things play out. One of our biggest aha's was to become aware of our relationship patterns. This has helped us make better choices and be more deliberate in who we date.

Finally, we saw how wishful thinking will bite us in the ass every time. We all fell in love with a fantasy instead of the flesh and blood person in front of us. We now do our best to see men as they are and not as who we wish they were or who we think we can change them into.

As a result of all the sharing in the Maplewood Divorce Club, we learned so much about ourselves and became better people. But in the early days of the club, what most of us felt was confused, scared, and in need of a friendly face.

WHO ENDS A MARRIAGE MORE OFTEN—MEN OR WOMEN?

Women ask for a divorce 70 percent more often than men, according to the American Sociological Association. This has been true for more than a century. Over the past 125 years, wives have consistently filed for divorce more than husbands, according to the 2014 *Relationships in America* survey from the Austin Institute. How did things work out for these women? Divorced women in large numbers revealed in the survey that they're happier now than they were when they were married.

One of the first members of the group, Denise, had known for years that she and her husband, Mitch, were good roommates but the passion was MIA. This truth was inescapable during the tropical vacation she booked to save their marriage. Denise found herself in Jamaica at a fish fry sitting across from Mitch, steel drum music in the background and a rumrunner in her hand, feeling just as alone as when they would sit in painful silence in their living room watching the ten o'clock news. When they returned from the trip, Denise asked Mitch to begin marriage counseling but it left them feeling even more estranged.

The first time Jamie came to the Maplewood Divorce Club, she had just left Doug, her husband of eleven years. The incidents of being mistreated by him had been multiplying in frequency and intensity. The more he drank, the meaner and more controlling he became. She'd finally had enough.

Eleanor told us that she never would have chosen to leave her marriage. When her husband, Harold, broke the news to her over tea, she simply couldn't accept it, even though he had been telling her he was unhappy for years. She didn't think he would really leave her.

When a relationship unravels, you're left with a lot of questions. The great mystery is how a union that starts with a bride and groom in love, surrounded by friends and family, full of joy and promise, can end with the realization that it's just not going to work. A couple that once treated each other with thoughtfulness and tenderness now avoids eye contact. If a marriage starts with a bang, it can end with a shouting match, followed by a whisper that asks,

"What happened?" "What was that?" "Who was that?" "Who am I without him?"

Separating from your spouse can feel isolating; often your best friends and family don't understand what you're going through. But consider this: Each year more than a million women like you get divorced in the United States, and they're wondering who will help them get through it. The answer is, we will: Jill and Suzanne, along with our circle of friends—ten women in the Maplewood Divorce Club who have already gone through separation and divorce and come out better on the other side. In our stories, you're sure to find someone whose situation is similar to yours, whose example can guide you through difficult decisions, and who will comfort you and make you laugh when you least expect it. You will meet women who will remind you that you will feel better again. As dramatic and heartbreaking as the end of a marriage can be, the good news is, we made it to the other side, and so will you.

> "The only thing worse than not having sex was for Mitch and I to sit in a room with the therapist, a virtual stranger, *talking* about not having sex."
> —Denise

WHEN YOU LEAVE HIM
"I had unrealistic expectations."

The summer before Jill left her husband, she began training for the New York City Marathon. An athletic and upbeat social butterfly, Jill, in her thirties, was also disciplined. She followed a strict schedule, running every other day for hours without headphones. While she ran, she did a lot of thinking. "You know you have a lot to stew over if you're running for hours without music," she says now.

As Jill ran, she noticed that she was mentally tallying up reasons to leave the marriage. "That's a dangerous rabbit hole to go down," she says. The biggest source of her upset was the realization that she and her husband were arguing all the time—the romantic, carefree, happy phase was over and discord was the new norm. While for most, it's a natural evolution from honeymoon to real life, Jill grew up in a home with parents who never had fights or even disagreements in front of her and her older brother.

"My parents acted like permanent newlyweds," Jill says. "Of course, I saw other parents fight and people on TV argue, but I had very little experience being in the middle of conflict." She now realizes that it's unusual to be raised in an environment without any yelling or disagreements, but that was her model for relationships. As a result, Jill expected her marriage to be like her parents' union.

It's not surprising that conflicts arose: Jill and her husband had different parenting styles, along with contrasting ideas on how to spend their money and what to do with their free time. Even their opposing political views became a sticking point. Over time, the differences created a crack in her marriage, one that continued to widen. Jill kept her problems from her friends, fearing that talking about them would make them harder to ignore.

Eventually Jill shared her growing concerns about her marriage with her family. They urged her to stick with it. They knew Jill had been charmed by her husband's romantic gestures. After all, he had proposed, jokingly, the very first time they met. She loved his creativity, blue eyes, and dimple (yes, there's only one). Jill would come home from work to find that he'd left gifts for her with her doorman—handmade cards, love poems, jewelry.

Her family didn't want her to throw in the towel. "Try harder," they said. "Everyone has disagreements." And even: "It would be a huge mistake to leave him." Jill took the well-meaning advice to heart and decided to keep trying.

When her daughters were visiting their grandparents over the summer, Jill wondered if her husband would want to do something together during this rare time alone. On the day before the girls returned, he suggested they go out to dinner. Over drinks, Jill mentioned that a good friend was getting married in San Antonio in the fall, and suggested they use frequent flier miles for a fun getaway. Rather than pick up on the request for a romantic weekend trip, her husband picked a fight; Jill promptly asked for the check, feeling discouraged and disappointed.

"I now know that any serious relationship has ups and downs, but not seeing this side of marriage growing up, I was unprepared for the day-to-day conflict," Jill says. "It may sound naïve but I thought we were going to continue to live out the romantic fairytale of our courtship. When real life got in the way, I was lost." Jill was having a hard time handling the stress she felt as a result of all the fights with her Prince Charming. She thought some time apart might provide clarity . . . and peace.

Jill was a ball of nerves the day she decided to talk with her husband. She chose to tell him while their two young daughters were asleep and they had

BEST PRACTICES FOR HAVING "THE CONVERSATION"

Breaking up is painful and messy. The conversation may not go as planned. Still, there are worthwhile goals to keep in mind if you will be the one to initiate the talk.

Make sure you're safe. If your husband has a history of violent or erratic behavior, break the news to him in front of a therapist or neutral party or in a public place. You can't control how he reacts, but you can control the environment in which you choose to have the conversation.

Try not to blindside him. Ideally you have discussed what you feel is lacking in the relationship. You don't want your divorce announcement to be the first time you're clueing him in that you're unhappy in the marriage. The more he's surprised by what you say, the longer it will take him to accept the changes. The less he accepts your decision, the more he will try to talk you out of leaving.

Break the news gently. Be succinct and compassionate. Remember that you once loved this man and it's not going to be easy for him to hear that you're leaving.

Set the right tone. A key opportunity you have in this initial conversation is to set a kind tone for an amicable divorce. Treat him with consideration, respect, and honesty, and he just may do the same.

Be clear about what you want and follow through. Wait to have the conversation until you're sure of what you want. Some women tell their husband they want a divorce, and then make love, fall asleep in each other's arms, and agree to go on a trip to Hawaii, even though they know in their heart that they want out. Don't continue to act married out of guilt if you don't want to be married.

Be prepared for the stages before acceptance. In many ways, divorce is like losing a partner to death. Your husband may go through one or many phases of shock, denial, anger, depression, or bargaining before coming to accept that your relationship is over.

privacy. With her pulse pounding in her ears, she explained simply that she wanted to take time to think over their relationship. She was going to move to the third-floor bedroom to get some perspective. Her husband was surprised and upset. To him, conflict was normal and he thought she was being too sensitive. He didn't ask many questions and after a few minutes left the room to digest the news.

Jill and her husband went to marriage counseling once a week, hoping to work through some of their challenges and save their marriage. However, they made little progress in solving their problems. In fact, the sessions seemed to make things worse when they got back home. "I remember feeling like I had the emotional strength of a one-ply tissue," Jill says. "I was exhausted from all the conflict, withdrawn, and was starting to get depressed. I believed that physical and emotional distance from my marriage would help me feel better." Jill continued going to couples counseling for a few more months but soon realized that what she wanted was not only some peace and a room of her own; she wanted a divorce.

"My whirlwind romance in the city."

Suzanne and her future husband fell in love a few months after they met. Theirs was a whirlwind romance. A native New Yorker with a wide smile and an equal mix of energy and determination, Suzanne was swept off her feet by this smart, kind, and funny man whose integrity made a big impression on her. It didn't hurt that he looked a lot like James Dean. Suzanne knew she had met the man she wanted to spend her life with.

Both journalists—he was working as a TV news producer, Suzanne was a magazine editor—they bonded easily over their love of words, music, and film. He made Suzanne mixed CDs, brought her coffee in bed every morning, and made her laugh. One of the first of their many creative projects together was collaborating on a documentary film about the Mermaid Parade, a celebration of surf and summer held annually in Coney Island, Brooklyn.

The couple grew even closer when the terrorist attacks hit New York City on 9/11. Suzanne's soon-to-be husband had been commuting to work in New York from New Jersey. After the attacks, the trains were shut down. He wound up staying with Suzanne for a few weeks, which turned into his never leaving. They planned a wedding for the following year. Suzanne was ready to settle down and have a baby. She saw no reason to slow things down.

After they moved to Maplewood, New Jersey, and their son was born, the giddy thrill of new love carried them for a few years. However, they soon discovered that they had very different ideas about money, about work, and even about communicating. While Suzanne liked to talk things through when there was a conflict and resolve things as quickly as possible, her husband needed time to process his feelings and would often retreat and not communicate at all. Much as she tried to accept this, Suzanne often felt abandoned and resentful. Their opposite styles of communicating led to fights over trivial things. Add in difficult work schedules, a new baby, and lack of sleep, and the distance between them continued to grow.

Her husband dealt with their conflicts by spending more time at the pub with his buddies. Suzanne threw herself into her work. Still, neither wanted to give up on their marriage. They went to couples therapy on and off over several years. They tried to compromise, see each other's point of view, and make things work. Despite all their best efforts, ultimately they were unable to find a common ground.

On particularly challenging days, Suzanne would close the door to her office at work and give herself a cry break. She felt frustrated and disappointed that she couldn't figure out how to make things better. "We fell in love and thought everything would work out," Suzanne says. "We didn't take the time to understand what each of us thought marriage would be like. It turned out we had very different expectations."

> "Although we loved one another, we were bringing out the worst in each other, not the best." —Suzanne

One evening when Suzanne was working in her home office while her husband was watching TV on another floor, she was struck by how they had both been hiding from each other for a long time. She realized that the silence and the distance between them were growing wider and more painful. Therapy and heart-to-heart talks had not changed things. As much as Suzanne wanted her marriage to last and to keep her family together, she knew they had reached an impasse.

On July 4, about ten years into the marriage, though she didn't have a speech prepared, Suzanne told her husband she wanted to separate. "I told him that in spite of our best efforts, we weren't able to find a way back to each other. We were fighting more and drifting further apart. It wasn't a good environment for our son, or for any of us." Later that summer, after several more conversations, she moved out.

"I escaped when he was on a business trip."

Jamie

A die-hard people pleaser who avoided confrontation at all costs, Jamie made the decision to sneak out of her house rather than face her abusive husband, Doug. The soft-spoken, freckle-faced thirty-something redhead was afraid of her husband's temper and never told him she was leaving and taking their two kids. She shudders when she remembers the night she and Doug were driving home after a friend's wedding. Doug had had a few too many martinis, so Jamie was driving. It was late. She made several wrong turns. They were lost. Exploding in anger, he yelled in her face while she was driving, calling her an idiot and demanding she pull over. She pushed his face away, told him to stop screaming at her, and said he was too drunk to drive. He retaliated by yanking out a clump of her trademark curls. She was in shock—and in pain.

> "I was terrified of how he would react but I felt I had to escape."
>
> —Jamie

At that moment, a switch flipped in her mind. Though his temper was no surprise, nor was his drinking, this was the first time he had expressed his rage physically. Jamie was going to make sure it was the last. She secretly looked for a place to live and found a furnished two-bedroom apartment across town, immediately signing the leasing paperwork. She planned the move for a night she knew her husband would be on a plane to Arizona for a work conference. She had left her own job early that day, telling her boss in the production department at the advertising agency that she had a family emergency. When Doug got home to an empty house, he called Jamie, furious. This was the start of a contentious divorce that lasted years.

"I want a man who can't keep his hands off me."

Denise

Our friend Denise had known for years that her marriage was broken. The beautiful Kerry Washington look-alike had eloped with Mitch, the nice guy she had met after years of disappointing dates (including with Troubled Tom, who chose their third date to show her his house arrest ankle bracelet that restricted him from going to the new bar she wanted to check out). "There was always some major problem," Denise said. "I was so tired of dating. Mitch was so sweet. Everything seemed to fall into place with him."

IT MIGHT BE TIME TO GO WHEN . . .

- The bad times outweigh the good.
- There is no lasting conflict resolution. You have the same fight again and again.
- You have tried living for other things besides your relationship . . . and that didn't work.
- Your kids are exposed to a lot of conflict.
- Your kids are seeing you—their role model—being mistreated, devalued, or disrespected. You worry that they will seek out this type of relationship when they grow up.
- Loving each other has taken a backseat to finding fault, resenting each other, and the biggest romance killer of them all, expressing contempt.
- You realize you can't accept things as they are, and nothing you have done to improve things has worked.
- You have become hopeless and depressed about the relationship.
- You are scared for your safety.
- You are being lied to; he has a secret life.

But one child and ten years later, Denise, an African American woman in her forties, could not deny that something crucial was missing in her marriage. She found herself staying late at her demanding job as a pharmaceutical company marketing director, all the while resenting Mitch, who worked sporadically installing home stereo systems. She was also annoyed that he neglected his health and put on forty pounds. It got to the point where Denise couldn't stand to hear the sounds Mitch made when he slurped down milkshakes and gobbled fast food.

Denise rehearsed her exit speech in her head for weeks. She condensed all she was feeling into three sentences: "I want to be in a passionate relationship with a man who can't keep his hands off me and who I can't stop thinking about. We've never had that. I appreciate what we do have and don't want to lose you as my best friend." Denise felt relieved to finally get this off her chest, but her husband was still in love with her and didn't want to lose her.

While Denise had been thinking about leaving for a long time and had already emotionally detached from Mitch, he couldn't accept the news. He was devastated and took his story of hurt all over town, doorstep to doorstep. "The whining, the telling everyone he bumped into about what had happened was a typical Mitch reaction to bad news," she says now.

Denise learned that there could be a stark contrast between what you're feeling and what your spouse will feel once told of the divorce. Mitch, who had had no inkling that she was dissatisfied, questioned how she could be over him. She had been processing the break for months while she was still married. She realized she was so focused on what she needed to do for herself that she had not been sensitive to how he would handle the news. Looking back now, Denise says, "I wish I had been more compassionate about the fact that he was grieving the end of our marriage and needed time. I had been through that months before and was done."

WHEN HE LEAVES YOU
"Try leaving with two flat tires."

Eleanor

Our friend Eleanor, in her fifties, was known for her stylish silver bob and for sporting a tasteful cardigan twinset along with an air of entitlement. One Sunday afternoon she was looking forward to the weekend tea ritual she enjoyed with Harold, her husband of twenty-five years. She had baked muffins with blueberries from their garden and was eager to have his help solving a few baffling clues from *The New York Times* crossword puzzle, as was their habit since their daughter, Brie, had left for college five years earlier. A judge in the county courthouse, Harold is a thoughtful, quiet man who speaks in the deliberate style of a reasoned member of the court. "My dearest Ellie," he began slowly, "I have something very difficult to say. I have given it a great deal of thought. I believe our marriage has been over for quite some time. To that end, I think it is time we go our separate ways. I plan—"

Before Harold could finish delivering his verdict about their marriage, Eleanor picked up a Limoges teacup and threw it against the wall, sending shards everywhere.

"Are you kidding me?" she shouted so loud her neighbors could hear. "You're leaving me? I don't believe this!"

With that, she got a utility knife out of a drawer and went outside, slamming the door. She proceeded to slash the tires on her husband's Mercedes. Problem solved. "Try leaving with two flat tires," she taunted.

Eleanor poured some tea into the lone teacup on the table and put it in front of Harold. "You don't want a scandal," she said. "You'll change your mind if you get a good night's sleep. Now finish your tea and enough of this nonsense."

Harold looked pained. "You haven't been very happy with me for years. I'm surprised you're this upset," he said quietly. "I have tried to talk to you about separating. It's time. I'm in love with someone from work."

That night, Eleanor found herself alone in their king-size bed. Harold slept in the guest room. She kept thinking about their conversation. She had to admit that he had told her many times before that he wanted to leave, but she had ignored him, hoping their problems—and his wanting to separate—would go away. "I made everything worse by not listening to his concerns and taking them seriously," she says now. "I put my head in the sand. I took him for granted." Eleanor stared at the ceiling, aware that everything Harold said was true. She knew the marriage wasn't perfect, but she liked their home, their town, and the life they'd created. And she simply never thought he'd have the courage to leave.

"The day my husband came out of the closet."

 Gina, an Italian American hairdresser in her thirties, pregnant with her first child, loved to talk while she worked, hearing all the latest gossip from everyone who sat in her chair. She never imagined that one day she would have her own dramatic tale to tell.

Gina had been straining to organize a neglected closet, since bending over was difficult in her third trimester, when she noticed what looked like a loose wallboard cut down the middle. She slowly lowered her unwieldy pregnant body to investigate. She jiggled the board, imagining she would find some discarded toys from a previous owner's children in a long-forgotten hiding spot. Instead, she stumbled upon a stash of gay porn.

After crying all afternoon, Gina confronted her husband, Clayton, the second he walked in the door. "I really didn't know what to think, but I hoped it wasn't his, or that maybe he had a fetish but was still into me," Gina said.

Her husband listened without moving a muscle. When Gina was done talking, he took a deep breath, looked her in the eyes, and seemed to summon all his strength. "I love you, and I really wanted to make this life work, but I can't," he said. "I'm gay." The truth had come out—and so had her husband—and there was no turning back.

"He's in love with a Broadway actress."

A difficult truth about relationships is that we can never really know what the other person is thinking if he doesn't clue us in. Iris, a Chinese American stay-at-home mom in her late thirties, knew that her husband wasn't around much but had no idea that he was considering leaving her—until he actually did.

Iris's world got turned upside down one random Wednesday evening as her three young daughters ate chicken, mashed potatoes, and corn on the cob. Flint came home from work and sat down at the table without taking off his coat. "I can't do it anymore," he said. "Rough day?" Iris asked as she placed a plate of food on the table. "I want a divorce," he blurted out in front of the kids. "I've been seeing someone. She's a Broadway actress. We're in love."

> "I slept next to this man for most of my adult life. I couldn't believe that while I was thinking about what to do with the girls over the weekend, he was thinking about how he was going to leave. He planned it all out, and I had no idea."   —Iris

Iris was in shock. She couldn't believe what she was hearing. The rest of the evening, she felt like she was underwater, with everything blurry and hard to decipher. She fixated on the fact that this woman acted on Broadway. Why did she need to know that? When the shock wore off a few days later, Iris felt she was being discarded after nine years of marriage. She kept this a secret from everyone she knew for more than a month, barely able to face what had happened, let alone have others feel sorry for her. She spent this time hiding out at home, crying over family photos and digging for information online about the new woman in her husband's life.

"I read the texts from his mistress."

Carlotta, a blue-eyed blonde who could pass for Reese Witherspoon's sister, had suspected for years that her husband, Bill, had someone on the side. In fact, Carlotta was driving her spin buddy, Suzanne, and her other friends nuts with her constant need to be reassured that her husband wasn't having an affair. It's all Carlotta wanted to talk about. The late-thirties mom to Bailey, fifteen, kept asking: "Why is he working late so often? Why won't he talk to me? Why does he keep his iPhone with the screen down, ringer off, but right by his side all the time?"

When Suzanne didn't see Carlotta at the gym for almost a month, she texted her a few times. Not hearing back, she decided to go visit her in person. Suzanne took one look at her friend's red-rimmed eyes and disheveled hair and realized Carlotta's worst fears had probably come true.

"I don't know what I was dreaming, but I woke up in the middle of the night convinced I had to check his phone," Carlotta told Suzanne. "I can't explain it, but I had a gut feeling. I knew his password was either his favorite sports team or the dog's name. The very first message that came up was from her."

"From who?" Suzanne asked.

"His whore!" Carlotta shouted. "Her name is Allyson. Her messages were awful. She wrote, 'I'm crazy in love with you, baby!' He wrote back, 'Me too.'" When Carlotta confronted her husband the next morning, he seemed relieved. "He wanted to be with her but was waiting until Bailey graduated from high school," Carlotta said. "He was just biding his time with me." Carlotta crumpled as Suzanne hugged her, reassuring her that she wasn't alone.

"We didn't even make it to our first wedding anniversary."

When Meghan noticed her wife, Joan, withdrawing from the relationship, she chalked it up to work stress. A busty, petite woman in her twenties with a purple-tinged choppy bob and low self-esteem despite her many talents, Meghan had just begun training to be a massage therapist. Newlyweds, she and Joan had recently moved to Maine so that Joan could take a job as head chef at a well-regarded restaurant.

They were in their new house only a few weeks when Joan said there were rumors going around that she was having an affair with Kelly, the book-keeper at the restaurant. Joan assured Meghan there was nothing to the gossip. "People can be so catty," she said. "They're trying to cause trouble since I'm new and they're jealous they didn't promote from within." Sounded like a reasonable explanation.

Soon Meghan noticed that Joan was going to the gym a lot and had lost interest in sex. She had also stopped picking up her cell phone when she was at

> "I feel so betrayed. I did everything for Joan. I can hardly breathe without her. I think about her all the time. How could she prefer to be without me?"   —Meghan

work. Meghan wondered what was going on but was afraid to ask. By the time Joan sat her down a few months later, Meghan feared the worst. "I don't want to be married anymore," Joan said coolly, as though she were tired of the chili special that she'd created for the new lunch menu. "I've rented a house by the lake to think about what's next for me."

Meghan needed air. She went outside to clear her head. Without even realizing it, she walked for well over an hour. Meghan thought about a million questions she wanted to ask Joan. "I was in love. I didn't want it to end," Meghan said. "I was also in shock." She didn't want to give up on Joan, especially as they were just starting their new life in a new state. But when Meghan returned home from her walk, Joan was gone. Meghan sat down on the floor and cried.

"He told me he was leaving in a note."

How you handle yourself after you get the news is important. Sometimes, rage can get the best of you, like it did for our friend Amali. In her late twenties, Amali was a tomboyish Indian IT consultant with a long, swingy braid of jet-black hair. It was natural for her to turn to her computer after she found the stinging note that her husband left on the kitchen table.

On a scrap of paper, he had scribbled a note filled with his typical lousy spelling:

> *"I'm moving back to Chicago. I'm not cut out for mariage. It's just to hard. You'll be better of without me. I'll let you know wear to send my things. You can keep our Star Wars colectables. I'm sorry."*

Enraged, she immediately posted a picture of the note on Facebook and Instagram. In her caption, she said: "Sugi left me. If anyone sees him in a red Honda Civic, text me where he is so I can tell him what I think of him. Don't be shy about cursing him out and telling him what a coward he is."

PITY PARTY OF ONE

Everyone has someone on their Facebook feed who only posts depressing messages. Don't be that person. Our friend Carlotta once posted this status update: "He says I now have a fat ass and he never loved me." Before you type your way into trouble or despair on Twitter, Facebook, and the like, please ask yourself the following:

1. Could this post get me in trouble? Am I slandering my ex? Name-calling? Exposing sensitive information? Publicly threatening him?

2. If I read this in two months, will I regret it? Does it make me look like I am taking cheap shots at him? Do I come across as depressed or unhinged?

3. Am I using Facebook to hurt someone else? Don't be vindictive. Rise above. When it comes to live tweeting your breakup, way, way less is more. If you don't have anything nice to post, don't post anything at all. Make sure your updates are worth supporting—not pitying. You'll thank us in six months.

Go ahead and change your status to "it's complicated," because, believe us, sister, it certainly is.

Creative use of crowdsourcing to find your husband who left you? Sure, we give her props for that. Inciting others to verbally attack her ex? That went too far. A few clicks, a screenshot, or a good old-fashioned copy and paste of a thoughtless post can be all it takes to get in some hot water. Sugi's in-box filled up quickly with friends and acquaintances telling him what was up. Amali found out where he was, all right—at his attorney's office. She received a cease and desist letter by courier the very next day.

TRIAL SEPARATIONS

Often when couples come to an impasse in their relationship, they separate for a while to "try on" being apart. This separation may last weeks, months, or even years. Sometimes one spouse is waiting for the other to decide how he or she feels, which can leave the other in a difficult limbo. Trial separations can be a step on the way to divorce or they can be a period for self-reflection that brings a couple back together.

"I don't want to stay with him, but I'm terrified to be on my own."

With her Audrey Hepburn–esque short bob and big brown eyes, Renée, in her early sixties, had been waiting for something to change—for her husband Hector's over-the-top work schedule as a cardiologist to slow down, for him to become emotionally available to her, or for her to get the strength to leave him despite their thirty-plus years together. She had been longing to connect but felt continually rebuffed. "He seemed to find everything more interesting than me—his heart patients at the hospital, golf, whatever it was he was doing on his computer," she says. "The more I pressed him, the more he withdrew."

Retired from her job as a flight attendant for more than a year, she missed traveling and having an exciting escape from the frustrations of her daily life. She daydreamed about going on a cruise to see the world. Renée finally admitted to her close friends that she had done the math: She spent only about seven waking hours a week with Hector. His all-consuming work meant he was really married to his job, not to Renée. "Is this really how I'm going to spend the rest of my life, alone most of the time, trying to get his attention?" she lamented.

Even though she was unhappy, Renée was too terrified to leave the familiar for the unknown. That is, until she received a mysterious text.

"How's ur day going, R?" the message read.

"WHO IS THIS?" Renée demanded.

"Larry. From Houston. We talked online. I was wondering how that fund-raiser you were posting about went?"

Renée had met Larry in an online forum for people involved in grassroots projects to help feed needy children. They had traded phone numbers so they could exchange resources and information.

"It was a huge success," Renée responded right away, happy to have someone ask her about the event and to have a chance to boast about all the money they raised.

And they were off. They started texting in the morning, checked in most afternoons, and said good night in the evening. It stopped bothering Renée so much that her husband was MIA because she had a new man paying plenty of attention to her, even though he was a man she'd never set eyes on and knew next to nothing about. Though initially Renée dismissed her new text pal as a work-related colleague, she realized that when she didn't hear from him, she felt irritable. In fact, she missed him. "I knew it was silly to miss a man I'd never even met, but I did," she says.

When Renée confided to Eleanor that she was falling for a man she had been texting who lived fourteen hundred miles away, Eleanor told her about the special she'd seen on TV about "cat fishing." Eleanor explained that there are troubled people who make up identities to dupe lonely, unsuspecting men and women into online romantic relationships that can last months without anyone ever meeting. Often these people are hiding something and believe they would be rejected if met in person.

Renée ignored the warning and found herself daydreaming about Larry all the time, feeling emotionally connected to him, and making imaginary plans to travel the world together to help feed starving children. It wasn't until Renée also started fantasizing about divorcing Hector that she saw the truth: "I was having an emotional affair," she says. "I realized I had other options, and I finally felt ready to leave Hector."

Renée waited up for Hector, who was working late at the hospital that night, and asked him how he thought things were going between them. He said things were fine. Renée told him that she had been feeling his absence for a long time and had started communicating with a man online. She wasn't sure what was going to come of it, but she felt certain that her connection with Hector had been eroding for years. "You're married to your work. I hardly ever see you," Renée said. "I don't want to keep living this way." Hector listened intently. He saw this as a wake-up call, a problem they could solve, and suggested they go to marriage counseling. Renée agreed to give it a try, but in her heart she wanted some space to evaluate her relationship with Hector. She wanted a trial separation, even though she knew it might set the wheels in motion irreversibly.

"My hormones caused my affair."

For our friend Pilar, a late-forties Cuban American mother of two tween sons, a feeling of panic about her life slipping away led to her decision to leave her husband. She worked as a high school English teacher, wore a pixie cut, and favored high heels,

THINGS TO DO NOW

I n the early days of separation, you may feel so shell-shocked that it's all you can do to just make it through the day. We'll get into specifics on money, communication, taking care of yourself, and more in the coming chapters, but for right now, here are a few key actions to take.

❏ Set up alerts on your joint bank account for transactions of $500 or more. If he starts moving money around or taking out larger sums, you want to know about it.

❏ Try to make sure you have money set aside to last a few months while you begin to get your finances settled.

❏ Make a list of all your bank accounts and financial assets. Print out your most recent statements.

❏ Confide in a trustworthy friend. Do not hold everything inside because you feel too embarrassed. We all have faced hard times.

❏ Keep it simple. This is not the time to volunteer to be PTA president or go for that promotion at work. Keep things as pared down as possible.

often looking half her age. The morning her gynecologist told her she was exhibiting signs of perimenopause, she had received an AARP membership card in the mail, which she immediately tossed in the trash. "I didn't realize it at the time, but I think I was having a midlife crisis," Pilar says today. "I started picturing myself in a retirement community for active seniors." Her twenty-year marriage to Justin, her college sweetheart, was stable but stagnant.

When an attractive young English teacher started to shamelessly flirt with Pilar in the teachers' lounge, she found herself unable to resist the attention. "I needed to know men were still attracted to me," Pilar admits. After-work drinks with coworkers eventually led to a fling at his apartment. Confused about what this meant for her marriage and her family, and overcome with guilt, Pilar confessed her affair to Justin. She told him she needed to figure out what she really wanted, and asked for a trial separation. Pilar felt relieved that she admitted the truth and opened the door to leave. Justin was devastated.

~~~~~~

❑ Be direct. Ask for honest and clear communication from your soon-to-be ex and offer the same.

❑ Don't bury your head in the sand. Face your challenges and the reality of your situation.

❑ Take care of your health. Eat three meals a day. Sleep as much as you can. Try not to call in sick to work unless you really need to. Stick to your routine if possible.

❑ Beware of trying to dull the pain. Merlot can't make your troubles go away. Don't add a raging hangover to your list of what ails you.

❑ Stay active. Try to break a sweat every day. It will do wonders for your mood and help you work out some of that stress.

❑ Breathe. Deep breaths will trick your body into feeling relaxed—and your mind and heart will follow suit.

❑ Find support. Don't be afraid to seek professional support from a psychologist or psychiatrist. Divorce is a major life event. It's okay to need help getting through it.

TELLING FAMILY AND FRIENDS ABOUT THE SPLIT

As hard as it is to share personal news about the state of your marriage, you will need to tell your friends, family, coworkers, and more. The way you let others know about your separation will depend on how close your relationship is. We have found the best approach when speaking with acquaintances is to come up with a simple explanation about what happened that you're comfortable delivering. Think about what Hollywood press agents say when announcing the latest celebrity divorce. It usually goes something like this: *Gwyneth and Chris arrived at this decision together. They continue to respect each other and are committed to doing what's best for their children and their family.* Iris had a two-line explanation she used with acquaintances and nosy neighbors: "We discovered we weren't the right fit. It's been difficult, but we're doing okay."

Though it's possible to be detached when talking to acquaintances, it's a lot harder with family and close friends who are pestering you for information.

Prepare yourself—everyone will have an opinion. Many will think they know what's best for you. Even though it can be difficult to hear what they have to say—such as, "We never liked him anyway," or "You're too old to get divorced. Hang on to him with all your might," and even "You're no picnic yourself, you know"—just listen. Let them talk. The less you argue, the easier it will be for you. While you have been processing this split for some time, they're just getting the news and trying to make sense of it. When you have heard all you can handle, it's fine to let them know that it's enough discussion on the topic for that day.

Separating from the in-laws, if you were close, can feel like yet another big loss. They need to pick a side, and it's likely not going to be yours. Denise had always been close to her mother-in-law, but after she announced she wanted a divorce, her mother-in-law made her feel like a villain. "Our relationship got a little better after the dust settled, but it was never the same," Denise says. "I miss cooking together on holidays and the easy rapport we had." Jill and Suzanne both wanted to maintain a relationship with their respective in-laws. Jill let her in-laws know that she understood that they would need to support their son and distance themselves from her during the divorce. However, she also told them they would always be welcome in her home and in her life. Suzanne also had an open-door approach with her extended family. She was happy when her son's birthdays, performances in plays, piano recitals, and other special events, as well as holidays, included his grandparents, uncles, aunts, and cousins on both sides of the family.

EMOTIONAL ROLLER COASTER WITH LOOP-DE-LOOPS

You're likely feeling adrift and isolated during the early weeks of your separation. Often the people we're used to turning to for support and advice, like our families and close friends, don't quite know what to say to comfort us. If they have never been divorced, they may be at a loss for the right words. Other times, "couple friends" will take sides, and some acquaintances will flat out ignore you or pretend you're invisible because they're so worried about saying or doing the wrong thing. It can feel as if you're untethered from many of the usual anchors in your life and unwelcome in places that used to be shelters in the storm. Your closest friends will know that rather than platitudes, you need

Resources **Three Books to Help You Feel Better Today**

The Art of Uncertainty: How to Live in the Mystery of Life and Love It by Dennis Merritt Jones. Though we may crave some predictability and order, this book helped us discover how to embrace uncertainty in this time of flux.

Me Talk Pretty One Day by David Sedaris. Pick up this short story collection on those days when nothing in the world seems funny.

Smart and insightful, the book will help you laugh and remember that one day, even if it's not today, you will feel okay again.

The Art of Happiness in a Troubled World by the Dalai Lama and Howard C. Cutler, MD. Discover the power of community and solidarity. Learn that happiness resides within you, whether you're married, single, or divorced.

actual help, such as inviting your kids on playdates so you can have some free time or bringing you dinner. The most helpful gifts they can offer may be to connect you with other friends they know who are divorcing and to let you know they're there for you no matter what.

Furthermore, the "I love him, no, I hate him" volatile mood swings can make you feel like you have an extended case of PMS. The bad news: This is going to take longer than a twenty-eight-day cycle to resolve. The good news: You're among friends who know what you're going through. We will help you ride the emotional waves you experience during this period of transition until your feet are on firm ground again.

What I Wish I'd Known

Amali

"I was impulsive after my husband left me. I wish I had thought before I acted. I bad-mouthed him all over town and did a lot of damage. He hurt me, and I wanted to hurt him back even more. It took a long time for both of us to move beyond the terrible way things ended. I wish I'd understood then that he and I would one day find our way back to being friends." —Amali

Chapter 2

THE KIDS: HANDLE WITH CARE

"Divorce isn't such a tragedy. A tragedy's staying in an unhappy marriage,
teaching your children the wrong things about love. Nobody ever died of divorce."
—Jennifer Weiner, *Fly Away Home*

Your kids are passengers in your divorce journey. They ride shotgun as you travel through this confusing time, bearing witness to how you handle the tumult. What they really want is to relax in the backseat while Mom and Dad both sit in the front, navigating the family wherever they need to go.

It can be helpful to realize that while you have an adult view of your marriage and its complications, your children most likely will not understand why the family can't keep living together. Our friend Iris felt her heart break each time her girls tried to get her back together with their dad. If you left your husband, your kids may think your reasons weren't good enough, as was the case for Pilar. If your husband left you, your child may blame you for not being nicer to their father and believe you caused him to take off, as was the case with Eleanor. When she told her daughter, Brie, about the divorce, the twenty-three-year-old had little sympathy for her mom's hysterics. She was living away from home in Virginia and told her mom that she'd witnessed the cool and detached way Eleanor had treated Brie's dad and she wasn't that surprised he had found someone else and left. The words stung Eleanor, whose already strained relationship with her daughter seemed more fragile than ever.

We can't know what our children are experiencing when they hear the news of our separation, no matter what their age, but a parenting class we attended helped us get a glimpse into the perspective of younger kids. In New Jersey, parents who file for divorce are required to complete a seminar at the courthouse. About one hour into the workshop we attended, the social worker in charge said, "Okay, everyone up and move. If you're sitting in the back, go to the front. If you're on the left, go to the right." Comfortable where we all were, everyone muttered to themselves as we picked up our belongings and relocated. After we settled in, the social worker said, "You didn't like that, did you? You imagined spending your whole two hours in that seat. You were comfortable. You didn't want to change. That is just a tiny peek into how your children are feeling every day and every weekend as they shuffle back and forth between two households." We got the message.

There's no way around the fact that when your kids learn you are divorcing, it's likely the most dramatic thing they have experienced in their young lives. While some parents carefully plan the talk, searching for exactly the right words, others hope for on-the-spot inspiration. No matter how you handle it, whether you have a tidy speech or you stumble and stammer, it's going to take time for everyone to fully understand the ramifications of what you have said, and to recover.

THE NO-TALK TALK

Jamie moved out at night, packing up a suitcase and throwing in as many of her most versatile clothes and essential toiletries as she could cram in and still zip it shut. Next she hustled into the kids' room and asked them to fill their backpacks with their favorite toys, books, and games while she packed their clothes. The boys, Lucas and Harry, ages five and seven, asked if they were going on a trip. Jamie said they were, without elaborating.

Jamie didn't feel ready to answer a lot of questions. She remembers feeling that if she said what was happening out loud, she would lose her courage. Instead, she chanted it in her mind, "We're leaving. We're leaving. We're really leaving."

During her eight-year marriage, Jamie had become adept at tolerating an abusive home environment. She would physically steel herself whenever her husband walked in the room, keeping her eyes in a downward glance so as to disappear just a little bit. Of course, the tension in the house impacted everyone, not just Jamie. She started to notice that her boisterous boys were adopting her mannerisms of downward glances when they were around their father, and that they winced when he yelled at them for what he viewed as their many offenses. She had an epiphany that perhaps "staying for the sake of the kids" didn't make much sense in her case.

She moved the boys to their new apartment across town. It was a pricey choice for her income as a part-time employee at an advertising agency, but she felt she needed a furnished place. She had to rely on her own savings because Doug, the main breadwinner, had always insisted on keeping separate bank accounts. Still, the rental was worth it to Jamie: "I wanted to make this home a place where the boys felt safe to be themselves, a place where we could all relax and figure out what our new normal was going to be."

It took about a week for the boys to ask, "When are we going back home?" Jamie wasn't ready for their question but let them know that the apartment would be home while she and Daddy sorted out some of their problems. She assured them that they would see their dad soon.

She started to do the things the boys had dared not ask for back at the house under Doug's critical eye, like themed dinner night (think Taco Tuesdays), designating a "Breakfast for Dinner" night, preparing pizza from scratch, and dirtying every square inch of the kitchen. Having mismatched towels in the bathroom was now possible. They all felt freer in their new home.

At last Jamie and her sons lived in a peaceful environment. She looked forward to creating new memories for her boys, memories in which she was a fun-loving, happy mother rather than a meek, cowering woman consumed by fear. For Jamie, *leaving* for the sake of the kids, and taking action to be the mother she wanted to be, made her feel empowered and better about her family than she ever had.

Key Takeaway: Jamie discovered strength she didn't know she had. She also noticed how much her kids were taking their cues from her. Now that she was more relaxed, the kids were calmer as well.

YOUR EX BREAKS THE NEWS WITHOUT YOU

Carlotta

Carlotta went into a free fall after her husband confirmed what she had feared for years: He was having an affair and wanted to leave her. She soon found herself bitter, bitter, bitter with a dash of spite. The woman who used to start the day with a Spin class with Suzanne turned into a *mombie*—a mom zombie who was a shadow of her former self. Showering was no longer important. Why bother? Doing the laundry felt overwhelming. Food had lost its taste. This period, which Carlotta dubbed her "Great Depression," had an eyewitness—Bailey, her fifteen-year-old daughter.

A few weeks after her husband left, Carlotta realized that she hadn't said anything to Bailey about where her dad had gone. When Carlotta asked Bailey to sit down for a minute as she handed her daughter her backpack for school, Bailey dutifully took a seat. She knew it must be important, since they hardly talked anymore—her mom seemed to be sleeping the days away.

"I know it's been a few weeks or maybe a month since your dad was here, I'm not really sure," Carlotta began, realizing she hadn't thought this through at all. "Turns out he's living with Allyson, a whore he's been sneaking around with for years. He's in love with her. You know, it's painful to even say the words." Carlotta broke down in tears. "I don't know what we're going to do."

Bailey rolled her eyes. "What's wrong with you, Mom? I mean, seriously. Dad took me out for pizza and told me everything," she said, adding, "If you want Dad to come back, stop wearing those gross old pajamas."

As her daughter slammed the door, Carlotta realized she was at an all-time low. Her husband didn't even bother to include her in the talk with their daughter. What's worse, she didn't even know the conversation had taken place.

When Suzanne's texts to Carlotta went unanswered, she decided to stop by. Carlotta's Jack Russell terriers, Jack and Diane, were yapping as usual. The door was open. As she walked in, Suzanne found Carlotta sitting in the dark in the living room, amid piles of unopened mail and clutter, the shades drawn. Carlotta looked bedraggled, her beautiful blond hair a greasy mess. She was wearing stained pajamas and exuding "I give up" energy.

"Thanks for stopping by," Carlotta managed. "I'm afraid I'm not such great company these days. Everything is just"—she started to cry—"too much." Carlotta told Suzanne that she felt it was physically exhausting to exist. "I wish it would all stop," she said. "Trying to clean up this house. Paying the bills. Walking the dogs. Getting groceries. How often does Bailey need to eat dinner, anyway?" Carlotta asked.

Surveying the mess in the room, Suzanne asked her, "How is Bailey doing?"

Carlotta had been so consumed by her own loss that she couldn't answer the question. "I don't know," she admitted. "He told her the news without me."

Carlotta later learned that Bailey was going through a very rough time herself. She was not only processing her dad leaving, but now it seemed she was being "left" by her mother as well. At first, Bailey thought that if she could just hold it together, her mom would snap out of it, her dad would realize he was being a jerk, and everything would go back to the way it was. She started bringing her mom food in bed, doing the dishes, and running errands.

NEED A LIFT?

Pick up Kelly Corrigan's magnificent little green book, *Lift*, written as a tender letter to her children. *Lift* takes its title from hang gliding, a pursuit that requires flying directly into rough air, because turbulence saves a glider from "sinking out." This becomes a metaphor for all challenging endeavors, including one of the most rewarding of all, parenting.

Corrigan offers a rich sense of intimacy and speaks to the unique experience of loving someone as much as we do our children. At times funny, tender, and tough, this memoir of motherhood can help you gain perspective and appreciate the gift of your kids. It's the kind of book that reminds you of all the micro moments filled with magic that every mother experiences.

But after a few weeks of living in the house without her dad and with her mom moping around weepy
and depressed, Bailey got angry. Everyone was doing
whatever they wanted—but her! All the structure in
her home life had crumbled.

> "It's really hard to keep it together when you feel like your whole world is falling apart."
> —Carlotta

Bailey started acting out in the clothing she wore
to school. After all, her mom was still in bed when she
left in the morning. Maybe someone else would pay attention to her. The day
she wore a ripped super-mini skirt and a barely there tank top, Carlotta never
picked up the phone—or retrieved the voice message—when the school called.
Bailey kept pushing the envelope, seeing if her mom would object to anything
she did. She dyed her hair pink, wore heavy black eye makeup, and got a nose
ring. During lunch and after school, she started hanging out with the crowd
that smoked and experimented with drugs. When Bailey's dad asked her to
lunch for her birthday, he barely recognized the angry teenager who stared at
him across the table with her arms crossed.

He called Carlotta later that day. "Have you seen what Bailey is wearing
these days?" he shouted into the phone. "Where did she get those clothes?
She looks like a juvenile delinquent. Why are you letting this happen?
What in the world is going on over there?" Carlotta didn't have the energy
to argue but remembers replying, "I have no idea." *Click.* She hung up the
phone and turned up the volume on *Judge Judy*. At least there was justice
somewhere.

One night when Carlotta was asleep, the dogs ran into her room and
wouldn't stop barking. Carlotta rolled out of bed and followed them down the
hallway to see what was going on. She opened the door to Bailey's room and
found the window wide open, the bed empty.

Alarmed, she phoned her ex and asked him to drive around and look for
their daughter. Bailey finally strolled in around 2:00 a.m., smelling of beer and
cigarettes. This time, Carlotta was waiting for her. Instead of yelling or lectur-
ing, Carlotta grabbed her daughter onto her lap and held her. "I'm sorry, baby.
I'm so sorry." Bailey let her mom hug her, and she started to cry. Carlotta had
already lost her husband; she wasn't going to lose her daughter, too.

Carlotta knew she had to pull herself together and that she had to get
them both help. They started going to family therapy sessions. Bailey went

alone and also with each of her parents. Having a safe place to talk about all that she was feeling, including a lot of anger at her parents, made it possible for Bailey to stop acting out. Carlotta discovered that she had been directing all her anger at herself and decided it would be healthier to instead direct it at her husband, Bill, and his mistress, Allyson. This shift left Carlotta with a lot more energy. Instead of moping around, she now spewed venom and storm clouds everywhere she went. She had a long road of recovery ahead.

> 🔑 *Key Takeaway:* Carlotta learned that it wasn't all about her. When her daughter, Bailey, started acting out, Carlotta saw how much she was affected by the divorce and was able to find reserves of energy and compassion to focus on her daughter and get her the help she needed. As a result, mother and daughter were able to shift from being estranged to helping each other heal.

YOUR KIDS THINK YOUR REASONS FOR LEAVING AREN'T GOOD ENOUGH

Pilar

It was up to Pilar to talk to her sons about the separation alone. Justin had been giving her the cold shoulder for the past two months, ever since she'd confessed to him about the fling she had with a younger teacher at work. His response was a complete retreat. Pilar got the silent treatment, and if he had to answer her, he spoke in as few words as possible with no eye contact.

She decided to have the talk with her kids during a four-hour car ride to visit her parents. She explained that in the years since she and their dad had met in school, a lot had changed. "Adults can grow apart," she said. "I need space to find myself. I don't know who I am anymore. The only time I'm by myself is when I'm in the bathroom!" She let out a sigh of exhaustion. "The bathroom?" Alejandro, fourteen, shouted. "Mom, TMI, TMI!" Matias, ten, covered his ears. "Everyone needs something *from* me all the time. Now I need to do something *for* me." (Although she overshared, Pilar refrained from telling the boys that the something she was doing for herself was a twenty-seven-year-old teacher at school.)

TIPS FOR THE TALK WITH YOUR KIDS

Avoid the blame game. However angry you might be, don't blame your spouse for the breakup in front of your kids and avoid arguing in front of them. Also keep to yourself any details about an extramarital affair or financial problem that are not appropriate for children. If Dad calls Mom a "liar" or "cheat," they begin to see themselves, half the product of Mom, as part liar, part cheat.

Keep it short and simple. Remember to keep the explanation age appropriate. They most likely will not stay focused during a long and drawn-out lecture. Convey the information as simply as possible, and let them know they can ask questions and continue to talk about it.

Let them have their feelings. Some kids will cry and scream. For others the reaction will come later. Some will ask many questions. Others may be silent. There is no right way to react. Do your best to be available to your kids whenever they are ready to talk about it.

Tell them together if possible. Though some couples are unable to do this, if you are able to present a united front to your kids, it can help them feel more secure about all the impending changes.

Alejandro and Matias didn't like what they were hearing, and let her know. The older boy immediately started yelling: "If you're not happy, do something fun. You always blame everything on Dad." Following his older brother's lead, Matias added, "Yeah, Mom. Do something fun. Like you always sit in the house when we all go snowboarding. Why don't you just come with us?" As if they hadn't said enough, Alejandro added, "You're the worst mom ever."

Pilar kept her gaze on the road, but her vision became blurry. Tears streamed down her face. She didn't want her boys to see that they'd gotten to her, and she couldn't formulate a sentence, so she turned on the radio. A little while later, Alejandro asked what she meant by finding herself. Pilar tried to explain how she had put her own needs last for so long that she didn't even recognize herself anymore. She just wanted some time. Nothing she said helped them understand. The rest of the ride passed mostly in silence while the boys sulked.

HELPING YOUR KIDS HANDLE THEIR FEELINGS

When you get divorced, your children will experience a wide range of emotions, from sadness and disappointment to anger. Here are ways you can help them cope.

Empathize. Let your child know that you understand that it's hard for them. Validate their feelings.

Know your role. It isn't to shield them from disappointment. Help them find something positive to focus on, and model appropriate behavior when you're feeling disappointed. Help them acknowledge the feeling and accept it.

Help them find something they're good at. This can encourage them to pour their energy into constructive activities that will help build their self-esteem and keep their focus on the positive.

Reassure them. Even though you're in the middle of a lot of changes, let them know that your love for them is constant.

Encourage them to talk to you. Make time to explain things to them as many times as they need.

Widen their support network. Let their teachers, coaches, and guidance counselors know that they're going through a big transition. Consider having relatives or friends visit more often to provide love and understanding.

Say yes when you can. They're experiencing a big No. Whenever possible, say yes to their requests that make them feel they can still get things they want, such as hanging photos of the absent parent or including everyone in a special occasion.

Less than a week later, when they were back at home, Matias started wetting his bed. Pilar thought it might be a temporary setback, but it continued. Every morning he would wake up embarrassed and upset, his sheets drenched. Pilar talked to her son's pediatrician, who explained that stress and anxiety could cause a child to regress. He suggested some simple steps, such as no drinks for her son two hours before bed, encouraging him to use the bathroom before bed, and letting him know it was okay if he had to get up in the middle of the night to use the toilet. She also added night-lights in the hallway to make sure he was comfortable walking to the bathroom in the middle of the night. To make cleanup easier and less embarrassing, she got a waterproof overlay, a washable underpad, a plastic mattress protector, and pull-ups for her son to wear to bed.

The pediatrician suggested Matias might want to talk to a child psychologist to sort through what he was feeling. The therapist explained that her son could not control what was happening, so blaming or punishing him for wetting the bed would not be appropriate. He added that it was fine to reward him when he was dry in the morning. The therapist encouraged her to be very gentle during this time, since bedwetting can damage a child's self-image and confidence. Pilar took his advice, reassuring Matias that it was a common problem and that she knew he would be able to overcome it. Within five months, his bedwetting stopped. Pilar was convinced that therapy, some of the bedtime rituals, and the passing of time helped Matias to process the separation and to conquer bedwetting.

Key Takeaway: Pilar learned the value of asking for help. She was glad she quickly turned to professionals to get to the bottom of her young son's regressive behavior. Seeking support during the early months of her divorce made it possible for her to help her son in ways she never could have alone.

THE ONLY PART THE KIDS HEAR IS "NEW BUNK BEDS"

Iris and her husband, Flint, managed to sit in the same room together long enough to tell their three girls, Anne, two, Lilly, six, and Jiang, eight, that they would no longer all be living under the same roof. "Your mother and I have grown apart, but we both still love you as much as ever, and we'll do—" her husband began. "Your father wants a divorce," Iris interrupted, unable to act like it was a mutual decision. She couldn't believe he wasn't changing his mind when staring at the innocent faces of their beautiful girls, who were looking up at them expectantly. "Your father has made his decision, and he's moving out," Iris said, glaring at him. She needed to place the responsibility where it belonged. "I know this is hard, but you'll be getting the bunk beds you asked for," she said. "You'll spend half your week with me and the other half with your father."

The girls barely reacted. Within the hour, however, they had many questions. They wanted to know if they would get two bunk beds, one in each home. How would they decide who got to sleep on the top bunk? Could they get pink? Is it possible to fall off the top bunk? The whole divorce message was gibberish, but the words "new bunk beds" came through loud and clear.

As soon as they started splitting their time between their mom's and dad's homes, Lilly and Jiang's efforts to get their parents back together kicked into gear. They found the box with their parents' framed wedding pictures and put a few around the marital home Iris was in. On Christmas, all they wanted from Santa was for their parents to get back together. They requested the same for their birthdays. They barely spoke to their dad's new girlfriend, Margot, hoping they could break up the relationship.

"It's painful to have my girls beg me to get back together with the man who betrayed me. He made it impossible. It's so hard to explain to them in a way they can understand why we'll never reconcile." —Iris

Flint felt guilty for having an affair and became a Disney Dad, who was all about ice cream, good times, and trips to the American Girl store, spending money like wild trying to buy a permanent place in their hearts. He left homework, structure, square meals, getting enough sleep, even sunscreen to Iris. He took the role of "good cop," and that meant the discipline and the role of "bad cop" went to Iris. She was also left to pick up the pieces when Disney Dad showed up late for his parenting time or, worse, didn't show up at all. Iris was emotionally and physically zapped from being an around-the-clock supermom to her three children.

Iris also took on the role of communicating to the girls whenever she could that she and their dad were not going to patch things up. She felt flooded with guilt each time they asked her to get back together with their dad, but she stood firm with the message. "Your father and I love you very much, but that will not happen," she would say simply.

🔑 *Key Takeaway:* Iris learned the importance of not bad-mouthing her kids' father. She reminded herself not to burden her daughters with the details of what had happened. She let them know it was his choice to leave but didn't talk about the other woman or how upset she was.

YOUR CHILD DOESN'T REACT . . . TILL LATER

Suzanne took her son to one of their favorite spots by the beach to tell him about the changes that were about to rock his six-year-old world. Her husband wanted to have his own talk with him about the separation. It was late August, and school would be starting soon.

She and her son rode their bikes to the point on the New Jersey shore where Shark River forms a bay before it empties into the Atlantic Ocean. They stared out, fascinated as always by the old-fashioned bridge joining Avon-by-the-Sea and the neighboring town as it opened for tall boats. They loved to see the man in the tower descend when a large boat approached. He would close the bridge to cars by pushing a big gate shut; lights would flash and a bell would sound. Then he'd pull a lever to open the bridge, allowing boats to float through to the other side.

Seeing a toddler sitting on the backseat of a bicycle that her mom rode over the bridge reminded Suzanne of how her own mother used to ride her around on the back of her bicycle. Feeling a mixture of regret and determination, Suzanne told herself that as much as she had wanted her marriage to last a lifetime, she had to accept that this wasn't the way it worked out. She noticed the seagulls, the surfers, and the lifeguards.

Suzanne knew she couldn't put the talk off any longer. "Sometimes people who love each other grow apart and can't agree on things no matter how much they want to or how hard they try, so they decide to live in separate homes," she began. Her son stared at her, saying nothing. "That's what's happened for Daddy and me. He's going to stay in the house, and I'm going to move into an apartment. You're going to live part of the week with each of us." Suzanne paused and looked in her son's eyes. He wasn't reacting. Was this registering at

IS DIVORCE BAD FOR KIDS?

Studies suggest that kids recover quickly after the initial blow of learning their parents will divorce. Researchers at the University of Virginia found that many children experience short-term negative effects from divorce, especially anxiety, anger, shock, and disbelief. However, these reactions typically diminish or disappear by the end of the second year.

Most children of divorce also do well in the longer term, into their teenage years. Studies find only very small differences in academic achievement, emotional and behavior problems, delinquency, self-concept, and social relationships between children of divorced parents and those from intact families, suggesting that the vast majority of children endure divorce well.

all? "You're the most important part of our lives, and we're going to take care of you. But Mommy and Daddy aren't going to be married anymore." Her son finally spoke. "Okay, Mommy. Can we go in the water now?"

A few days later, Suzanne's son asked whether she and his dad still loved each other. She assured her son that they did. And it was true. Suzanne and her husband still loved each other; they also knew they couldn't live together. Later, when his dad spoke with him, it was clear that he had not taken in what was said. He thought his mom would stay in the house and didn't understand she would move into an apartment. He wasn't sure where he was going to live. It took several more conversations for him to sort out what was going to happen.

Following the news, the smiley boy who loved to tell jokes and made friends everywhere he went changed. He seemed sad and upset, and for the first time, he hit a good friend on a playdate.

When school started a few weeks later, Suzanne spoke with her son's teacher, who recommended a family group run by the school social worker for children "in transition," whether it was due to divorce, the death of a parent, or another big change. In the group, he was able to talk with other kids, draw pictures, and ask questions. It seemed to help. Of course, some of the many new words he was learning in the group were cause for confusion. When he said he

Resources   Divorce Bookshelf: Must-Reads for You and Your Kids

There are many books on helping kids through divorce. Here a few that we and our friends found helpful, both for ourselves as parents and for our kids.

Books on parenting during divorce

Putting Children First by JoAnne Pedro-Carroll. Written by a clinical psychologist, this book offers research-based strategies to promote your child's emotional health and resilience during divorce.

Divorce: Techniques Helping Kids Cope with Their Parents Separating by Victoria Poindexter. Short and to the point, this book highlights ways to keep your child's well-being as the focus. It emphasizes the importance of honest communication and reassurance.

Parenting After Divorce by Sarah Booker. Most parents don't mean to neglect their child during or after their divorce, but it can happen. This book gives clear instructions on how to care for the emotional and physical needs of your children despite your own turmoil.

Coparenting with a Toxic Ex by Amy J. L. Baker and Paul R. Fine. Find a positive parenting approach to dealing with a hostile ex-spouse. Learn how to protect your children from painful loyalty conflicts between you and your ex-husband.

Books for kids about divorce

Two Homes by Claire Masurel. This reassuring story focuses on what is gained rather than what is lost when parents divorce. The main character, Alex, has a place in both of his homes and embraces the changes with an open and optimistic heart. Ideal for preschoolers.

What Can I Do? by Danielle Lowry. At first, Rosie tries to get her parents back together. When that doesn't work, she joins a group at school where children with divorced parents share their feelings and helpful ideas about how to cope. Recommended for kids age eight and up.

The Divorce Helpbook for Teens by Cynthia MacGregor. This warm guide is geared to younger teenagers who are struggling to answer tough questions during the early stages of divorce, including what they can do to feel less depressed, how to say no to parents who want you to carry messages to the other parent, and more.

Mom or Dad's House? A Workbook to Help Kids Cope with Divorce by Erainna Winnett. Therapeutic art and writing exercises help kids ages six to twelve get their feelings out, learn how to deal with those feelings in appropriate ways, and build their self-esteem.

now knew what a stepmother was, he explained that it was his mom's sister, his aunt, whom he considered a second mom. Hmmm. Suzanne explained what a stepmom was, and they would have many other conversations clearing up misunderstandings.

Soon her son started talking about how he was feeling. He said the dinner table was lonely with two people instead of three. If Daddy wasn't going to live with them anymore, he wanted a dog. They settled on fish first, with the promise of a dog later. Suzanne complied when he asked her to put up a family photo in his room. The family photo reminded him that his parents still loved him and each other.

Key Takeaway: Suzanne learned that it took more than words for her son to make sense of the news. It took actually moving to a new place for him to understand the impact of the split. The more she encouraged her son to express his feelings, the more a weight seem to lift from his shoulders.

YOU DO ALL THE TALKING

Jill felt the pressure of telling her children the news of the separation. It seemed like she was about to be the source of all the unhappiness and angst in their little lives, and she wished there was a way around it. The girls were four and five at the time, and after Jill and her husband talked about different approaches to broach the news, they decided to read them a book a friend had recommended called *Was It the Chocolate Pudding?* by Sandra Levins. Written from the point of view of a child who has just been told by his parents that they're divorcing, the book illustrates how this little boy mistakenly thinks that the reason his parents fought, then separated, and ultimately divorced is because he smeared chocolate pudding on his baby brother. Once the parents discover his misguided notion, they're quick to comfort him and assure him that his behavior did not have anything to do with their separation.

As Jill read the story, she'd glance at her girls, sitting side by side on the living room couch, with their legs swinging back and forth. Like so many times and so many stories before, they were listening to the tale, unaware that reading this book was bringing a chapter of their lives to a close.

After the story, Jill and her husband looked at the girls. He didn't say anything, so Jill started her speech. "Daddy and I love you both very much, but Mommy and Daddy are having some grown-up problems. Sometimes grown-ups need to have some space to figure things out, so Mommy got an apartment nearby. You will spend time there with me, and time here with Daddy." Jill looked to her husband to see if he wanted to add anything. Silence.

Whatever Jill was expecting, it wasn't what she got next. "Okay," chirped one little voice. "Um, okay," said the other. And just like that, they were off the couch and going to play. Jill remembers walking into her older daughter's room and asking her if she had any questions. "Not really," she replied.

It was then that a new understanding came over Jill. All her kids had known was togetherness. "They had no context for being separated—for what I was trying to tell them," Jill says. After she moved out, with help from her neighbors, her mother, the girls, and even her ex, it all began to seem more real to her and to the girls. "This isn't like the house." "Why are we here?" "We have to share a room?" The time for the questions from the girls had come, and Jill did her best to answer them, one by one.

Jill told her daughters' teachers what was going on at home, and soon learned that there were two other children in her older daughter's class whose parents were divorcing. She reached out to those moms for playdates, thinking it would be good for the girls—and for her, too. The moms and their kids are still close family friends today. Setting up playdates and making new friends who can relate to "not having Daddy live with us" all the time helped to normalize the situation for Jill's girls.

Key Takeaway: Jill learned that setting up playdates with other children whose parents were divorcing helped her girls feel less different. It also enabled Jill to make new friends who understood what she was going through and provided her with a lot of support. When she overheard her kids talking about divorce over tea party playdates, she was glad they were exploring the changes through their games.

YOUR HUSBAND DOES ALL THE TALKING

Denise

Denise and her husband, Mitch, told their seven-year-old son, Andre, together, after dinner, with Mitch doing most of the talking. Feeling guilty about initiating the divorce and worried about how her son would take the news, Denise felt she didn't have it in her to tell him. Staying away from the word *divorce*, Mitch explained: "Your mom and I have talked about this, and we've decided that we aren't going to be married anymore. We actually made this decision three months ago, and you can see we still get along. We will continue to live under the same roof until your mom finds a house nearby. We'll both still see you all the time."

Andre immediately burst into tears and then started hyperventilating. When he finally was able to calm down and catch his breath, he shouted: "Why didn't you tell me three months ago when you decided? Then I would be over it by now." Denise was surprised that as young as her son was, he

EXPLAINING DIVORCE TO YOUR CHILD'S FRIENDS

Denise was volunteering for a classroom party at school and talking to Andre's classmates as she handed out the cupcakes. One little girl named Olivia said, "I know everyone in your family. I know Dre. I know you. I know your husband, Mitch . . ." Denise interjected, "Dre's dad isn't my husband anymore." Without missing a beat, Olivia said, "You can't keep a man?" Denise was flabbergasted. "Oh, no, that's not what happened. Trust me, Olivia, I can keep a man. I've kept plenty a man very happy back in the day." And then Denise remembered she was talking to a seven-year-old and that she wasn't on a witness stand defending her womanhood.

When your separation comes up with your kids' friends, keep it simple and age appropriate, such as, "We are separated, but you're still welcome to come over and play." It's also a good idea to let the parents of your children's close friends know about your divorce because your child will likely be talking about the split with friends at school.

understood that though he was feeling a lot of pain, he would get past it in time. But right at that moment, he was angry. He stormed up to his room and slammed the door, shouting, "I hate you both."

Denise and Mitch sat in the living room trying to figure out how they could help their son. Denise said she would make herself more available to volunteer at Andre's school. Mitch said he would spend more time reading with him. They would continue to discuss long-term strategies.

Since Andre didn't want to talk about what he was feeling, Denise suggested to Mitch that they see if keeping their Sunday night routine of heading out for ice cream after dinner might comfort him. Though Andre couldn't process what was happening, on this Sunday night, he enjoyed having the distraction of a chocolate chip ice cream cone, a reminder that even on a bad day, there were still simple pleasures to be had together as a family.

> *Key Takeaway:* Denise learned that keeping routines and family traditions intact when possible would go a long way in helping her son feel more secure after the separation. She and Mitch got more involved in their son's activities and amped up their efforts to schedule playdates and visits with his grandparents. In turn, Andre started opening up more about his feelings, drawing pictures, and writing about the divorce in school.

TAKE THE PARENTING PLEDGE

Put your hand over your heart and repeat after us: "I, [state your name here], do solemnly swear to place my children first by not putting their father down in front of them. I will choose my words carefully when I speak to my children about their dad."

DON'T CONDEMN. If you are angry with him, you might think, "He doesn't deserve my kindness!" Perhaps you're right. But your children do. Save your complaints about your ex for your shrink, your girlfriends, or your mother, who never liked him anyway.

DON'T CRITICIZE. Those little confused cherubs of yours are half him, half you. To criticize him is to criticize them and make them feel bad about themselves. They also may feel like you're asking them to take your side. So zip your lips and accept that both their parents aren't perfect. You and their dad have good and bad qualities. This will become more than obvious to your kids as they grow up.

EMPATHIZE. If your ex disappoints the kids by not showing up, don't criticize him, but do empathize with their feelings.

DON'T QUIZ your kids on what they do at their dad's house, and don't use them to communicate with your soon-to-be ex. Just because they're going back and forth between two homes doesn't mean they should literally be your go-between.

What I Wish I'd Known

Carlotta

"I wish I'd known that Bailey wouldn't stay mad at both of us forever. She's more resilient than I realized. I regret that I lost sight of her needs while I was grieving the loss of my marriage, but I'm glad I got us into family therapy."

—Carlotta

Chapter 3

LAW & DISORDER

"The best way to predict the future is to create it."
—Abraham Lincoln

T hough Iris's husband, Flint, walked out the door lugging a massive suit-case, with his favorite LeBron James jersey thrown over his shoulder, it wasn't until she hired an attorney that her divorce started to feel real to her. "I kept dreaming he'd come back, full of apologies and regret," she says. "Even though I was furious at him, I wanted to wake up and find him beside me. When weeks turned into months, and he stopped depositing his paycheck into our joint account, I knew I needed to hire a lawyer." Since she wasn't working, Iris scrounged the money for her lawyer's retainer fee by selling her engagement ring and getting a loan from her sister. She wanted to know what she was entitled to receive, immediately and long term.

Renée couldn't believe that she had made an appointment to consult with an attorney. A few months earlier she and Hector had agreed to try mar-riage counseling, but there was always a last-minute medical emergency at the hospital that kept him from attending. Renée used the sessions to discuss what it meant that her husband wasn't making their marriage a priority even now that it was in crisis. "I always knew that his job as a cardiologist wasn't nine to five, but I didn't think it would be twenty-four/seven," Renée said. "There was no time for me." Renée suggested to Hector that they take some time apart to decide what they each really wanted, and she consulted a lawyer about a separation agreement.

About half of all couples who divorce in this country hire a lawyer. We did; so did many of our friends. It's the only way you can be sure you fully understand the laws that will impact your divorce, because they vary from state to state, and let's face it, they're confusing. We wanted to learn our rights when it came to alimony, child support, custody, property, and more.

> "I'd always been leery of lawyers, but it was reassuring to know someone was looking out for my interests."
> —Iris

It was no surprise that while working out the nitty-gritty of our divorces, unexpected emotions cropped up. If either spouse is having a difficult time accepting the reality of ending the marriage, he or she may refuse to agree to basic compromises and try to drag out the process. It's a way to maintain a connection, no matter how tenuous. Eleanor's divorce took three years to be finalized because she missed Harold and looked forward to each collaborative divorce session as a chance to spend time with him. To prepare for their first meeting, she got her silver bob dyed a platinum blond and traded in her signature cardigan for a low-cut top. She brought freshly baked chocolate chip cookies, Harold's favorite, to sweeten the mood. Harold's all-business demeanor didn't discourage Eleanor from doing everything in her power over the next few years to maintain a connection.

In this chapter we will address your biggest concerns, such as: Will I get my fair share of the assets? How are custody decisions made? How long will my divorce take? We also share our best advice on what to look for when you hire an attorney, how to reach interim agreements with your husband while you're waiting for your divorce to be finalized, and what type of divorce to choose. As you read our stories, you will feel strengthened knowing that others have experienced what you're going through now, and that the more we faced our challenges head-on and understood them, the better we felt able to tackle them.

HOW THE HELL AM I GOING TO PAY FOR ALL OF THIS?

Getting a fair share of the marital assets is a top concern for many. If you're a stay-at-home mom like Iris, or not working like Meghan, who was training to be a massage therapist, or working part-time like Jamie, your immediate worry may be paying this month's bills. Jamie faced a unique challenge because Doug had always insisted on separate bank accounts. These women needed money from their MIA spouses, who were the main breadwinners. They filed an application for pendente lite relief with the court. This is a temporary support order for an agreed-upon amount of money that you would receive monthly until your divorce is finalized. This interim support helped our friends maintain their financial status quo and spelled out the ground rules while their divorces were pending. A pendente lite order can also dictate who will live in the family home, how the bills will be paid, and more. You will need an attorney to file for pendente lite. (See our tips on hiring an attorney on page 49.)

If you've never hired an attorney before, as was the case for Suzanne and Jill, you may be surprised to learn that you usually need to plunk down anywhere from $2,500 to $7,500 as a retainer before a lawyer will start work on your case. If you can't tap savings, ask a close friend or family member for a temporary loan or explore creative ways to raise funds.

SIZING UP YOUR DIVORCE OPTIONS

The type of divorce you choose will determine the professionals you need to hire. Key factors to consider include how friendly or antagonistic your relationship with your soon-to-be ex is, the size of your marital assets, the complexity of custody arrangements, and if you feel there may be hidden assets. If you're trying to save money and you can still communicate well, you may opt for mediation or collaborative divorce, like Jill, Suzanne, and Gina, or even a do-it-yourself divorce like Denise. If you and your husband can't communicate, as was the case for Iris and Jamie, or your assets are significant, like Eleanor's, the process may be more drawn out and may even involve litigation or arbitration.

Carlotta

Worried you may pick an approach that isn't the right match for you and your spouse? You will know soon enough. It quickly became clear that face-to-face meetings were not going to work for Carlotta's collaborative divorce because she was unable to contain her rage over Bill's affair. At the first meeting with her ex and both their attorneys, Carlotta showed up thirty minutes late, looking disheveled and ready to fight. "The alarm didn't go off," she said by way of explanation as she sat down. "It's two o'clock in the afternoon, Carly," Bill shot back. "You don't get to call me that anymore. It's Carlotta," she fumed. "Now that you're finally here, let's get started," Bill's lawyer said as he handed out a list of key issues to discuss. Carlotta was immediately overcome with emotion and the reality that the divorce was really going to happen. "This is bullshit!" she screamed, looking into Bill's eyes. "How could you leave me?" With that, Carlotta stood up, threw her cup of water in Bill's face, and stormed out, tears in her eyes, rivaling the best *Real Housewives* showdown. There would be no second meeting. Instead, the lawyers opted for conference calls.

Below, we detail some of the leading options, and what worked best for us and our circle of friends. We only wish we knew someone who bought a string bikini and headed to the Dominican Republic for a quickie divorce—if you're adventurous enough to try this option, send us a postcard. Just bear in mind that DR divorces aren't legal in most states in the US.

Do-It-Yourself $

This approach works well for couples that get along, have a simple financial picture, and generally agree on custody arrangements. It was well suited to Denise and Mitch, who wanted to keep things as simple and painless as possible. "I didn't divorce Mitch because I couldn't talk to him—I just didn't want to have sex with him anymore," Denise says. "We didn't have complicated investments. We knew we could talk through everything and save money."

If you have an amicable partnership like Denise, get a calculator and start brainstorming with your husband. If you can agree on all the terms sitting at the kitchen table with your soon-to-be ex, by all means do so. Make sure you cover custody, alimony, child support, health care, marital assets, property division, and more. When you're all done, take your draft to a paralegal to have them draw up the official contract. If you don't want to use a paralegal, a number of websites can help you prepare divorce papers online. For an uncontested divorce, check out sites like completecase.com, legalzoom. com, and divorceformz.com. Since this is such an important document, we strongly recommend that each spouse hire their own attorney to review the final contract before you sign on the dotted line.

Mediation $$

In divorce mediation, you and your husband hire a neutral third party, called a mediator, to discuss and resolve the issues in your divorce. Mediation can generally save you about half the cost of an attorney. A mediator helps you work together to reach an agreement. However, a mediator doesn't represent either you or your spouse, or give you legal advice. Therefore, if you can't sit in a room with your spouse, can't talk through things calmly, your spouse is a bully, you have trouble speaking up for yourself, or you have a complicated financial picture and need representation, this probably isn't the choice for you. In addition, if your spouse doesn't really want a divorce, this approach can drag on for years. Jill and her ex were unable to reach an agreement through mediation and ultimately wound up hiring individual lawyers. Meghan and Joan were able to mediate their divorce. They not only saved money but were also able to work together on the agreement. Be smart and have your own attorney read through your mediation agreement before you sign it.

Collaborative divorce $$$

You and your spouse each hire a lawyer to represent your interests and give you advice, with the goal of reaching a divorce settlement without going to trial. This is the approach Suzanne and her husband took. They each hired an attorney to advise them in negotiating a settlement agreement. They met with their attorneys separately, and also met together with their attorneys to hash things out. Picture the four of you sitting around a table, deciding everything from how to split assets to creating a parenting plan. They ultimately appeared in family court so that a judge could sign the agreement and make it official.

Arbitration $$$$

Arbitration isn't an approach couples choose initially, but in highly contentious divorces where no agreement can be reached, it may be where you end up. This was the case for Jamie, who agreed to arbitration because she saw it as the only way to stop endless bickering that went on for years, without any agreement to show for it. In fact, one of the few things she and Doug could agree on was that arbitration was a welcome chance to have their case heard and resolved, once and for all. An arbitrator is usually a lawyer or a retired judge, whom you pay hourly. Your lawyer and your spouse's lawyer will know lots of arbitrators and will probably be able to agree on someone who would be appropriate for your case.

Jamie and Doug each selected an arbitrator recommended by their attorney, and the two arbitrators selected a third to round out the panel. This trio of arbitrators reviewed the facts of the divorce and made a decision, acting in the role of the judge at a trial. While the fee will vary, hiring several attorneys can make this option especially costly. Depending on the state, arbitration can be binding or nonbinding. It's important to know which type of arbitration you're agreeing to so that you don't go through a costly process only to find out that your soon-to-be ex won't sign off on the panel's decision. "I was nervous because I knew the arbitration panel's decision would be final," Jamie says. "I didn't get everything I wanted, but I thought the decision was a good compromise and I was relieved the endless back and forth was finally over."

Litigation $$$$$

Litigation is a legal term meaning "carrying out a lawsuit." It doesn't mean the divorce necessarily winds up in court. But if both sides dig in their heels instead of cooperating, the threat of going to court is usually a good incentive to come to terms. Eleanor and Harold ultimately wound up litigating after mediation stalled. Negotiations fell apart when Eleanor learned from her daughter, Brie, that Harold had moved in with his girlfriend, Eva. That's when Eleanor refused to agree to anything. Harold, who was pressured by Eva to finalize his divorce, realized mediation wasn't going to work. Opting to litigate to move things along, Harold hired a highly skilled but not overly contentious negotiator. He knew as a judge himself that a combative approach would only prolong the pain and make legal fees soar. Eleanor selected a combative attorney, feeling she wanted to be ready to fight.

If you're like Eleanor and Harold and you can't come to a reasonable settlement with your spouse, then going to court might be the only way to resolve the issues. If you do end up in court, a judge who knows very little about you and your family will make the final decisions about the custody of your kids, your property, your money, and more. Harold knew this better than anyone. However, he also knew Eleanor and didn't want to give up another three years of his life fighting with her.

HIRING THE RIGHT PROFESSIONAL HELP

Once you know what kind of divorce you will likely have, it's time to hire the right support. A good starting point to finding an attorney, mediator, or paralegal is through a recommendation or referral from friends or family. Ask around and start gathering names of people to consider and to avoid. Jill found the mediator she hired through a family friend. Gina went with a

BEWARE OF BILLABLE HOURS!

Be sure you consider the following when hiring and working with an attorney:

Every minute is billable. Renée was surprised to learn that the attorney she consulted to learn more about her divorce options—should that be in her future—had a $400 an hour rate that was broken down into fifteen-minute billable time blocks. A short email requiring a "yes" or "no" answer cost her $100. She realized it made more sense to gather several questions before contacting her attorney.

Attorneys without a support staff. Suzanne hired a female solo practitioner but soon discovered the disadvantages of a one-woman show. Her attorney didn't work with a paralegal or an associate, who would have had a lower hourly rate, so Suzanne found herself paying the same rate whether her attorney was filing a motion, sending an email, or photocopying a brief—a costly mistake. Her attorney also wasn't easy to reach.

Attorneys who stir the pot. Some lawyers may try to make a contentious split even more so to rack up billable hours. An attorney friend told us about a colleague who would keep matters stalled until he had pocketed $20,000 per divorce case.

recommendation from one of her salon clients. Denise found her paralegal through a neighbor. After you have collected a few names, have in-person interviews with two or three prospects. They will all have different styles, and you can tell a lot about whether you want to work with someone when you meet face-to-face.

When Jamie met with a highly recommended local attorney, she realized he didn't appear strong enough to represent her in a powerful way in what she knew would be a contentious divorce with Doug. Jamie eventually found the right lawyer for her through her dentist. Amali interviewed several attorneys before she chose one who took time to answer all her questions thoughtfully. She was looking for an amicable process and had quickly nixed the first person she met, an aggressive attorney who suggested she file for a permanent restraining order before he even heard any details of her case just to "set the stage for the divorce."

POPULAR MISCONCEPTIONS

Many women we know mistakenly thought that splitting up would mean splitting everything down the middle. Renée assumed that if she and Hector were to divorce, the value of the home and vacation property she and Hector enjoyed would be divided fifty-fifty. It turned out that Hector was the sole owner of their beach house in Puerto Rico, which had been given to him when he turned eighteen, long before he married Renée. That meant Renée was not entitled to half the value. She learned that there is no rule that automatically entitles each spouse to half of the marital assets. A fifty-fifty split, or something close to it, depends on many factors, including whether both spouses are earning similar salaries, the length of the marriage, as well as the earning potential and health of each spouse.

> "It was tough to discover that a house I'd thought of as mine for over thirty years actually wasn't."
>
> —Renée

Of course, men aren't the only ones to pay alimony. Denise, the family breadwinner, discovered that all guidelines pointed to her paying Mitch both alimony and child support. This oversight meant she had to start from scratch with the monthly budget she had already carefully drawn up. Eleanor assumed she would

YOU DON'T NEED TO GO TO LAW SCHOOL, BUT . . .

Before you read this chapter, you may not have known that pendente lite is a temporary support order that can be a critical
lifeline, since a divorce can take years to finalize. Here are some more
terms you'll want to understand:

Property Settlement Agreement (PSA) Commonly known as a
separation agreement, this is the detailed official agreement that
a married couple reaches about how they will move forward during separation and divorce. It includes the parenting arrangements,
child support, alimony, property and debt distribution, and more.
(This agreement is called a PSA in New Jersey. The name may vary
in your state.)

Qualified domestic relations order is a court order giving one
spouse a share of the other spouse's pension or retirement funds.

Relief is whatever you or your husband ask the court to do, either
dissolve the marriage, award support, enforce a prior court order, or
divide property.

Alimony or spousal support is a legal obligation to provide financial
support to a spouse after separation or divorce. The spouse with the
lower income can pursue getting alimony from the other. Alimony
counts as income, and you will be taxed on the alimony you receive.

Child support is arranged as part of your settlement. Your mediator
or attorney will use established guidelines to calculate this payment. It's based on your incomes, expenses, and parenting schedule.
Overnight visits with the children are counted monthly to help come
up with the number.

automatically receive tax-free alimony for life because she had been married
more than ten years and she had never held a job. To her dismay, she learned
that no set number of years of marriage automatically entitles you to permanent alimony. What's more, alimony is considered income and is taxed.
She found out that the longer the marriage lasted, the more likely you are to
receive permanent alimony. However, courts consider many factors along with

PUNISHING HIM OR HURTING YOURSELF?

Get clear on your motivation before you go the route of punishing your ex. When we're filled with "he's wrong/I'm right" anger, it can be all too easy to fall down the slippery slope of filing motions against each other or reporting to your attorney every frustrating thing your ex has done to the tune of $300 an hour. Once the bills start to arrive and you see that your complaining has cost you the equivalent of a brand-new Honda Odyssey, you will have a new definition for "petty cash."

Carlotta didn't care about much in the first year after her split, but she did want to make sure that Bill shared her pain. Looking back, she regrets allowing her emotions to guide so many decisions. "I thought I was dragging out the divorce to punish Bill, but I was really punishing and hurting myself," Carlotta said. "He had moved on."

the length of your marriage, such as your spouse's ability to pay, your age and health as well as that of your spouse, maintaining the "marital standard of living," and more.

Jamie thought she would easily get full custody of her boys because Doug worked full-time while she worked a part-time job at the ad agency, and she had evidence of his drinking problem. Her attorney explained that custody is actually determined by what a judge considers to be "the best interests" of your children; there is no guarantee that the children will automatically live solely with their mother. Jamie wound up getting primary residential custody, meaning the boys lived with her most school nights. However, she had joint legal custody, so that both she and Doug were involved in all decisions affecting their children's health care, schooling, and where they live.

Another popular misconception is that a divorce can get finalized within a few months. For our friends, the average was closer to two years, mainly because it took time for both sides to stop disagreeing and start compromising. It's wise to get ready for a marathon, not a sprint. Meghan realized about eight months into the haggling that she was having trouble mustering the energy to hash things out with Joan. This almost cost her, until her friends encouraged her to take a more active approach. "I was so tapped out emotionally and in every way that I was agreeing to a lot just to end the back and forth with Joan," says Meghan. "I almost gave up important things, like the log cabin."

These are strong reminders of the importance of consulting an attorney about how the laws and guidelines in your state apply to you. Don't assume that what happened to your best friend's cousin in Toledo will apply to you if you live in Wichita. Knowledge truly is power.

> "Not signing papers or agreeing to terms didn't stop Bill from being happy with another woman. It just slowed down my own healing process and my own ability to get past the split."
>
> —Carlotta

SHOULD YOU GET A SEPARATION AGREEMENT?

Some couples opt to draft a legal separation agreement, usually a temporary fix (though you could stay legally separated forever if that's what you both choose). This agreement makes sure you have access to liquid assets and stay on his health insurance plan or he on yours. It can cover such items as the division of assets and debt, alimony, child support, and visitation. Of note, it can also limit your liability if your husband racks up debt after you separate but before you actually divorce.

You can find examples of separation agreements online at sites like Findlaw .com and Nolo.com. If you and your soon-to-be ex don't get along, like Jamie and Doug, or Iris and Flint, reaching a legal separation agreement can prove time consuming, frustrating, and expensive. Denise and Mitch, however, compromised and talked things out, drafting and signing their separation agreement in two weeks. If you're testing the waters of a trial separation, like Pilar and Justin, or Renée and Hector, you may or may not want to draft a formal agreement. Pilar went to Findlaw.com for help drafting a temporary separation agreement that she and Justin signed.

The finish line for most couples is to sign a final divorce decree that spells out all things financial for the future. This can take months, or even years, depending on the complexity of your finances and how well you and your husband can compromise.

DIFFERENT TYPES OF CUSTODY

Wondering how the custody arrangement for your kids is going to turn out can be the most emotionally fraught part of your divorce. In most cases, you will end up with joint custody, meaning you and your ex will share time with your child and share in making decisions about your child's care, including the school they attend and medical decisions. One parent needs to be chosen as the "parent of primary residence," generally the parent who has the child for the most overnights. If parents who share custody fifty-fifty can't agree, the court will determine the parent of primary residence. This is the home that is considered the child's residence when it comes to determining the school the child is zoned for and other matters. The types of custody include:

JOINT PHYSICAL CUSTODY. Both parents share their respective homes with the child, and the child stays with each of them according to a predetermined schedule or agreement. The schedule for the overnights does not have to be fifty-fifty.

JOINT LEGAL CUSTODY. Both parents are involved in the long-term decisions that impact their child's welfare, including issues relating to health care, school, sports and activities, and more.

SOLE CUSTODY. One parent has decision-making authority over the child, in addition to providing the child's primary residence. The other parent is almost always awarded some form of visitation.

When the court rules in favor of joint custody, parents work together to determine a parenting schedule. Many states require a written parenting plan, but even if your state doesn't, it can be helpful to put your schedule down on paper. Suzanne and her husband crafted an agreement that allowed for schedule changes and flexibility. "We were committed to doing what was in our son's best interest," she says. "We tried to accommodate each other's schedule changes and requests whenever possible."

The agreement, no matter how you reach it, will bring about big shifts. Suzanne had not spent a day apart from her son since he was born six years earlier. "The first night I didn't have him, I was on the phone all evening with my sister in California because I didn't know what to do with myself," Suzanne says. "In time, I would use days apart from him to run all my household errands or see my friends." Jill couldn't imagine what two days apart from her girls in the middle of every week would be like for her or her daughters. The emotional component can be far more difficult than the practicalities of whether you see your child on alternate days or weeks. Still, being apart from your kids can have its upsides: Jill and many other single moms we know used the time to process the divorce and take care of themselves, and later on, to start socializing.

WHAT YOU NEED TO KNOW ABOUT CHILD SUPPORT

Child support is one of the few legal terms that is exactly what it sounds like. It's the monetary support one parent receives to help care for and provide for their child. Take note that the parent who pays child support can't claim it as an income tax deduction and the parent who receives child support will not see it taxed as income.

Which parent receives child support? Child support obligations depend on the custody schedule and the financial situation of both parents. When one parent has sole custody, the other typically pays them child support. When parents have joint custody, child support is based on how much each parent earns and the percentage or breakdown of time the child spends with each parent, including how many overnights.

How much child support will I receive? Child support guidelines exist at the federal level due to the Child Support Enforcement Act and also at the state level, with variations state to state. Be sure to understand the specifics in your state. You and your spouse will be asked to complete detailed forms listing all your finances and expenses, which the court or your attorney will use to calculate child support. Most states consider the following to determine the formula for support:

1. The income and the ability of the parent expected to pay and how many other support orders (i.e., other children) this parent has.

2. The financial needs of the children, including health insurance, day care, education, after-school activities. and special needs.

3. The income and needs of the parent with custody of the child.

4. The child's standard of living before the divorce. Most courts recognize that it will be difficult to maintain the exact same standard as before the divorce because the parents' income now supports two households.

5. The child's own resources (if perhaps he or she has a trust or an inheritance).

HOW TO DRAFT AN EFFECTIVE PARENTING PLAN

A key part of the separation agreement is the parenting plan. The court requires parents who divorce to have this document, along with divorce paperwork. Depending on the jurisdiction, separated parents may also enter into a parenting plan without going to court. The most detailed parenting plans will spell out everything from bedtime routines and time spent with relatives to when

TAKE A LONG-TERM VIEW

Jamie's attorney advised her to consider not only present needs but also what she wanted five years out. "I knew I wanted to move closer to my parents in Chicago by the time the kids started middle school, so that they could help out with the kids," said Jamie, whose boys were five and seven when she left her marriage. "Even though that was a few years away, my lawyer said I needed to start planning for it now."

She tried to include language in her original parenting plan that would allow her to relocate to another state, but Doug would not agree. She wound up pursuing sole custody due to what she saw as his violent and negligent behavior as well as his escalating drinking problem. Eventually she prevailed and won sole custody.

Many of our friends wound up back in court after their divorces were finalized because they didn't think about their future needs or include enough detail in their parenting plans. Do your best to think ahead.

it's okay to introduce a new romantic relationship to the child and more. The level of detail in these plans generally reflects how cooperative or antagonistic parents are. It's best for couples at odds to have as much as possible spelled out to limit interaction and disagreements. This helped Jamie and Doug, Carlotta and Bill, and Iris and Flint have fewer blowouts. If you have a cantankerous ex, like Iris did, who went through a phase of calling the cops at the drop of a hat over ambiguity in their original agreement (*"Snow days are my days because I have the sleds! Give me the kids—or I'm calling the cops!"*), the Property Settlement Agreement (PSA), which includes the parenting plan, is what you will be showing the police when they arrive at your door during a custody dispute. That's why the less room for interpretation, the better.

In contrast, Denise and Mitch, and Suzanne and her ex, had less detailed and more flexible parenting agreements, knowing they could talk through issues as they arose. As a rule of thumb, we have seen that the most successful parenting plans tend to be those that are specific and put the kids first. The items below are only the tip of the iceberg, to give you an idea of what can be included in your parenting plan.

LIVING ARRANGEMENTS. The biggest decision is whether the child will live mainly in one residence or move between two homes. If a child is dividing time between two homes, it's a good idea to specify times, days, locations, and the people responsible for pickup and drop-off. Other considerations include how to make it easier for your child if they forget items at the other parent's home. Do they carry clothes between homes? For Iris, with three children, this was particularly challenging. "Something was always missing, whether it was tennis shoes or a teddy bear," Iris says. "We had to have two sets of certain essentials, such as rain gear, jackets, hats, and gloves."

VACATIONS, HOLIDAYS, AND SPECIAL DAYS. These are going to be tricky. You will want to specify whether you rotate holidays each year and which holidays are more important to one parent than the other. How will you handle your child's birthdays, and the parents' birthdays? Many opt for online tools to help keep track of schedules, including Google Calendar and Our Family Wizard, which you can access on a smartphone.

HEALTH CARE. Who will pay for the child's health insurance? How will decisions be made about medical and dental issues? What about vaccinations or other preventative treatments? Who will take the child to medical appointments? If your child is ill and needs to stay home from school, who will take time off work?

TRAVEL. Who will keep the child's passport? How much notice will be given to the other parent about trips out of the country? Do both parents need to sign off on every trip? Jill put in her parenting plan that her girls would be able to spend two weeks every summer with their grandparents. It's up to you whether you include such specifics or not.

COMMUNICATION BETWEEN PARENTS. Iris spelled out in her parenting agreement that Flint was only to email her, no more than twice a day, only between 9:00 a.m. and 9:00 p.m., and to call only in case of emergency. Agreements can detail what information has to be communicated to the other parent, including school updates and travel plans; whether communication should be by email, text, or telephone; and the frequency.

BUILDING A CUSTODY CASE . . . IF YOU NEED TO

If you're looking to get sole legal and physical custody of your kids, like Jamie or Iris, but your ex is opposed, this will be challenging because it isn't the norm. Jamie believed she should get sole custody because of her husband's drinking habit; he overindulged on a regular basis, and it impacted the boys. Her attorney set her straight: "Kids have a right to have a bad dad or a bad mom." He explained that she would need to build a case that Doug was a danger to their sons. Overall, judges are looking for parents who encourage and facilitate a healthy lifestyle. If you feel that your child is in physical or psychological danger, the burden of proof will fall on your shoulders, as it did for Jamie.

Physical well-being takes into account your child's routine, sleeping habits, eating schedule, medications, and any special-needs considerations. Psychological well-being encompasses the environment that the child is exposed to and the experience that the child has with that parent. Judges are looking for parents who put their children first, who don't try to negatively

Resources — Legal Information

Womansdivorce.com. This site includes information about all aspects of divorce, from the time you split to the aftermath. It offers state-by-state legal information and links to forms you may need.

Divorcenet.com. This site clearly presents legal information about custody, child support, alimony, and more. Especially useful is a state-by-state breakdown that includes the factors a judge may consider when deciding custody. Each state has its own rules about what is in "the best interest of the child."

Divorce Attorney Crash Course by Philip Andrews. This book offers valuable information about picking the right attorney and how to work effectively together.

impact a child's relationship with the other parent, and who have a safe, structured, and loving home environment.

1. AVOID "HE SAID/SHE SAID" AND GATHER ALL THE PROOF YOU CAN. Iris believed she had evidence that would show her ex was unfit to have joint custody. She felt he harassed her and had been negligent when he left their three young children, ages two, six, and eight, home alone for ten minutes while he ran an errand, something neighbors had witnessed. He also fed them junk food and neglected to give their girls the proper treatment when they got lice at school. Iris's attorney told her that she needed stronger evidence to have a chance at winning in court, including police reports, phone records to indicate harassment, and more.

2. KEEP ALL HIS TEXTS AND EMAILS. Jamie downloaded the PhoneView app to easily print threatening text messages from her ex. Before she wrote anything to him, she would ask herself how it would look to a judge. Her advice: "Write in a calm, factual manner, sticking to the issues at hand, without name-calling. Don't have phone conversations with your ex. Keep everything in writing in case you need proof of the way he speaks to you."

3. ASK YOUR FAMILY AND FRIENDS TO WRITE CERTIFIED LETTERS ATTESTING TO WHAT THEY HAVE WITNESSED. Jamie found that these letters went a long way in establishing her case. "Be sure to get the exact wording from your lawyer for the bottom of the statements so that they hold up in court," she says. "Have each person sign and date their letters." After Jamie received a phone call from the after-school program saying Doug smelled of alcohol when he came to pick up the kids, she asked the director to write a letter, which she did.

4. HIRE A PRIVATE INVESTIGATOR. If you suspect that your ex is doing drugs, abusing alcohol, or engaging in other behavior that could negatively impact your children, consider hiring a private investigator to help you document this. Keep in mind that this is an expensive undertaking. If you're considering this in order to prove adultery, bear in mind that many states now have no-fault divorce, which means that evidence of your ex's affair will likely not impact your custody case.

5. KEEP A DETAILED DAILY DIARY. Write down everything your ex does that isn't in the best interest of the children. Keep this diary in a safe place that the children will not see and that cannot be misplaced or easily destroyed. Iris backed up her diary on the cloud and on a hard drive.

What I Wish I'd Known

"I didn't know how challenging it would be to get a parenting plan changed once both parents have signed it. I wish I had included more detail, including who is responsible for dropping the kids off and picking them up each time they're staying with a different parent." —Jill

Chapter 4

TEMPORARY CHAO$

"The only way out is through."
—Robert Frost

Money, worry, and a whole lotta change. It may be hard to imagine how everything is going to work out. The income that comfortably covered one household may be stretched thin over two. You might need to jump-start your career to increase your earnings. Or you may find yourself suddenly pinching pennies because you will be paying alimony and child support.

No matter how confusing or daunting your financial picture appears, it's going to come into better focus and become more manageable. We've been there, and we figured it out. This challenging, uncertain time is temporary. We reminded each other that chaos can be the birthplace of new financial lives of abundance. Think back to those Greek creation myths you learned about in middle school. Chaos preceded the creation of the universe. The tumult you're experiencing is an opportunity to start to visualize your new financial life, full of possibilities, and then to begin to create it.

By now you've likely hired a lawyer and determined your immediate financial needs. As you start to think about big decisions on the horizon—perhaps selling your house or other assets or finding work—realize that you don't have to take them on all at once, but getting a handle on what you need and what's ahead will help you feel more prepared. First up, we help you tackle the tasks you need to address right away, like opening your own bank account. Next, we show you how to create a budget that makes sense for your circumstances. We'll help you brainstorm ways to make some cash if you need to while you embark on a new career or safeguard the one you already have. Jill's new career helped her realize that she could take care of herself and that her earning potential exceeded what she ever imagined. Suzanne saw a chance to refocus her career on projects that she found more meaningful, while she also taught her son the lesson her mother had taught her about the power of financial independence. Don't be surprised if during this period you discover, as we did, that opportunities arise when you least expect them.

LEAVE ROOM FOR LITTLE MIRACLES

 When Jill moved out, she hadn't worked for five years. She'd left her advertising copywriter job to care for her girls and hoped to continue to be a full-time stay-at-home mom for her daughters. "Going over our finances with the mediator," Jill recalls, "it became clear that, ready or not, I'd need to get a job and start making money right away."

While she was racking her brain about how she could have a flexible job that allowed her to earn enough money without the grueling hours she'd had at the ad agency, a little side gig selling jewelry provided an answer. Fate stepped in, as it likes to do, and put Jill in the home of Robert, a local top-selling real estate agent who happened to have sold Jill and her soon-to-be ex their house many years earlier. Jill was working a Stella & Dot jewelry party for Robert's wife, who enjoyed hosting get-togethers. Jill interacted with the guests, styling them, and ultimately sold quite a bit of jewelry that evening. This did not go unnoticed by Robert as he passed by the women gathered in his dining room.

The next day, Robert invited Jill out for pizza to make a pitch. He talked about his real estate business, the schedule flexibility, and how he thought this could be the perfect next step for Jill. "After all," he said to Jill, "what's the difference between, 'This necklace looks great on you' and 'This house looks great on you.'" Jill was convinced to give it a try. In about a month, she got her real estate license, after logging seventy-five classroom hours and passing a state exam. Jill was now able to work flexible hours near her home with unlimited income potential.

After you separate, you may need to go back to work or enter a new field because it provides a higher income or a flexible schedule, health benefits, or the ability to stay close to home or not have to take business trips. Keep your mind, your eyes, and your options open to see what job leads come your way, whether they're from your cousin, a neighbor, a former coworker, or a college friend you have reconnected with on Facebook.

FIRST THINGS FIRST

Amy Poehler, one of our favorite comedians, compared her divorce experience to spreading everything she cared about on a blanket and then tossing the whole thing up in the air. "The process of divorce is about loading that blanket, throwing it up, watching it all spin, and worrying what stuff will break when it lands," she noted. Dividing a shared life into his-and-hers piles can feel daunting, but you can break it down, one task at a time. Here are some immediate actions you will want to take to help you launch your own independent financial life.

DIVVY UP JOINT BANK ACCOUNTS. First up, you will need access to cash. Some couples make a trip to the bank together, as Jill did with her husband, splitting the contents of their joint accounts in half. Iris, afraid her husband would spend their accounts down, removed about half the funds from their joint accounts on her own. In other cases, dividing joint accounts will be worked out through lawyers. If you close your joint account, be sure to make a note of all automatic withdrawals and arrange to have them redirected to another account so you don't damage your credit rating.

CLOSE OVERDRAFT ACCOUNTS, EQUITY LINES, LINES OF CREDIT, AND CREDIT CARDS YOUR SOON-TO-BE EX HAS ACCESS TO. It may take a while to have automatic deposits and withdrawals rerouted to a new

CHILD'S PLAY: TEACHING KIDS ABOUT MONEY

Suzanne

Suzanne considered trying to shield her six-year-old son from the period of financial turmoil that followed her separation. However, she quickly saw the benefits of involving him in this supremely teachable moment.

She let him know that they would be in savings mode, eating out less and making fewer purchases for a little while. And since Suzanne's ex was staying in the house, her son would be living half of the time in an apartment with Suzanne until she could afford to get another house. It all seemed like an adventure to him, and he was on board. The fact that the apartment building had a pool and kids his age was a big plus.

Suzanne also explained how she had earned extra cash at various points in her life, including working as a cocktail waitress and videotaping weddings while in school. She would be seeking extra work now as well. We have to be flexible in life, Suzanne explained, and do what the situation requires.

She took on some extra freelance work doing technical writing, which paid a good hourly rate. It wasn't all penny-pinching: They planned a

account or stopped altogether, but it's a good idea to separate finances as soon as possible. Make sure that all accounts with joint liability are closed.

OPEN YOUR OWN BANK ACCOUNT. It's a major step toward financial independence when you open a new bank account in your name alone. Deposit whatever immediate cash you have—ideally you will deposit enough to cover a few months of expenses so that you have some breathing room while you get your finances in order.

GET A FINAL SNAPSHOT. Review your check stubs, automatic withdrawals, and credit card statements so you can start to understand how much you're spending.

IF YOU'RE ON A FAMILY PLAN, GET A NEW CELL PHONE PLAN . . . ASAP! This may involve swallowing a hefty fee to get out of your current plan.

vacation in Peaks Island, Maine, with Suzanne's brother and his family at his summer home. During this getaway, Suzanne's teenage niece, who had launched a profitable golf cart rental business on the island a few summers earlier, talked a lot about her dream of becoming a Steve Jobs–type entrepreneur. She even hired Suzanne's son to help promote the golf cart business to tourists visiting the island for the day.

All the talk about being an entrepreneur and figuring out creative ways to earn money resulted in everyone in the family brainstorming businesses they could launch together and getting money-inspired nicknames. Suzanne's mini mogul niece was appropriately nicknamed Old Moulah. Her soccer star nephew was Young Money. Suzanne's young son was Lil Cash. Suzanne was Lovely Loot. Her brother was Ancient Dough, and his wife, Pretty Penny.

Soon, talking about money and ways to earn and save became entertainment. Suzanne's decision to include her son in some money matters and the family's open conversation about entrepreneurship allowed him to begin his financial education early.

Accept this and move on. You don't want your soon-to-be ex to have access to your texts and phone calls.

SECURE HEALTH INSURANCE COVERAGE. If you were on your ex's health insurance, you will need to negotiate whether you and your children will stay on his insurance or not. If not, research your options. The Affordable Care Act has opened up all sorts of plans.

GET A CREDIT CARD IN YOUR NAME ONLY. This is another major step toward financial independence, since it will allow you to start to establish a credit history as a single person. If you have income, whether you are working or getting alimony, you can apply for a credit card. Do your research and steer clear of cards with a high interest rate—especially if you might not be able to pay off the balance every month. If you have trouble getting your first card, consider getting a secured credit card. That's a card that requires you to make

DREAM OF THE DAY YOU CAN SHARE IT!

When money is tight, it's hard to imagine that you will ever be in a position to give some of it away. But we like to dream about the day when we are financially stable and able to share our wealth with those less fortunate.

According to research, women are more likely to donate, and donate more, than men in similar situations. The Women's Philanthropy Institute at the Indiana University Lilly Family School of Philanthropy has found that women and men give differently. In one study, baby-boomer-and-older women gave 89 percent more to charity than men their age, and women in the top levels of income gave 156 percent more than men in that same category.

Part of the reason is that women and men view money differently. For men, money may represent power, achievement, or prestige, while women tend to view money in terms of personal security, freedom, and a way to achieve goals. A 2013 U.S. Trust survey on women and wealth found that women are nearly twice as likely as men to say that giving to charity is the most satisfying aspect of having wealth. Someday soon you will be making enough money to be able to spread it around.

a deposit with a bank or credit union account and then gives you a credit limit equal to the amount you have on deposit. A secured card gives you a chance to prove yourself without putting a bank at risk.

BUY A NEW CAR. If you and your husband shared a car, one of you may need to buy a new one (even if it's a used car). Consult with your attorney about the best approach. The rule of thumb is that you want to save big expenses until the divorce is final, not only so that you know what you can afford but also so your former spouse will have no claim on your new purchase.

MAKE $ENSE OF YOUR DOLLARS AND CENTS

Your attorney will want a picture of your expenses. If you haven't already, look carefully at your check stubs, automatic withdrawals, and credit card statements. Understanding how much you spend each month is a key step to making a budget. If you're a veteran budgeter, you'll know what to do to map out your income and expenses. But if, like many of us, you let your financial picture be a little hazy, it's time to get things into focus.

Though your future expenses and earnings may not be clear yet, drafting a budget can help you get a picture of what you spend, what you can afford, and what you need to earn.

You'll want to put on some music—we suggest something upbeat that will help make this task more fun. Though drafting a budget when you're in a state of flux can feel frustrating and even painful, by the time Gina finished her budget, she felt proud that she was being responsible and finally opening her eyes to day-to-day living expenses. As a hairdresser with a cash-based business, Gina ran her salon, but she'd left running the home finances to Clayton. She had no idea how much they spent each month and wasn't sure how to factor in the cost of a new baby. What's more, she had relied on Clayton to have a good credit score. Now she faced the challenge of building up her own credit.

As the family breadwinner, Denise took pride in her ability to pull in a hefty income and provide every luxury for her and her family. When she drew up a new budget that included a second home in addition to paying Mitch alimony and child support, she realized her luxurious lifestyle would be put on hold. "The financial comfort I had worked so hard for was gone," Denise said. "When my income was slashed

LEAVE EMOTION OUT OF THE EQUATION

To have the best possible outcome, approach the financial aspects of your divorce as dispassionately as possible. Pretend you're making a budget for your sister or a friend. When you're emotionally exhausted, you might be inclined to make compromises that aren't in your best interest. Remember: In divorce, there are no do-overs, and you could be stuck with the consequences of a bad decision you made because you just couldn't deal. Instead, set your emotions aside, and keep your eyes on what really matters: a secure financial future.

STRESS LESS

Thinking about how you will afford your new life can make the most zen of us panic. Here are three easy ways to lighten up.

1. LOL—Watch a comedy on your laptop or invite some friends over to binge-watch an entertaining TV series you've missed. Every time you laugh out loud, more oxygen travels to your organs, increasing blood flow and lessening stress.

2. Sing a song—Crank your favorite tunes on your iPod in your car or sing in the shower. It will lift your spirits and benefit your heart and immune system.

3. Chew gum—Who knew that you could freshen your breath while you also reduce stress and anxiety. Gum also helps improve mental performance.

dramatically, I had to make a lot of sacrifices, even though I was still working just as hard."

Eleanor

Though Eleanor was far from strapped for cash, she had never written a check in her life and didn't know anything about budgeting, let alone how much money she would need in retirement. When a pipe burst in her basement, she called an emergency plumbing service. When the plumber asked for $400, Eleanor handed him her checkbook. "Be a doll and fill out the check for me, would you, Nick?" she asked. Nick the plumber stared at her in shocked silence for a minute. Shaking his head he said, "Lady, I'm an honest guy. But the world isn't full of us. You're going to have to learn how to write a check. Or get another husband." Nick pulled out a pen from his pocket with his business logo on it and filled out Eleanor's check, explaining what all the lines were for as he wrote. When he was done, he left the pen and a stack of business cards. Eleanor had a new favorite plumber. For her, there was a steep learning curve in dealing with her finances. By leaving money management to Harold, she thought she was sidestepping a potentially stressful and unpleasant task. She discovered that understanding her finances and planning for her future were crucial. She would have to make the effort.

Regardless of your situation, you don't need complicated software to create a budget. Grab a notepad, sharpen up your number-two pencil, and let's get to it.

STEP 1: List your current income. This includes any income you're earning through a job, alimony, or child support. You will also want to list any savings that can be tapped in case of emergency.

STEP 2: List your expenses. Start with regular monthly expenses, and be sure to include nonessentials, such as vacations, eating out, hairstyling, mani-pedis, your morning latte, a gym membership, and more.

HOUSEHOLD EXPENSES. List your rent or mortgage payment. Are insurance and taxes included in your monthly payment? Also list power, gas, water, garbage collection, lawn care, pest control, home maintenance, home phone, cell phone, cable/satellite TV, and internet. If you might be moving, here is a rule of thumb: An affordable mortgage would be between two and two and a half times your annual income, and landlords generally want your monthly income to be three times the amount of your monthly rent.

FOOD. Groceries for you and your kids, plus school lunches.

CAR/TRANSPORTATION. Car payments, insurance, gas, parking, maintenance (oil changes, repairs, tires). Train or bus pass.

BIG-TICKET EXPENSES. If you will need a second car, because you and your spouse shared one car, include that expense here. Ditto for estimated income taxes and a security deposit for a rental apartment.

CHILDREN. Remember, expenses grow as your children grow. It's not just what they eat and wear and need, it's also allowances, birthday party gifts, school trip fees, and maybe activities like tae kwon do, summer camp, and math tutors.

INSURANCE. Will you continue to be covered under your husband's health insurance plan? What about life insurance and disability insurance?

DEBT. Are you still paying off student loans? Have you borrowed money from your 401(k) or other retirement plan? Think about joint debt as well as your own debt. Do all you can to learn about your soon-to-be ex-husband's potential hidden debt or hidden income. If you think this is an issue, consider hiring a forensic accountant ASAP.

MISCELLANEOUS EXPENSES. Include clothing, laundry, dry cleaning, uninsured medical expenses (copays, eyeglasses, prescription drugs, dental, orthodontist). This is where you can also list gifts.

VACATIONS. Whether you're saving up for a big getaway with the kids or simply driving to see family, include opportunities for fun and downtime in your budget if you can.

UNANTICIPATED EXPENSES. This is your emergency fund for that new boiler, fender bender, or roof leak.

SELF-CARE. This could include gym membership, hair salon, nail salon, therapy, and more.

FUN MONEY. Going to the movies and dinner and meeting for drinks. Just because you're cutting back doesn't mean you should eliminate all entertainment. We always thought the French had the right idea when they offered the unemployed the same discount on movie tickets that students received. After all, who needs the lift of a movie more than someone who is having a hard time?

Resources Budgeting 101

The Spender's Guide to Debt-Free Living by Anna Newell Jones. Written by a popular blogger, this book shows you how to go on a spending fast. It promises to help you go "from broke to badass in record time." The goal: live debt-free.

Youneedabudget.com. This popular site, known to fans as YNAB, offers budgeting tools to help you get a financial tune-up. There's a fee, but the site promises you will save bucks the first month you use it.

Mint (online and app). This free site and app promise to help you manage your money and your budget better every day. Be aware of privacy and security issues that have been raised with sites such as this, and do your own research.

$IMPLE WAYS TO $AVE

Maybe you come from a long line of coupon cutters but you've never picked up the habit. Guess what? Now's the time to take those opportunities to slash your spending and start saving.

Consolidate credit cards. Get the best rate—and then pay off one bill instead of five.

Barter. What skills or services can you offer in exchange for something you need? Amali stays overnight once a week to babysit at Iris's house while she works the night shift. In exchange, Iris has Amali, who lives alone, over for family dinner every Sunday night. Gina cuts Pilar's hair in exchange for Pilar helping her balance her business account.

Collect groupons and coupons. Go online before you buy anything over fifty dollars and see if you can find a coupon, discount, or promo code first.

Shop at the end of the season/off season. What you pay for a swimsuit during "resort season" in March is three times what you pay at the end of July when stores are clearing out summer stock for fall.

Ask about deals. Always ask the salesperson if there's a sale coming up and if they can do better on the price. You may find out the big sale on winter coats starts in just two days and they will hold the coat for you. Don't be shy. Most salespeople will be glad to help you save some cash.

Be a loyal customer. If you frequent a store or shop, you may find yourself getting some perks. Jill was offered a free bottle of Chardonnay to sample because she often shops at the Village Wine Shop in town.

Beware of drinking away hard-earned dollars. You may want to start carrying around a water bottle or your own thermos of coffee like we did. A five-dollars-a-day latte or smoothie habit can run you almost $2,000 a year. Think before you drink.

STEP 3: **Subtract your expenses from your income.** Total up your income and expenses, and do the math. If you make $5,000 per month and spend $4,500, you will have $500 of wiggle room. However, if you spend more than you make, you will need to find ways to cut expenses and/or increase what you earn.

STEP 4: **List expenses you can cut or reduce.** If your expenses exceed what you earn, decide which noncritical items you can eliminate. Until you get back on your feet, consider cutting all expenses that aren't absolutely necessary. This may include smaller items like dining out. It may also include bigger lifestyle changes, such as moving to a smaller place to live or downsizing your minivan. If your town charges for trash collection, switch from two cans to one can to cut your bill in half. Do you really need both a cell phone and a landline in your home? Going to the salon every six weeks instead of every four for a root touch-up will save you four appointments a year. Can you pack a lunch for work and school? Consider calling your creditors and negotiating lower payments. Many will be willing to work with you to make sure you don't fall behind.

> "I thought budgeting was going to be a drag—tedious and depressing—but when I actually got into it, it was kind of like a game. I enjoyed working the system." —Jamie

STEP 5: **Realize the changes don't have to be permanent.** Once you have been on your own for a few months, you will be able to better gauge how far you can stretch your income. If drafting a budget makes you painfully aware that you have to live a spartan existence for a while, have confidence that over time you will figure out how to increase your income. Living frugally won't be forever.

JUMP-STARTING YOUR CAREER

Jill launched a new career in real estate. Suzanne took on freelance technical writing and editing gigs to do after hours because they paid a high hourly rate. Amali started setting up computers in people's homes after hours and on weekends to bolster her savings. Iris signed up for a few online courses to update her nursing license, passed her state exam, and accepted a job at a local hospital on the night shift. This bolstered her ego and her bank account, ensuring a steady paycheck and health benefits for herself and her children. "I started to see a future that wasn't tied to Flint," she says. "I proved to myself I could earn my own money."

Regardless of your circumstances, it's important to stay optimistic and realize there's always a way: You could get a job in retail; work as a waitress, dog walker, or virtual assistant; start an errand business; be a nanny or a kid chauffeur. To cut costs you might barter with a friend for child care or get a tenant to move in, as Meghan did. She was still taking courses to be a certified massage therapist and needed to supplement the pendente lite she was receiving from Joan. You get the idea. There are many options when you believe that you can do whatever it takes to take care of yourself.

Quick New Careers

Here are six interesting jobs that in most states require only six months of training (or less).

1. PHLEBOTOMIST

THE JOB: Draw blood samples from patients for medical tests, transfusions, or research.

WHAT YOU NEED TO DO: 80 hours of training, state certification by your state department of health services.

THE MARKET: Jobs are plentiful in hospitals, doctors' offices, and clinics.

ANNUAL SALARY RANGE: $24,000–$37,000

LEARN MORE: Bureau of Labor Statistics (bls.gov/ooh/healthcare/phlebotomists.htm)

2. HEALTH/MEDICAL INTERPRETER

THE JOB: Help non-English-speaking patients communicate with doctors, nurses, and other medical staff. You need to be fluent in a second language. Employers include medical facilities and interpreter agencies.

WHAT YOU NEED TO DO: Certificate programs range from 40 to 400 hours.

THE MARKET: It's an expanding field.

ANNUAL SALARY RANGE: $35,000–$60,000 depending on skill level

LEARN MORE: National Board of Certification for Medical Interpreters (certifiedmedicalinterpreters.org)

3. PARALEGAL (SOMETIMES CALLED LEGAL ASSISTANT)

THE JOB: Assist lawyers with admin and research work, including court and document prep.

WHAT YOU NEED TO DO: There is no universal certificate for paralegals, and training programs vary; some go with on-the-job training.

THE MARKET: Jobs are plentiful. However you break in, it's a lucrative field.

ANNUAL SALARY RANGE: $40,000–$50,000

LEARN MORE: Center for Advanced Legal Studies (paralegaledu.org/how-to-become-a-paralegal)

4. REAL ESTATE AGENT

THE JOB: To show apartments and houses, often on the weekends.

WHAT YOU NEED TO DO: Pass the real estate school test and the state exam. It can involve as much as 180 classroom hours in Texas, 75 classroom hours in New Jersey, and 45 hours in New York. Check the requirements in your state.

THE MARKET: You will easily get hired as an independent contractor.

SALARY RANGE: The sky's the limit—it depends on how many deals you close (on average, agents close four deals a year) and what your split is with your broker (typically, you get a fifty-fifty split starting out).

LEARN MORE: National Association of Realtors (realtor.org)

5. COCKTAIL WAITRESS/BARTENDER

THE JOB: Mix and/or serve drinks. Bonus points if you can remember what everyone is having for refills, especially as they get intoxicated.

WHAT YOU NEED TO DO: Take a weekend bartending course and get a certificate or go through a brief training program at the restaurant that hires you.

THE MARKET: People love to drink. They always have and they always will. What's more, this job is recession-proof.

SALARY RANGE: Both jobs can pay over $200 cash a night at higher-end establishments. Generally the nicer the place, the more expensive the drinks, the more you will earn.

LEARN MORE: Career Overview (careeroverview.com/food-service-careers.html)

6. CERTIFIED NURSE ASSISTANT

THE JOB: Doing simple tasks helping the nurse and the patients.

WHAT YOU NEED TO DO: The typical Certified Nurse Assistant (CNA) training takes approximately six weeks, but you can also find programs that take more or less time.

THE MARKET: The health industry is booming.

SALARY RANGE: Around $200 a day

LEARN MORE: National Network of Career Nursing Assistants (cna-network.org)

SAFEGUARDING YOUR JOB DURING YOUR DIVORCE

If you already have a job while you're going through the upheaval of your divorce, it's important to protect it. You will want to make sure the challenges going on in your personal life don't spill over into your professional life. You will be spending time preparing legal paperwork, meeting with your attorney, and dealing with the day-to-day drama and changes that come with a divorce. Do your best to compartmentalize so that your work doesn't suffer. If appropriate, speak with

> "When I told my boss that I was getting a divorce, I didn't go into her office in the throes of the turmoil. I waited until I had a plan and could present it in a simple and straightforward way that wouldn't result in extra work for her."
>
> —Suzanne

your manager about changes you may need to make during this transition.

Suzanne made sure she had a plan before she went to talk to her boss about her divorce, so that she could confidently say that the impact on her work, if any, would be minimal and temporary. She had backup child care in place and was using personal days to move into an apartment. She had one request: to adjust her hours so that she would start and end earlier each day, so as to be available to her son earlier in the evening. The request was granted. "What helped was keeping it professional and unemotional, sticking with the facts and providing solutions, rather than burdening my boss with my personal problems," Suzanne says.

A few pointers . . .

SAVE SOME OF YOUR VACATION AND SICK DAYS. During the divorce, you might need to take partial or whole days off to go to court hearings, meet with your attorney, participate in mediation sessions, and more. If you can, save your vacation and sick days to attend to these matters.

LIMIT DIVORCE-RELATED WORK IN THE OFFICE. Filling out divorce papers, emailing back and forth with your attorney, or arguing with your spouse via text while at work will only upset you and distract you from getting your job done. Keep your personal life out of the shared photocopier for all your coworkers to see. Doing so will also help avoid unnecessary gossip around the office.

REFRAIN FROM TAKING PERSONAL CALLS. Though some items may feel urgent to resolve, ask your spouse and divorce attorney not to interrupt your workday with questions about the divorce or the kids that can easily wait until you leave the office. Jamie made this request after her manager issued a warning to her for taking too many personal calls while she was at work. She followed up by asking for a meeting with her manager in which she shared that her divorce was the reason for the personal calls but she would make sure she saved them for after hours. When her manager told her how much the company valued her work, Jamie took the opportunity to ask for more hours, which she eventually was able to secure.

What I Wish I'd Known

Suzanne

"I wish I had seen the dry freelance work I took on to pay the bills as the opportunity it really was. It was while taking walks and talking about these writing assignments that Jill and I connected over our love of writing. We started to toss around the idea of a more creative project we could do together that grew out of our experiences during our divorces. You never know where opportunity lurks. That dreaded freelance job became a stepping-stone to writing this book." —Suzanne

Chapter 5
A PLACE TO CALL HOME

"The only way to make sense out of change is to plunge into it,
move with it, and join the dance."
—Alan Watts

O n one of her morning power walks, Denise noticed a For Sale sign in the yard of a charming Cape Cod–style house only a few blocks away from her marital home. It had been about three months since she and Mitch told Andre they were separating. Denise and Mitch had agreed that she would continue to live at home until she found a place within walking distance so that it would be easy for Andre to go back and forth. Denise excitedly called her favorite Realtor, Jill, who made an appointment for her to see the house that afternoon. It passed the Andre test, with its finished basement and nice backyard with climbing trees. Denise loved the sunny kitchen and living room and the oak floors throughout. They put in an offer that was accepted within the week.

Whether you move out of the marital home or not, what you think of as *home* is going to change. For Denise, the move helped her embrace the changes that were already underfoot. After Pilar moved out, she loved how orderly her new apartment was. "I found it relaxing to leave the apartment clean in the morning and come home to find everything still in its place," she said. For Jamie, her apartment was a concrete symbol of her determination to make a fresh start.

Many women enjoy decorating their new spaces, even if they're transitional, so they feel cozy and comfortable. If you stay in the marital home, like Eleanor, Carlotta, and Gina, you may take steps, as they did, to reclaim the space, rearranging furniture, deep-cleaning, painting a few rooms, or even switching bedrooms. Buying a new comfy chair or even bright pillows can be acts of self-love. Setting the dinner table in a festive way can create a joyous feeling, despite other pressures we may face. Filling your home with plants and meaningful personal objects, like family photos or other mementos, can help you and your children feel more relaxed and settled.

We hope the stories of how our friends made the decision to stay in the marital home or move out, and how they navigated selling, renting, or buying, will help you get a better picture of your options so you can embrace this time of change as the start of something great. Find out how we overcame challenges, such as lack of employment and poor credit, and took different paths to finding a new home, whether we rented, bought, or moved in with friends or family.

LEAVING THE MARITAL HOME

There are pluses to moving out and into a new place. On the top of the list is the appeal of a fresh start and, of course, a place with no memories of your ex. While some women are chomping at the bit to get a new place, like Pilar, others took a few months after deciding to separate to feel ready, like Suzanne and Jill.

Before you move out, do your homework to make sure that by leaving you're not forfeiting your parental or property rights. Before you go anywhere, research the laws in your state, talk to your lawyer, and if you have kids, draw up a parenting plan with your soon-to-be ex (see page 56). This will spell out a visitation schedule for the children and will state that both parents agree that the parent moving out is not giving up their rights in any way.

The fact that one spouse stays in the family home at separation doesn't necessarily mean that spouse is more likely to be awarded the house when the property is divided. State laws require marital property (defined in the broadest terms as property acquired during the marriage) to be divided either equally or "equitably," meaning fairly. As we mentioned in chapter 3, many factors are considered when making this determination. Before you move out, don't forget to value, photograph, and document all the furnishings, art, jewelry, and other big-ticket items you own, especially if an agreement has yet to be reached for divvying up these items. The spouse moving out should only take personal items and furniture from the home that the spouse who's staying agrees to, such as the guest room bed or the family room sofa.

Renting an apartment

Jamie

Jamie had been carefully planning her exit strategy, so she knew she would need about three-and-a-half-months' rent to be able to move into an apartment, including the first month's rent, a real estate agent's commission (one month's rent), and a one-and-a-half-month security deposit. She also knew she wanted to move into a furnished apartment to simplify things. Since her husband insisted on keeping their finances separate, and her part-time job didn't allow her to save that kind of money, she asked her best friend and her sister to loan her the $6,000 she needed to make her break. Her landlord required her to have a cosigner on her

CHECKLIST—IF YOU'RE LEAVING THE MARITAL HOME

- ❏ Have a clear understanding of the monthly housing payment you can afford.
- ❏ Be sure to draft and sign a parenting plan.
- ❏ Break tasks down into manageable steps so that you don't take on too much at once.
- ❏ Take time to add warm finishing touches to your new home to make everyone feel more comfortable, even if it's a temporary landing spot.

lease, and thankfully her sister was ready and willing to sign her name on the line for Jamie. If you aren't moving into a furnished apartment or home, you will also need money for movers and new furnishings for your place.

Buying a house

Suzanne

Suzanne rented an apartment for a few years before she bought a house. When she was ready, her first steps were to make sure she had enough money for a down payment and to contact a mortgage broker for a pre-approval. Next, she researched different neighborhoods in her town. Eventually she chose a yellow cottage-style Colonial with a private cul-de-sac location, abundant natural light, and a butterfly garden in the front yard. Once her offer for the home was accepted, the mortgage process began.

Suzanne had forgotten how much paperwork is involved in the home-buying process. "Make sure you have the energy and time for the mortgage application process," she says. "The first

> "There are lots of mortgage options, and it really helped me to have a broker who took the time to answer all my questions."   —Suzanne

few weeks, it felt like a second job to me. I was signing a lot of forms and digging for past tax returns." Once she signed the contract for the new house, Suzanne packed up her apartment, taking time to declutter, and hired movers. On the morning of the closing, Suzanne did a walk-through of her new home with one of her best friends, took her bank check for the remaining balance to her attorney's office, and signed the final paperwork. About two hours later, she had new house keys and a big smile on her face.

Moving even if you don't have a job yet

Even if you're not employed, if you're getting alimony, you can likely move into a rental because you're showing income. For example, if you're slated to receive $65,000 a year in alimony for the next ten years to be the main caretaker of your kids, a landlord will consider that your salary. You will need to provide your prospective landlord with a signed copy of your support order or divorce decree spelling out your monthly or annual income.

If you have no job and no support order or alimony, you will likely need to get a guarantor/cosigner. This is someone who has the savings or the income to pay the rent for you and agrees to back you up should you be unable to pay your rent on your own. Showing proof of funds (such as a bank statement) and writing a letter of introduction to the landlord can help you seem like a more trustworthy tenant.

Handling bad credit

Be prepared for the real estate agent to run a credit check. If you have a poor credit rating as a result of your divorce, you will likely need a guarantor/cosigner and a letter of explanation. With the help of a credit repair professional, you can typically improve or remedy bad credit in six to nine months. Gina stayed in the modest home she had shared with Clayton and never gave her credit a second thought. That is, until the day she went to trade in her two-door Chevy Camaro for a more family-friendly SUV.

As a candidate for a car lease, Gina's lack of credit was a big concern when the salesman reviewed her paperwork. Gina's cash-based salon benefited her at tax time but definitely not at the car dealership. If you have credit issues, there is no shame in getting professional help from a credit repair company. Since Gina had no independent credit history, she applied for three different credit cards and started using them and paying them off every month to help establish a good credit score. If you're looking to move and your credit score is low, writing a letter of explanation to the landlord and offering to pay a few months up front can help convince them to rent to you.

Moving back in with your family

Iris had some big decisions to make. When Flint opted not to pay the mortgage and play hardball with the divorce settlement, she realized she would likely need to put her house on the market and move. The mortgage payments felt like a giant dollar sign looming

"At first I found it humiliating to be moving back in with my parents. But it turned out to be a great solution. My kids had more time with their grandparents, and my folks stepping in made it possible to relaunch my career. It's not to say there weren't rocky moments, but mostly it was good for everyone." —Iris

over her head. Iris had already decided to get her nursing accreditation so that she could go back to work. She asked her parents, who lived a few towns over, if she and the girls could move in with them for about six months, while she got back on her feet. Iris told them about the missed mortgage payments, Flint's girlfriend, and her plan to go back to work and save up some money. Her parents agreed and volunteered to babysit three days a week (but "not on my golf day, Iris," her dad joked). Iris hugged her parents and started to make plans to move back home.

Setting up house (again)

After you secure a place to live, you will need to furnish it. Jill viewed her apartment as a temporary landing place, so she opted for hand-me-down furniture from friends and thrift stores. Pilar's coworkers advised her to use the "swap/free" page on her town website to quickly and inexpensively get a dresser, table and chairs, sofa, and more for her new studio apartment. If you're considering leaving most of your belongings behind in the family home, you will be setting up a whole new house. This means you may need everything, from a TV to a toaster oven to tongs for turning your chicken wings. Even if you buy your supplies at IKEA, the costs of starting over can really add up. This is an expensive undertaking, so consider negotiating with your ex to secure some key items to take with you if you move out.

STAYING IN THE MARITAL HOME

Initially, the decision to stay is often fueled by emotion. The reasons you may want to stay could include your connection to the house, garden, children's school, and neighbors. Or perhaps you just don't want one more big thing, like a crosstown move, on your plate during the divorce. Many women we know—including Renée, Eleanor, and Gina—couldn't fathom leaving their homes. Other friends didn't want to leave but financially were unable to stay, which was the case for Meghan and Iris. There is a difference between what we can handle emotionally and what we can afford financially—make sure you consider the economics of your choice. Sometimes whether we stay or go will come down to four simple words: What can I afford?

Making the house yours in name and deed

There are two ways to stay in the marital home. Either you're awarded the home in your divorce settlement, like Renée, Meghan, and Gina were, or you buy your husband out, as Amali did. She wanted to stay in the condo so she bought Sugi out, using a quit-claim deed. This essentially meant that Amali bought Sugi's name off the deed, and in exchange he "quit" his claim to the home.

A quitclaim deed is often used when houses aren't sold but ownership is transferred, such as in a divorce, inheritance, or if it's a gift. Harold transferred ownership of the family home to Eleanor using this approach. The potential downside of a quitclaim deed is that it doesn't guarantee that the property is free of any easements, liens, or other encumbrances on ownership. If you're fully aware of the status of your home, this may not be an issue. But if you think it could be an issue, consider a warranty deed, the strongest type of deed. It guarantees that the seller holds clear title to the property and has the right to sell it. No matter what, if you're going the route of transferring property, speak to your attorney to ensure that you understand the difference in your jurisdiction and what makes the most sense for you.

To figure out the value of your property, you can use a licensed appraiser or a real estate agent. To price the condo, Amali and Sugi agreed to use both

CHECKLIST—IF THE MARITAL HOME IS NOW YOURS

❏ Change the locks.

❏ Ask your ex to have his mail forwarded.

❏ Transfer all utilities and home accounts so they're in your name only.

❏ If you have kids, stick to the parenting schedule to help ensure that your ex doesn't think he can drop in or pop by anytime because he used to live there.

❏ Reclaim the space by decorating, painting, or changing up your home so that it reflects who you are today.

SAGE ADVICE

If you stay in the marital home and want to get rid of any residual bad energy, buy a bundle of silver sage online and follow this ancient Native American tradition. Open a window and light the sage. Keep your purifying intention in mind and wave the bundle of burning sage in front of all windows and doorways. "Heads up, this can smell like marijuana," Amali notes.

and average the two quotes. They hired a bank appraiser who charged a few hundred dollars and used "sold" homes to establish the value of their condo. In contrast, Jill, their real estate agent, prepared a Comparative Market Analysis (CMA) that used condos that had been sold, were under contract, or were currently listed for sale to establish the value of their condo. Real estate agents provide this service free of charge for their clients.

"Pricing is an art form," Jill said. "Make sure you have a trusted local real estate agent prepare your CMA. In my mind, a CMA is a more accurate predictor of the current value of your house than an appraisal because you're considering the 'active' and the 'under contract' listings, too. The 'solds' could be from six months to a year ago."

Amali and Sugi came up with $300,000 as the value of their condo. Amali paid Sugi about half of what they would have netted if they sold the condo at that price, depleting her savings; he signed the papers to give up his claim to ownership.

Get clear on who is paying the mortgage

Iris

When Flint moved in with his new girlfriend, a devastated Iris was left in the house with their three daughters. A full-time mom, she assumed Flint would continue to pay the mortgage until their settlement was reached. She was wrong. "He stopped paying the mortgage as a tactic to get me to agree to a lower settlement. I wouldn't budge, and he was threatening to really screw up our credit," Iris said, shaking her head. "I went to my lawyer right away to see what my options were." Her lesson: Don't assume he won't hold the roof over your head, over your head.

Early in the separation, when each spouse's financial responsibilities are murky, it can be tempting to assume your ex will continue to pay the bills, especially if he is the one who left. This isn't always the case. So, how can you protect yourself if you're counting on your ex to pay the mortgage? If you have a temporary support order or any written documentation that your ex has agreed to pay the mortgage, take that to your lawyer to file for an emergent motion. (In New Jersey, this means the court will hear your case in less than two days.)

The court will likely order him to pay should he be financially able to. The next time he doesn't pay, he will be in violation of a court order—a serious offense. If he isn't paying because he doesn't have the money, then you will need to speak to your attorney immediately. You can file a hardship claim with your lender and potentially work out a modified payment schedule or a temporary freeze on your mortgage payments if the lender agrees to recognize your hardship. You will need to prove your financial hardship—expect the bank to ask you for documentation. You will have to resume your mortgage payments once the freeze period granted by the lender ends. If neither you nor your soon-to-be ex plan on resuming paying your mortgage, consider selling the home and moving to a new place that's more affordable for you. With the help of their lawyers, Iris and Flint decided to sell their house and worked out how to split the proceeds.

You want to stay, but you aren't sure you can afford to

If you can't imagine parting with your marital home, you may take on a second job, figure out how to dramatically slash your expenses, or get creative, like Meghan, so that you can find a way to make the numbers work and stay put.

Meghan was living in a new state and in the middle of training for a new career as a massage therapist when Joan left her. She was alone in a log cabin in Maine with no friends and plenty of debt. Meghan weighed her options. She didn't want to move again—she had barely started to get settled. What she did have was an empty second bedroom with its own full bathroom. Meghan crunched the numbers. She couldn't afford to pay the mortgage on her own, and she wasn't sure if Joan would come back or serve her with papers. She needed an interim solution.

RENTING OUT A ROOM

Think carefully about what you are including in the rent (utilities, parking, garden access, linens); the house "rules" you will be expecting your tenant to live by (for example, no sleepovers, no pets, no smoking); the ideal rental term (people will pay more for month-to-month because it's flexible); and the type of person you want to rent to (man? woman? age? profession? temperament?).

Get the word out. Post the notice on your local town website as well as sites like roommate.com and craigslist.org. Tell your friends, too.

Vet each candidate. Have them email you, then move on to a phone call, and finally to an in-person interview. Call their references and Google them online as an informal background check.

Once you find someone you like, make it official. Put your agreement in writing and both sign it. You can find sample rental agreements online.

Understand the tax implications. The rent money you receive is taxable income. Talk to your accountant.

Never one to shy away from an adventure, Meghan placed ads on her town website and put up fliers on kiosks in the village square looking to rent out her spare room. She wasn't too far from a university, so she directed her ad to grad students with "a quiet and friendly disposition." She asked for $800 per month, including utilities. "No pets, no smokers, no partyers, please."

Within a week, Meghan rented out the room to Carlos, a grad student who checked all the boxes in her ad. Carlos also filled the biggest need of all, which Meghan hadn't even considered: friendship. Meghan liked having two coffee cups in the sink again, the white noise of another person padding around the house in his socks in the evening, and someone to talk to and share occasional meals.

> "It's not just the mortgage. You have to have money to pay for the heat, electricity, wifi, water, and so much more." —Meghan

Making the marital home feel like your own

Eleanor couldn't dream of moving out of her home, but living there without Harold was a big adjustment. "I moved out of the master bedroom and started sleeping in the guest room. It was easier for me because it didn't feel like anyone was missing in that room. After a few weeks I realized that the best solution was redecorating to take back my bedroom." Eleanor called an interior designer who specialized in "Divorce Décor" and helping people get a fresh start after their split. The bedroom took on a different feel after Eleanor had it painted a sumptuous plum color and bought a new duvet cover and throw pillows.

For Gina, the challenge was to remove traces of Clayton that seemed to fill every room, whether it was knickknacks from their vacations or the artwork he'd selected. "I went through the house and removed items he had chosen that I thought he would want in his new home," Gina said. This also helped her start to feel that their home was transitioning into her home.

If you're staying in the family home that you have lived in for a long time with your ex, it can be a real transition to make it feel like "your" space. As

RECONCILING YOUR SINGLE-AGAIN LIFE WITH BEING A MOM

Once she got set up in her new apartment, Pilar routinely stayed up late, invited friends over weeknights, and went out dancing until the wee hours on weekends. It was as if her new studio apartment, a place Justin and the boys never visited, was an alternate universe from her home life with her family. "When I was at my apartment, I was a free woman who could dress how I wanted, eat what I wanted, and do what I wanted," Pilar said. "When I went back to the family house, I was a mom again. I talked differently, dressed differently. It was like living parallel lives."

After a few months of high-intensity single life, Pilar started to calm down and go out less. She was exhausted at work from staying up late, was spending too much money on drink tabs at swanky lounges, and was tired of the meaningless flirting with the new men she had met. Pilar knew she wanted to work on finding a balance so that she felt authentic regardless of which home she was in.

time goes on, slowly but surely, make choices in the home that will make it feel like your sanctuary and refuge. Our home is our world, and you deserve an amazing place to recharge and renew.

SELLING THE MARITAL HOME

If you can't afford to keep your family home, it can be challenging to let go of a place filled with memories. Your home is likely your most valuable shared asset, so deciding how to assess its value is extremely important. As discussed, options include an appraisal by a licensed appraiser (who will charge a fee) and/ or a Comparative Marketing Analysis (see page 85). "If your ex is suspicious of the valuations set by your real estate agent, you can get a second opinion from a real estate agent of his choice, and even that of a neutral third agent as well," says Jill. Interview the prospective agents. Be sure to have a consistent list of questions so that you and your ex will be able to directly compare the three different agents' responses.

When considering real estate agents, Jill advises picking someone who can communicate with both you and your ex and who is a top sales agent in your area—someone who has a lot of listings. Ask friends for referrals, and research all the prospective agents online. Do they have websites? Positive reviews? Stop by one of their public open houses unannounced to see how they conduct themselves. Most important, Jill advises, be honest with the real estate agent you select about your goals and the transition in your family. The more you tell them, the better they can help guide you and your ex and find you the rental or new home that you will be moving into.

> "If you don't know what real estate agent to pick, drive around your town and see who has a lot of 'For Sale' signs in people's yards. If they have the listings, then they have the buyer leads."
>
> —Jill

Jill recommends asking a prospective agent how he or she will handle conveying news about the listing to each spouse. Is he willing to always contact both parties so that neither is left out of the loop—whether by email, phone, or text? Iris and Flint interviewed Jill, and his chief concern was Iris and Jill's friendship. Jill spoke with them at length and reassured him that while it might feel like he and Iris were on different pages because of the divorce, they would all be working toward the same goal: quickly selling their house for the highest price, at the best terms. Flint was on board.

Talk to your real estate agent, as many factors determine what you will net, including what you still owe on the mortgage, second lines of credit, closing costs for your state, the commission you pay, and your attorney fees. Provide the information that your real estate agent requests so he can give you a projected net figure.

Saying good-bye

When you decide to sell the family home, you and your kids will have to say good-bye to a place that was a big part of your lives. Years after their house was sold, Jill's daughters still say, "Hi, old house" when they drive by it, and talk about it fondly. When Iris's house was almost ready to close, she helped her kids memorialize their time there by taking pictures, having a pizza party on the porch before closing day, and letting each girl take her bedroom doorknob as a keepsake (of course she replaced them!). Iris left on a positive note, having her two older girls draw pictures for the new homeowners and writing a friendly card welcoming them.

Resources **Around the House**

Realtor.com. This site will help you whether you are looking to buy or sell. You can look up homes in your town to see the asking price to get an understanding of your market. The houses listed on this site are updated every fifteen minutes.

We2me.com. Jodi Topitz, a fine artist and creator of Divorce Decor™, specializes in redecorating a marital home after divorce, and helping you personalize your new house or apartment so you feel comfortable in your new space. You can look at her before-and-after photos and tune in to her "light at the end of the tunnel" decorating and coaching show

that demonstrates the power of a nourishing space after transitioning from we to me (married to single).

Home Improvement 1-2-3 by The Home Depot. This book will show you how to make home repairs so your handyman won't need to be on speed dial. It offers solutions for basic fixes and maintenance, as well as more advanced projects involving plumbing, electrical, and flooring. If you don't already have a toolbox, it's a good idea to get one stocked with the necessities: hammer, nails, tape measure, wrench set, screwdrivers, screws, level, duct tape, and an electric drill.

THE DIFFERENCE BETWEEN ALONE AND LONELY

Does living alone mean you're automatically lonely? This wasn't the case for us. While many of our friends in the Maplewood Divorce Club missed certain aspects of living with another adult, from a warm body beside us at night to someone else to take out the trash or help discipline a child, there was plenty to enjoy about living *without* another adult around. Jamie loved the freedom of setting the thermostat high so her apartment would be nice and warm, just the way she liked it. Pilar loved having the remote control to herself. "Two boys and a husband? My TV was always on ESPN. Now, every time I turn it on, it's on HGTV. Heaven."

Once Hector and Renée decided to proceed with the divorce, Hector moved out, because Renée couldn't imagine leaving the house that she had so painstakingly restored and decorated. She felt she would be leaving a little part of her soul behind if she did. She was now alone in their expansive five-bedroom Mediterranean-style home, but because Hector worked about sixty hours a week as a cardiologist and had spent most of his free time at the golf club, Renée was already used to being alone in the big house and didn't feel as lonely as Meghan, Gina, and other women from our group.

If you're worried that you will feel lonely because you have never lived alone before, try to distill your fear down to the root cause. When you know exactly what's bothering you, it's easier to strategize about how to solve the problem. Jill missed having someone to say hi to when she walked in the door. Getting a little black cat she named Jingles solved that problem. Now when she comes home, she always says, "Jing-a-ling, I'm home." Suzanne missed having someone to talk with over meals. When she didn't have her son with her, she often met up with friends or called one of her best friends or her sister to catch up.

Gina, who put on a good show of always being brave, realized that she felt unsafe at night when she was home alone. At a Maplewood Divorce Club meeting, she shared that she was feeling uneasy after dark. Amali told her that she had a sixty-dollars-a-month solution if she was interested. Gina definitely was. Amali called her friend who installs wireless home security systems and made an appointment for Gina to get an estimate.

Look carefully at what makes you antsy and see if there are simple solutions, such as a pet, a security system, or some adjustments to your decor, that will allow you to feel more relaxed at home. Learning how to take care of ourselves is an important part of our divorce journey.

What I Wish I'd Known

Pilar

"I wish I hadn't moved to a trendier town twenty minutes away from Justin and the boys. I moved because I didn't want to run into Justin when I was on a date. But it meant I spent a lot of extra time chauffeuring the boys back and forth to school, playdates, and their after-school activities. It would have been a lot easier to just meet up with a date in a neighboring town instead of me actually moving away."　　　　　　　　　—Pilar

Chapter 6

THE EX FILES: COMMUNICATING 101

---

*"The single biggest problem in communication
is the illusion that it has taken place."*
—George Bernard Shaw

You're now at odds with a person who knows exactly what buttons to push to see your anger soar from zero to ten. He knows that it makes you anxious when he's late. He knows how much it upsets you when he sends the kids to school with their hair in knots, looking like ragamuffins. He knows your Achilles' heel is your children's safety, and that Thanksgiving is your favorite holiday. He also likely knows exactly what you want out of this divorce, whether it's financial support so you can continue to work part-time, like Jamie, or that you want to keep the house, like Renée.

Of course, you have the same insider's advantage when it comes to getting under his skin. Add to this the fact that it's no easy feat to keep your cool when you're inside the emotional pressure cooker of negotiating a divorce settlement and you have, to put it mildly, a challenging dynamic. If there are children in the picture, you're also navigating highly charged custody decisions. These incendiary conditions can make even the most benign exchange quickly escalate into verbal fisticuffs worthy of Jerry Springer.

On those days when you're so fed up with your ex you could scream, it can help to remind yourself that you once loved him and, of course, he's not all bad. You will feel better at the end of each day if you set a goal for your interactions with him, such as to behave in a way that's civil and kind. This is especially critical if you have kids, because you're going to be in contact with him for many years to come. Iris calculated the exact number of years, months, and days until her youngest turned eighteen and fantasized about never receiving another email from Flint again. She was the biggest proponent of our sanity-saving communication strategies that have been time-tested and divorcée-approved. We're not saying these are easy to put into play, but we know they're worth trying; they worked for us.

INTERCOURSE (THE OTHER KIND)

Time and time again, we thought we were getting a point across to our ex only to discover later that an entirely different message was received. Through trial and error, we, along with our circle of friends, discovered tips that helped us communicate more effectively. For us, the foundation for smoother communication with our exes was deciding that letting some things go and safeguarding our serenity was usually a better choice than blaming him, being defensive, or "winning" an argument.

LESSON 1: Speak from the "I."

Ironically, it wasn't until Pilar and Justin separated that they decided to focus on improving how they communicated with each other. Pilar's biggest shifts were to speak from the "I" and to avoid using extreme words like *always* and *never*. Pilar knew she had a tendency to overdramatize things and blame her often-preoccupied husband when anything went wrong. "You never help plan the boys' birthday parties," she would say. Justin had pointed out that blaming him all the time for so many things made him feel like Pilar was trying to start fights instead of solve their problems. He suggested that Pilar try asking him for what she wanted rather than find fault with him. "Why not say, 'I'd appreciate some help planning Matias's birthday party'?" Justin suggested.

The next time Pilar felt like snipping, "You always bring the kids late!" she recast that critical statement. Instead she heard herself saying, "I would prefer that you let me know when you're going to be late with the kids—that way I can try to find ways to adjust our evening schedule." This got Pilar much better results because Justin didn't feel attacked and was able to take in her message. "Speaking from the 'I' worked really well for me," Pilar said. "I had been so ready to lay blame and rehash every fight we ever had. This kept me more focused on making my point and keeping it simple."

Pilar started pausing before erupting in anger at Justin when she felt he was going out of his way to make things more difficult for her. When she felt like saying, "You keep changing the schedule on purpose so that I'm always running around like crazy" she reframed it as, "I need you to let me know ahead of time when you want to change the schedule." This way, Pilar didn't assume that Justin had some secret nefarious motivation behind the way he was acting, and she wasn't making unfair generalizations. When he felt less attacked, Justin was able to see that he had not thought through the impact his last-minute schedule changes were having on Pilar. He learned that Pilar was taking on more hours as an English tutor in addition to her teaching job, so her schedule was less flexible than he realized.

LESSON 2: There's no such thing as winning a fight.

You may think you "won" a fight, but what did you really win? You still fought! You still chose to get all worked up and to exchange harsh words. Is this the best use of your time and energy? Suzanne realized that arguing with her ex cost her something—time, peace of mind, focus. She took responsibility for her part in their arguments. Instead of thinking, "He started it," she would notice when it seemed he was starting to argue and then decide not to join in. She also realized that when she took good care of herself and got enough exercise and sleep, she was less likely to pick a fight. "It takes two people to argue," Suzanne says. "Once I really took that to heart, I could detach and end a conversation or walk away to prevent a blowout. I noticed that he started doing the same thing. Neither of us wanted to fight anymore."

It was knowing how much damage fights had caused in their marriage that allowed Suzanne and her ex to do their best not to engage in disagreements—not in person, not over the phone, and definitely not in the most dangerous way of all, via text, when rapid responses can propel arguments into the stratosphere faster than you can send a "pulling your hair out" emoji. "Stepping back and taking a breath when things looked like they would escalate worked for us because we both wanted peace more than we wanted to be 'right,' or to have the last word," Suzanne says. Despite occasional slips, Suzanne and her ex did a better job of keeping their interactions civil, calm, and friendly.

LESSON 3: Email, text, and speak to him like he's a coworker.

Amali

If you wouldn't put what you're about to say in a text to your coworker, don't send it to your ex. This will save you from writing countless angry rants and pressing SEND when you know you shouldn't. By following this approach, Amali learned to pare down and fact-base her emails to her ex. Not only was this good form, so that he didn't have inflammable emails and texts that he could potentially one day use against her, it was also an effective way to speak to the issues at hand and avoid fights.

Carlotta

When you're talking face-to-face or on the phone, think of yourself as the driver of the conversation. You're trying to guide the talk from point A to point B either to get information or to solve a problem. Carlotta practiced this technique with Gina, asking her to react exactly as she thought Carlotta's ex, Bill, would. Bonus points to Gina because she altered her voice to a bass range. No matter what "he" said, Carlotta practiced staying calm and on point. But first they practiced a conversation with no driver and two angry people.

EXAMPLE 1: Carlotta says whatever comes to mind, and Gina (playing the role of Bill) responds in kind.

Carlotta: Four days a week isn't a fair schedule.

Gina, playing Bill: You don't think anything is fair.

Carlotta: That's not true! You're such a child!

Gina: No, that would be you.

Carlotta: You always get your way, and I'm tired of it. You need to step up.

Gina: Why don't you yell a little louder so the people down the block can hear you?

Carlotta: I wouldn't be yelling if you listened.

EXAMPLE 2: A conversation with a neutral driver (Carlotta) and an angry man (Gina as Bill):

Carlotta: I'd like to talk about Bailey's spring break schedule.

Gina: What?

Carlotta: I could have three days and you could have two.

Gina: You just want your way! Like always.

Carlotta: Actually, no. I would like the schedule to be the best it can be for everyone. I had an idea and I'd like to run it by you and see if you have suggestions, too.

Gina: You love to control everything.

Carlotta: I don't see it that way. I just want to talk to you about the schedule. Here is what I propose . . .

Carlotta is just dealing with the facts. She isn't letting herself be bumped off point. "He" insults her and goads her, but she doesn't react, and thus provides no fuel for the fire. The first time Carlotta tried to stay neutral in a conversation with Bill, she lost her cool, turning a conversation about where their daughter, Bailey, might go to college into her calling her ex "a lying scumbag." The next time, Carlotta did better, but Bill lost his temper.

After failing a few times, Carlotta learned to steer her conversations with Bill where she wanted them to go. Her advice: "Stay the course. Keep practicing. I stayed focused on the topic or question rather than letting my anger get the best of me."

Did "driving" the conversation take superhuman amounts of control for Carlotta? Yes, especially at first, because she *wanted* to fight with Bill. Was she happy she mastered this technique? Absolutely. Having a clear goal for your conversation (such as finalizing a decision on the timing of selling your house), and making sure you don't veer off course (which is very easy to do), can help you both stick to the task at hand, rather than reenact all the reasons you find each other so difficult. Your next stop may not be Puerto Vallarta, and you know you're not on the *Love Boat* anymore, but it doesn't have to be the *Titanic*, either.

LESSON 4: Set limits when dealing with a bully.

Jamie discovered that when her ex, Doug, prodded her, insulted her, or provoked her (and he knew how to do this better than anyone else), she could refuse to take the mistreatment and come up with solutions on her own. She was adhering to her parenting agreement because she presented him with choices and options. She was no longer going to be Doug's doormat.

> **Jamie:** Can you pick up the kids tomorrow since I'll need to work late—yes or no?

If he insulted her or yelled, she made it clear she wasn't going to talk to him: "I can see this isn't a good time for you to have a conversation. I will make other pickup arrangements for the boys. If you want to discuss this further, it needs to be when you're not yelling at me."

Jamie solved the problem without his involvement and showed him she was no longer going to be mistreated by him. Jamie's approach: If you can't simply end a conversation because, say, you need some information from your ex, restate your question, along with the options for a response.

> **Jamie:** When will you let me know about your summer vacation plans for the boys?
>
> **Doug:** I'm not sure.
>
> **Jamie:** Will you take vacation time in July or August?

When he again gave a nonspecific reply, Jamie said, "Let me know by the end of the month. I have to book camps, and if you don't provide me with the week you would like for their vacation, I will book seven weeks of camp, allotting for my vacation time only."

Iris had many opportunities to practice this technique, since communication breakdowns seemed to be the norm with Flint. She remembers when he declined to help with the estate sale at their home but kept calling her with complaints about how she was handling everything. "I was so tired of him arguing about absolutely everything as I got ready for the estate sale," Iris said. "He stopped paying the mortgage on our house and was living in a penthouse with his new girlfriend while I was taking care of our three kids, trying to get our house sold, and packing up boxes."

Flint wanted half of everything, even insisting on seeing an inventory of their silver. But when she asked him if he wanted to look over the contents of the house before items were sold, he never gave her an answer. "He refused to accept that we had eleven salad forks and must have lost one—yet he also wouldn't come by to see for himself or offer to help," Iris said. Rather than continue to argue, while also doing all the prep work for the sale, she stepped out of the fray. "I sent him a salad fork with the following note:

> *'The house sale is now your job. The estate sale is now your job. The kids and I moved in with my parents. Fork you.'"*

Iris knew that she was going above and beyond to get their home emptied and sold. When Flint was nitpicking over cutlery and refusing to help, she realized that removing herself from the situation entirely was the sanity-saving thing to do. Flint had no choice but to become more involved in the process.

LESSON 5: Vent more, complain less.

When talking with friends and family about all that you're going through, you want to be wary of sucking the energy out of the room with your tale of woe. If you become an energy vampire, friends may start to find you draining and exhausting. Of course, you want to get support and love from important people in your life. However, check yourself to see if you're venting to let out steam, like Gina, or stuck in a dark loop of complaints, like Carlotta, focused only on the problems and how you're powerless to solve them.

Gina had a lot to get off her chest as she came to terms with her husband Clayton's homosexuality. She felt betrayed, hurt, and deeply disappointed. She was also pregnant and having a hard time accepting that the family she imagined was not to be. She would let her friends know how she was doing but refrained from obsessing about it. "There wasn't a solution to my situation, but it helped to get things off my chest and be listened to," Gina says. After sharing how she was feeling, she would drop the topic, eager to move on to hear what her friends had to say was going on in their lives. This allowed Gina to hear funny stories others had to share.

Carlotta, on the other hand, was showing up everywhere as a dark storm cloud, talking only about Bill's affair with "the whore." She noticed friends limiting their time with her or, worse, not making time to see her or take her calls.

> "Even though I could have talked endlessly about Clayton, I didn't want every get-together to be focused on my problems. By sharing the floor with my friends, I was able to stay connected to them and I also got a welcome distraction from what I was going through." —Gina

"I was so hurt and angry that I was endlessly complaining about Bill," Carlotta says. She started to notice friends saying things like, "I understand how hurt you are, so why don't we talk about ways to get over him." It took Carlotta some time before she realized that complaining about how bad things were not only kept her feeling upset but was bringing everyone around her down, too. Carlotta began to save some of her pent-up complaints for her weekly therapy session. She soon noticed that she enjoyed her time with her friends even more when they had the opportunity to talk about everything under the sun—not just Bill's latest offense.

LESSON 6: Don't criticize or play detective.

Talking with our children in the early stages of divorce, when nerves feel frayed, requires vigilance so that we sidestep the temptation to bad-mouth their dad or use them to report back on their time with him. Criticizing your ex, in effect, is criticizing your kids. They are part him, part you. Don't make them feel bad about part of themselves or feel that they have to pick sides. Kids don't want to hear either parent say anything negative about the other parent. Do what you have to do to keep your mouth shut about your ex. If that means not talking for three minutes and deep breathing until your blood pressure normalizes, so be it. Punch pillows in your bedroom instead of calling him names or putting him down in front of your kids.

It's normal to be curious about your ex and his new life. You may want to know if he seems happy or even what he made the kids for dinner. Iris initially took it too far, asking her two oldest girls a zillion questions about Margot, the Broadway actress who lived with Flint. *Does she stay there all the time? Does she watch you by herself?* Iris thought her head would explode the day the girls told her that Margot liked to tuck them in and sing to them at night. Iris full on lost it, yelling, "How dare she?!" It was the sound of Iris's oldest daughter, Jiang, crying that snapped her back to reality. Jiang looked far too tired for someone only eight years old. Whimpering, Jiang threw her hands up and said, "I don't know what to say when you ask me questions. I don't know what the right answer is." Iris hugged her fiercely and apologized for yelling and for asking questions that made her feel uncomfortable. Your kids don't want to feel like they're in the middle of your fights with your ex or, even worse, spying for you. Take off your investigator's cap.

LESSON 7: You don't have to answer right away.

When you think he's trying to pick a fight or put you on the spot, don't engage. He might say: "Can my new girlfriend, Tiffany, show you her résumé? I told her you could help her get a job." Pause and say, "I will think about it." You have put off answering an uncomfortable request in person, and it's hard to argue with someone who says they will think about it. Later you can email him: "I've thought about it, and the answer is no."

Take a deep breath before speaking and before answering. Eleanor found this helpful when dealing with her infuriatingly calm husband, Harold. Though normally poised and composed herself, Eleanor felt like she was living on the edge of losing it after Harold left her. Taking a deliberate moment to breathe before speaking helped her gather her thoughts and measure her response.

Meghan also found this "take a moment before you answer" approach extremely helpful in her dealings with Joan, who despite leaving Meghan, had no qualms about asking Meghan for favors, such as driving her to the airport over an hour away, jump-starting her car when she had a dead battery, or delivering her mail to her. Meghan knew that she was still in love with Joan and was an easy target; by taking time to think before she immediately said yes, she was able to mull over the likely consequences of her choices. Meghan learned not to go with her knee-jerk reaction, which was always yes and usually resulted in Meghan feeling bad about herself for agreeing to Joan's latest request. This ultimately helped to bolster Meghan's self-esteem. She realized she was setting healthy boundaries about what she would and wouldn't do.

LESSON 8: Forgo the verbal knockout punch.

If you excel at witty banter and clever comebacks, that's great—but save them for your next cocktail party, not conversations with your ex. As Jill recalls, "These great zingers would just pop into my head and fly out my mouth. At first I couldn't help myself. But I soon realized that the momentary satisfaction I got from comebacks, like, 'You gave the kids a bath. Hold on, I can't hear you over the parade that's going by in your honor,' wasn't getting me anywhere. I was actually prolonging the fight and acting like a jerk." Jill's advice: Hold your tongue. Don't add fuel to the fire that's already aflame between you and your ex.

Carlotta faced a similar challenge. "One of the highlights of my day used to be coming up with a new put-down for my ex," said Carlotta. "I would start every email with a jab before getting to my point. Big surprise that when a text started out, 'Aye, aye, Captain Douchebag' he ignored the message." She realized that as briefly satisfying as it was for her to make a cutting remark at his expense, all it did was upset him and delay or prevent him from answering the question. Carlotta gave up the name-calling and the put-downs, because when she put Bailey first, there was no room for antagonizing, spite-filled messages.

LESSON 9: **Keep your cool.**

On the day Jill's divorce was scheduled to be approved by a judge, she and her ex, along with their attorneys, were all at the courthouse. "There's just one thing we haven't worked out," said her ex's attorney, sending Jill into a panic. Jill couldn't imagine what was left to hash out. His lawyer continued, "We forgot to include how to address health care moving forward." Jill's ex started to fume and insist that he wasn't going to pay for everyone's health care forever. Neither lawyer had any solution. Jill's lawyer started to pack up, as if he were going home and the divorce wouldn't be happening that day.

Jill realized that she had to stay calm or her divorce would be delayed again. In the face of everyone's frustration, Jill asked them to consider their options for resolving things that day. Only a few minutes later, they reached a solution: They simply added the words "to be revisited in two years." They initialed the changes and signed the agreement; about thirty minutes later, they were pronounced divorced. That would not have happened if Jill had gotten upset or caught up in her emotions. Focusing on finding a solution, instead of arguing about the problem itself, worked. If he's yelling or becoming angry, there's no reason for you to do the same. You're not on the debate team, and no one is keeping score during your conversations. Stay measured and in control of your emotions.

LESSON 10: **If you want to ask him back . . .**

If you've searched your heart and want your soon-to-be ex back, like Eleanor wanted Harold, express how you feel in a way that serves you. Eleanor tried everything to get Harold's attention, from showing up unannounced at the courthouse where he worked and wearing revealing outfits to mediation sessions, to making batches of his favorite cookies and inventing reasons to call him. *"Sorry to bother you at work, Harold, but I can't remember how to set the timer for the sprinkler system."*

Eleanor told Renée that she wasn't making any progress with Harold and time was running out. Eleanor knew he was planning to marry Eva shortly after their divorce was finalized. When his guilt would get the best of him, Harold would stop by the house at their teatime on Sunday, spending what used to be his favorite hour of the week with Eleanor. But on most days, he had no patience for her antics. He felt she was rewriting history and had never truly wanted him, only the lifestyle he provided.

Renée pointed out that Eleanor had threatened him, slashed his tires, tried to bribe him with cookies, and pestered him with phone calls, but what she hadn't done was actually talk to Harold about her feelings and ask him to come back home. Eleanor couldn't believe she was so blind to this simple, honest approach. Renée cautioned Eleanor not to beg him to come back. This might only push him away further. "Pick your moment carefully, and tell him one time how you feel," Renée said. "Let him know that you still love him very much, you want to stay together, and if he changes his mind, and if you're available, you would be open to talking about getting back together." Eleanor knew she would have to plan the conversation very carefully.

This approach encouraged Eleanor to be honest and to leverage the attribute that both men and women find the most attractive—confidence. Conveying your love without implying that you will be waiting around instead of living your life shows him that you know you can live without him. Even if you're not convinced of this yet, we will help you get there. For Eleanor, however, this was an approach that could have worked years earlier. By the time Harold had left, it was too late for them as a couple. If you're considering asking him back, don't make Eleanor's mistake by waiting too long.

LESSON 11: Be honest about how hard it is.

People tend to respond better when we take a gentle approach and show tenderness. When you're open with your ex about how tough the divorce is on you, he will likely be far more responsive than if you yell and scream about his missing a mediation session.

There's something bittersweet about moving on, even if it's what you want. When you can hold space in your heart for the person you once loved, you might find it easier to treat him well, even when you're having difficult conversations. Renée still offered Hector a drink when he came over and treated him kindly. "We were on the path to divorce, but at one point we really loved each other," Renée said. "I never forgot that." Letting your ex see how much he meant to you, even when you're both moving in different directions, honors the years you spent together.

STRIKE A POWER POSE

I f you've ever wanted to look or feel more powerful, watch social scientist Amy Cuddy's TED Talk, "Your Body Language Shapes Who You Are." One of the things she reveals is how taking a power pose (arms akimbo like Wonder Woman) for two minutes prior to an important meeting—or a conversation with your ex-husband—raises your testosterone and lowers the stress hormone cortisol. As a result, she says, you feel more empowered, get your ideas across more effectively, and are more likely to get what you want out of a negotiation.

LESSON 12: Look and listen for the good in your ex.

Denise

Follow the Golden Rule and treat your ex the way you want to be treated. That means you won't bad-mouth him around town, throw away his sports trophies to spite him, or be rude to his friends or family. Mitch initially had a hard time accepting that Denise wanted to separate and complained about it to anyone who would listen. Denise could have followed the trail of his tears and told her side of the story, defending her decision. Instead, she chose to take a step back. "I knew Mitch was telling anyone who would listen that I was selfish for leaving him," said Denise. "I also knew that he was hurting and it was his wounded ego talking." Keeping that in mind, Denise was able to be more sympathetic. She decided that she had lived most of her adult life looking for the good in Mitch, and she wasn't going to let the divorce change that. Denise knew that whatever we focus on expands, so she chose to focus on the positive with Mitch.

WHAT ROLE DOES YOUR EX PLAY IN YOUR DIVORCE DRAMA?

Conversations with your ex are going to be impacted by how you're getting along and the dynamic between you. Whether he shows up as the hero or the villain, here are some tips for keeping your cool no matter what role he's playing.

Sir Unreliable. When he's late again—or worse, forgets to show up at all for his parenting time—you may be tempted to scream bloody murder, even though you know this won't change anything. **OUR TIP:** If your ex is not dependable, make backup arrangements. Having a list of babysitters and friends who will take your kids last-minute if need be will keep you from scrambling in a panic.

Disney Dad. Accept that he has chosen the role of fun parent, leaving you in the role of strict parent. Don't waste energy trying to convince him to discipline the kids. Realize that you will need to extend yourself to pick up the slack. If you're doing most of the heavy lifting, though it may not be fun, know that it will benefit your kids in the long run. **OUR TIP:** If he's the fun parent, suck it up and be the conscientious parent. Remind your kids to brush their teeth and do their homework. Schedule orthodontist appointments. But also make time for fun activities, too, like going to the state fair, a picnic in the park, or roller-skating.

Heartbreak Harry. You can't help it, you're still in love with him. Every time you see him, you're hoping for a sign that he wants to try again. When he slips and calls you "babe" in conversation, you swoon just a little. **OUR TIP:** Use a Google calendar and email or text to avoid the potential triggers of seeing him, hearing his voice, or smelling his cologne.

Resources **Boost Your Communication Skills**

Getting to Yes: Negotiating Agreement Without Giving In by Roger Fisher, William L. Ury, and Bruce Patton. Popular in the business world for years, the step-by-step strategies in this book for resolving conflict and reaching mutually beneficial agreements can be used in personal relationships as well.

The 5 Love Languages by Gary Chapman. Learn how your primary relationship language, and the languages of the people in your life, color how you communicate and how you give and receive love. You will gain insights into all your interpersonal relationships.

Making Divorce Work by Diane Mercer and Katie Jane Wennechuk. Informed by the eight mediation tactics that were developed in the authors' practice, this helpful guide shows you how to keep discussions on point and rational to reach an agreement and preserve the positives that are left in your relationship.

Town Lothario. He's flirting with everything in a skirt. As much as your ex's antics may embarrass you, you have no control over his life and who he hits on. **OUR TIP:** Keep communication brief and focused on the kids and the divorce process, not his latest lady friend.

Mr. "I Want You Back." He may try to extend conversations and contact, show up with flowers, volunteer to fix stuff around your house, and respond spitefully when you move on. **OUR TIP:** If your ex wants you back and you're not interested, don't give him false hope. Be clear about what you want and limit your interaction with him.

What I Wish I'd Known

Renée

"My best talks with Hector would happen when I was honest about how hard the split was. This allowed him to admit that he was having a hard time, too, and generated a wave of goodwill."
—Renée

Chapter 7

YOUR EX AND THE WARM BODY REPLACEMENT

"To love oneself is the beginning of a lifelong romance."
—Oscar Wilde

A divorced or separated man who's reasonably attractive and financially stable might as well have a red neon Vacancy sign flashing across his now-wrinkled polo shirt. Time and time again, we saw newly separated men get snatched up faster than a pair of Jimmy Choos at a sample sale. We call the new woman who quickly appears on the scene the *WBR*, or *Warm Body Replacement*. She can be a fleeting woman your ex nuzzles up to on a lonely night, or she can stick around and turn into a permanent fixture. It's the ones with staying power who can make you the craziest, whether you wanted the divorce or not.

The common characteristic of the WBR is that your ex will hook up with her before your side of the bed has a chance to get cold. This was certainly true in our group members' experience. Jamie's ex remarried within six months of their divorce being final. Jill's ex welcomed a new baby in about a year. While they were not the first women that their exes dated, they sure showed up fast and partnered up with them in short order.

Whether you have kids or not—and whether you left him or he left you—the new woman in your ex's life can take up valuable space in your heart and mind if you compare yourself to her. "I can't believe she looks just like me—ugh!" or "I can't believe she looks nothing like me—ugh!" Learn from what we went through to find ways to let the obsession go and refocus your energy on more important things, like yourself.

WHEN HE LEAVES YOU

Watching your husband walk out the door can make you feel like an expired carton of milk that's beginning to turn. When you see him moving on (or moving in) with a WBR, your self-confidence can plummet as you elevate "what-iffing" to an Olympic sport.

Obsessing about the WBR can drive you to do some nutty things. But we've discovered from experience that there are many ways to harness strong feelings about an ex's new girlfriend, whether it's simmering jealousy and resentment (just ask Eleanor and Iris), burning curiosity (Meghan couldn't help but ask around town for crumbs of information about Joan's new girlfriend, Kelly), or murderous rage (Carlotta would be happy to expound). Without a game plan, it's easy to spiral into obsessive behavior, like our friend Eleanor.

Eleanor goes dumpster diving at the WBR's house

Eleanor

Suzanne had the chance to get to know Eleanor at a friend's block party. Carrying a glass of wine in each hand, Eleanor announced: "Suzanne! Nice to see you again. Sorry, these are both for me, honey. Since my husband left me, the only two men I can count on are Ernest & Julio Gallo!"

Eleanor proceeded to spill nitty-gritty details, and some of her wine, as she told Suzanne how hard things had been for her since Harold moved out. Eleanor said the only way she'd been able to make it through each day was with the help of her happy pills and Chardonnay. "Who here knows what it feels like to have the man who's slept beside you tell you he doesn't want you anymore?" Eleanor shouted, as her neighbors politely tried to ignore her. Dressed in a clingy skirt and revealing wrap top, Eleanor explained that she hoped to win Harold back now that she had a sexy new look. It wasn't hard for Suzanne to see that under her outrageous behavior, Eleanor was brokenhearted.

As a woman who had never worked outside the home and who had spent all her energy taking care of her husband and their now-grown daughter, and running their household, Eleanor felt she had lost more than a man—she had lost her identity.

> **"It's hard to recognize myself in all the outlandish things I did after Harold left."**
> **—Eleanor**

She couldn't let go of him and didn't know what to do with herself. It only seemed natural to her that she set out to gather information about the woman who had "stolen" her husband. When her curiosity got the best of her, she Google-stalked her ex's WBR, Eva, who, it turned out, was just as sultry as her name suggested. Soon Eva had become Eleanor's obsession.

Eleanor went on to confess that her morning routine now included a drive-by of Eva's house to see if Harold's car had been parked there overnight. Suzanne started to worry that her new friend might get herself in trouble. She urged Eleanor to try out a morning exercise class instead of doing drive-bys. "I just have to know what's going on over there," Eleanor said. "I can't help myself." Her need to know kept building until one day, Eleanor wound up in the WBR's backyard at dawn, "disguised" in a trench coat, straw hat, and gardening gloves, rooting through Eva's garbage for evidence of Harold's new life. One of the first items she found, amid Thai take-out cartons, was an empty box of condoms. "How can the man who claimed to have a low libido go through a value pack?" she wailed to Suzanne.

It took Eleanor's trespassing onto another person's property and rifling through her trash to realize the absurdity of her preoccupation with this stranger. "What in the world am I doing?" Eleanor finally asked herself.

 Eleanor's Aha: Though she acted out at first (combing through Eva's trash was a low moment), she realized she needed to start therapy so she could take a step back, get perspective, and examine her behavior.

Iris plots (not-so) sweet revenge

While Iris was living with her parents and pinching pennies, taking nursing courses online, and waiting for the marital house to be sold, her soon-to-be ex was maxing out their credit cards living a lavish lifestyle. "He's spending all our money on Margot and their new life together," Iris told Jill, who sat with her mouth open the day Iris laid out a very strange plan she had cooked up. "He's not going to get away with it!"

Margot, Flint's new girlfriend, was performing on Broadway in a play that was opening in a few weeks. Iris wanted to stand outside the theater and hand audience members flyers as they walked inside. "Here's what the flyer will say," Iris explained, as she read from a scrap of paper she fished out of her purse. "'By seeing this play, you are supporting Margot Weathers, a home wrecker who stole my husband and ruined my life. While I am destitute, living at my parents' in my teenage bedroom with our three children, my husband is shacked up with this floozy in a penthouse apartment. Donations welcome.'"

Jill realized her friend was going off the deep end. "We need to talk this through," Jill said, launching into all the repercussions this plan could have. "This will do permanent damage," Jill warned. "What if you guys can work things out?" Iris broke down: "He's not coming back," she said. "If he hasn't come back by now, he never will." To Jill's relief, Iris accepted her invitation to come over for dinner on opening night. Note to anyone who finds themselves in Crazy Town after their divorce: Be sure you tell a close friend about any plan you've hatched that involves destroying a WBR. Your friend will gently talk you off the ledge and help you regain perspective.

Iris's Aha: "I really lost it and was about to act in a very destructive way—and probably most destructive to me. It's embarrassing to think of how desperate I felt. I'm so relieved I didn't go through with my crazy plan."

Why Carlotta got "div-whore-ced"

Though it had been months since Bill left Carlotta for another woman in town, she couldn't move past the hurt and rage. Carlotta continued to refer to Allyson as "the whore," and everything that went wrong was Allyson's fault. When Carlotta stubbed her toe, she would yell, "Damn that whore!" When she knocked over a glass at dinner, the first words out of her mouth were, "I hate that whore!" When having brunch with her girlfriends, Carlotta would casually note that her ex was "spending Thanksgiving with the whore." Suzanne heard her complain to everyone, from the coffee barista to the waiter, that she didn't get divorced; she got "div-whore-ced."

One day Carlotta called Suzanne up and said, "Do you know that I will be thirty-nine years old next month?" Suzanne was wondering if Carlotta was hinting about having a birthday party when Carlotta added, "It occurred to me as I was thinking about my birthday that since he left me, I've been living my life like it's over, and I probably have forty more years to live."

It was when Carlotta finally took a long-term view that she realized her life wasn't even half over and she could still choose to move in a healthy direction. Did her husband leave her? Yes. Would she let his affair with the WBR shape the rest of her life? Not if she could help it. Did she want her gravestone to say, "Turned into a walking shadow of her former self after her divorce but managed to keep a pulse and control her bowel movements until she actually expired?" Hell no! She knew it would take time to get to acceptance, but she was open to trying something new.

When a man walks out, we want answers. We want to know *why.* Carlotta and so many of our friends learned that you might never be able to answer that question. Insisting on analyzing and figuring out his motivations can be a source of perpetual suffering. The only way to move on and be free of the torment is to start asking new questions: How do I want to spend my time? What makes me happy? Where can I go from here? Questions about yourself and what you want are the only ones that you can answer.

 Carlotta's Aha: She realized she was thinking more about Bill and Allyson than she was about herself and her daughter. She wasn't going to let a man leaving her be the defining moment in her life. Asking questions to advance her own life, instead of trying to figure out why Bill did what he did, helped her move on.

When the WBR is an H-I-M

Jill always enjoyed going to her hairstylist, Gina. She got to gossip, read magazines, and relax while Gina worked her magic. One summer afternoon, Jill showed up to see that Gina's wavy hair was pin-straight. When she asked about her new look, Gina explained that it was part of an elaborate plan to win back her husband, Clayton, even though he had announced that he was gay.

Gina caught Jill up on everything that had happened, and then explained that a deep conditioning treatment and blowout were part one of her seduction plan. Part two was taking a client's suggestion to buy maternity lingerie. Not surprisingly, neither of these approaches made a difference. "Even though he told me that he was gay, for a while I hoped he was just confused," Gina says now. "Or overworked. He may have been both of those things, but more than that—he was into guys, and that wasn't going to change."

Gina couldn't compete with the new WBR. "I needed to accept that the romantic part of our relationship was over, but it was so hard," Gina said. "It's crazy, but even though he packed up and moved in with Gary, I still loved him and wished things could be back to the way they were. I think it says a lot about how much he loved me that he tried for as long as he did."

Gina's Aha: She knew she had to let go of Clayton as her husband. Still, she hoped she would be able to keep him as her friend and her partner in raising their child.

WHEN YOU LEAVE HIM

Even if you were the one to leave, hearing about your ex's WBR can stir up a lot of uncomfortable emotions, including jealousy and resentment. For Suzanne, whose ex stayed in the family home, it was a surreal experience to see how much the house had changed after she left. "The first time I went to pick up our son after my ex's girlfriend had moved in, seeing her furniture mixed in with items my ex and I had selected was a powerful visual reminder of our separate lives." When Denise noticed that Mitch started wearing a pressed shirt when he left the house to go out on a date, she felt an unexpected pang of envy. Old T-shirts had been good enough for Denise. "To see him lose 20 pounds and work on being a new and improved version of himself for someone else was really hurtful," Denise said. "It's not that I wanted him back. I just found myself having a hard time seeing him move on." But move on he did. A few months after talking to Andre about the separation, Mitch tried online dating and started seriously seeing the second woman he met, Emily. Soon Mitch and Emily were inseparable. Denise was surprised by the emotions she felt—envy with a twist of hurt—when Mitch had actually found love before she did.

Jill's ex has an instafam with the WBR

Jill had been hearing a lot about the new woman in her ex's life from her kids and her ex. She seemed to be present every Daddy weekend. After a few months, Jill asked him over the phone if he was serious about her. "Yes, we are planning to be together and have a baby," he replied without missing a beat. *Flabbergasted* might be the only word to describe Jill's reaction. "I remember thinking 'I need a drink, and I need it right now.'" Perhaps it was the timing—about a year after their separation—or the fact that they still hadn't agreed to a divorce settlement. Either way, it was a lot to take in.

"Initially I didn't approve of his girlfriend spending so much time with my girls, but it seemed like they were moving full steam ahead and I'd better get on board," Jill says. She decided that if this woman was going to be her girls' stepmother, it was time to get to know her. "I sent an email offering to host a dinner at my house for my ex, his new girlfriend, and our children," Jill says. "The goal was to spend some time together and have a family meeting."

As the date for the meet-and-eat grew near, Jill worried about what to serve her ex's WBR, a strict vegan. Jill ended up making pasta and salad, along with hummus and carrots, and hoping for the best. The dinner went smoothly enough. The new couple wasn't touchy-feely, sensitive that this might be uncomfortable for everyone (somehow this helped make things less weird for Jill).

After dinner Jill asked everyone into the living room. "I gave a little speech to the new couple, inviting my ex's intended baby mama to reach out to me if she had any questions or concerns while the girls were in her care, and told her that if I do anything to upset her, to please tell me right away and I would straighten it out." Looking back, Jill considers the evening a success. She and the WBR even began a friendship that lasts to this day.

Jill's Aha: Though she initially resisted the idea of a new woman spending so much time with her girls, once she accepted that this woman wasn't going anywhere, Jill was able to relate to her as an important person in her kids' lives rather than a threatening or unwelcome presence.

Jamie's ex dates other mothers

 Jamie's divorce left her strapped for cash and prone to devising creative barter arrangements to provide her sons with some of the nice extras in life. When a good friend gave her a secondhand SUV, Jamie decided to sell her beat-up Toyota Corolla to a mom acquaintance from her kids' elementary school in exchange for a little cash and a year's worth of guitar lessons for her boys. The next month, her younger, Lucas, said in passing, "The guitar teacher tucked me in last weekend at Daddy's." It turned out the music teacher tucked in Jamie's sons on a rare "Daddy" night and then tucked in Daddy.

The next time Jamie drove by her old house, she noticed the guitar teacher's car (Jamie's old Corolla) parked in the driveway. Jamie's ex never mentioned that he was getting private lessons, too. This was the second woman she knew about whose kids went to school with their kids. Even worse, Jamie would learn about every yummy mommy her ex was dating not from him but from their children.

To say that Jamie didn't like her ex dating women she bumped into every day when she waited to pick up her kids would be an understatement. She actually would have preferred not to know what he was doing, and yet she was face-to-face with his parade of WBRs on a daily basis. Her therapist explained that it's not uncommon for separated or divorced men, accustomed to married life for so many years, to want to find a new wife ASAP. So they dust off their weapons of charm and head out to hunt for a replacement to settle down with so they can return to their "new normal" as quickly as they can. Many want fast results and choose women they bump into during their daily life.

Jamie understood why Doug was dating other moms, but that didn't make her feel any less embarrassed. When she decided to bring up the subject with him, he was surprisingly amenable to stopping because he saw that his dating patterns could impact the boys. Doug agreed not to date any of the divorced parents at their kids' school as long as Jamie agreed to do the same.

Jamie's Aha: Though she felt like Doug was looking for new ways to torment her by dating other mothers, she gathered her courage to speak up and ask him for a behavior change.

KEY TAKEAWAYS

Here's a quick recap of the lessons we learned about dealing with our exes' WBRs and new social life. Sometimes these are easier said than done, that's for sure, but we found it helped to be reminded of them.

- Do your best to shift the focus off him and onto you and your new life.
- Let go of all efforts to keep tabs on your ex's social life.
- Speak directly to your ex about the guidelines you will both agree to about introducing new romantic partners to the kids.
- Refrain from comparing yourself to the WBR.
- Understand what time of day you tend to feel the most vulnerable and have activities or phone calls with friends planned.
- Remember, happiness isn't finite—there's plenty to go around; his doesn't detract from yours.

What I Wish I'd Known

 "In those early days of our divorce when he was falling in love with Emily and I was still alone, I wish I'd known that his happiness takes nothing away from my own. It's like the comedian Louis C.K. said, 'No good marriage has ever ended in divorce.' It's really that simple." —Denise

Denise

Part Two
HEAL

There's no way around it—getting divorced feels incredibly sad and stirs up emotions that are unique to you. But there's also an upside. When you let go of how you thought your life would turn out, you make room for the universe to bring you something new and amazing. Discover ways to find peace of mind. Jump-start your self-care routine by following our TLC action plan. When you shift the focus away from *him* and back to *you*, the real healing begins.

Chapter 8

THE GOLDEN KEY: ACCEPTANCE

"I am not what has happened to me. I am what I choose to become."
—Carl Jung

C arlotta was struggling to accept that her husband had left her. She talked to her girlfriends and in therapy about how she felt stuck in the role of the wronged woman, unable to break free. The betrayal and profound hurt she experienced when she found out about her husband's affair gutted her, and she was having trouble recovering. "I thought we had an understanding, that we were connected in a way that would never allow either of us to do something so cruel to the other," Carlotta says. Despite her best efforts, she was spending a lot of time thinking about her ex and the new woman in his life, imagining how happy they were while she was alone and depressed. She wanted to be released from this obsessive thinking but was unable to stop. She felt like she was running on a hamster wheel, around and around, perpetuating her upset.

Like Carlotta, we all face an important choice after our divorces: accept what has happened and begin our healing journey or rail against it, depleting our energy and feeling miserable. If you're dwelling, replaying, or obsessing over things that went wrong in your marriage, then you're punishing yourself and likely suffering.

How did we start to heal? The most powerful tool we found to help lessen our distress and anguish about our divorces was acceptance. For Gina, this meant accepting that things didn't turn out as she had hoped. Eleanor finally accepted that she wasn't going to get back together with Harold. Pilar and Denise accepted the pain they caused their families and tried to make amends to them. Though it would take some time for Meghan and Iris to come around to acceptance, they recognized the stress that holding on to their anger and dis-appointment caused them. Jill and Suzanne discovered an unexpected upside to acceptance: It freed up energy. They directed that energy to new pursuits; that's how they came up with the idea to start a divorce club and write this book.

Choosing to accept what has happened can release you and help you feel more peaceful. It doesn't mean you and your ex didn't hurt each other. It means that you're admitting that there are things you can't change, focusing on things you can change, and not clinging to the past—all 192 pounds of him.

GETTING OFF THE HAMSTER WHEEL

Carlotta

Though Carlotta stopped calling the new woman in her ex's life "the whore," she still had a lot of anger and resentment to work through. After several months of weekly sessions in a therapist-run divorce group, however, she started to see her own role in her marital problems. Listening to other divorced women catalog their ex's faults reminded Carlotta how many faults she had found with Bill during their mar-riage. She was always trying to change him. Having barely worn anything but yoga pants and sweatshirts for so long after her divorce, she had to laugh when she remembered how she used to pick on him for the clothes he chose. "There were days he would wear dress pants with an old T-shirt to work," she says. "I was sure he was going to get fired." His habit of throwing pants over a chair and wearing them for several days in a row also maddened her. "I'd swap out the old pants for a fresh pair and throw them over the chair," she says. "He told me that he saw what I was doing and didn't like it. He said he was an adult and could dress himself." Carlotta disagreed.

These fruitless efforts to control Bill—not only how he dressed but also what he read, how he spent his free time—led to her unwittingly pushing him further and further away during their marriage. "I was really dissatisfied with Bill for a long time, and I let him know it," Carlotta admits. The more she saw that she played a role in their relationship failing, the less like a victim she felt.

Carlotta took a first step on the road to accepting her ex's relationship with his new girlfriend and calling a truce when she attended a school event with Bill for their daughter, Bailey, one of the few times she had seen him since he left. Bailey had been selected to take part in a prestigious sophomore debate team that made it all the way to the county finals. "Our rebellious daughter was excelling at something," Carlotta says. "Neither of us wanted to miss this, even if it meant we would see each other."

Getting ready to head over to the high school auditorium the Saturday afternoon of the debate, Carlotta didn't know if Bill would bring his girlfriend or not. She took a long shower, put on an extra coat of deodorant, and took a handful of Tums. She also took care to dress for the occasion, so she felt pulled together and confident.

Bill showed up alone and sat down beside Carlotta. Their elbows shared an armrest. They hadn't been this physically close since they shared a home. It was jarring to smell his cologne and hear his familiar raspy breathing.

As Carlotta watched their daughter on the stage, so articulate, smart, and persuasive, her residual anger began to melt away. "Something switched for me at that moment," Carlotta says. "I still felt a lot of remorse but no more anger. I realized I had a role in pushing Bill away."

After the debate, when Bailey saw her parents being civil to each other, and her mom looking better than she had in months, she suggested a celebratory lunch. The trio replayed every step of the debate, marveled at Bailey's poise and quick mind, and shared a few laughs. Carlotta was able to be in the moment, enjoying their accomplished daughter, instead of punishing herself by dwelling on past mistakes and hurt.

She realized that although her marriage felt black-and-white to her after Bill left, with him cast as the villain, there were more shades of gray than in that erotic romance trilogy. "When he was no longer the villain, I was no longer the victim," Carlotta says.

That afternoon together helped Carlotta understand that despite all the hurt, there was still enjoyment to be had together. "It was sunny, and we were all getting along for the first time in so long," Carlotta says. "I suddenly realized that we're all human, we all have our faults and make mistakes. I no longer wanted to blame him. I wanted to make the best of things and try to move on, setting aside how much Bill hurt me because the fact is, I'd hurt him, too."

EIGHT POUNDS OF ACCEPTANCE

As Gina prepared to welcome her baby, she received a lot of support from her friends and family. She was still full of sorrow and anger that her marriage had ended and what she'd pictured as family life was not to be. Still, Clayton was involved with Lamaze classes and doctors' appointments. He made it clear to Gina that while he was leaving their marriage, he had no intention of leaving their family. On the rare occasion when Clayton couldn't attend a class or an appointment, Amali or Gina's mom stepped in to go with her.

Gina was making a strawberry milk shake one afternoon when she got her first contraction, followed by a second. She called Clayton, who rushed over to take her to the hospital. Later that day, with Clayton by her side, and her mom and aunts in the waiting room, Gina gave birth to an eight-pound, dark-haired baby girl she named Valentina. Her many girlfriends were by the phone, waiting to hear the good news about mom and baby.

In the days that followed the birth, Gina was flooded with love for Valentina. She also felt a surge of compassion for Clayton. "When I first found out about Clayton being gay, I felt like I'd been living a lie," she says. "But this big-hearted man had lived an even more profound lie by denying a part of himself. He tried to make it work with me because he loved me." She knew his love wasn't a lie. He proved his love in his actions, coaching her through the birth, helping her set up the nursery, and making her grilled cheese sandwiches when she got home from the hospital.

Still, there were moments that Gina felt terrified about raising an infant alone. Some days when Clayton would say he had to go, she would feel panicked. In her low moments, Gina would give herself a pep talk, listing her many strengths, including running a successful hair salon, being handy around the house, and making the best lasagna around.

As she bonded with Valentina, Gina welcomed reminders of her strength. One afternoon, Gina's mom handed her a small box with a big bow. Inside, Gina found her grandmother's opal ring. "Now that you're a mom, I want you to have Nonna's favorite ring," Gina's mom told her. "Every time you look at the opal, remember that you come from a long line of strong women. Nonna raised me and your aunts all by herself after my dad died in the war. I know you're scared, but you can do this." Gina treasured the ring.

Clayton continued to show up, helping in any way he could. Gina counted herself as lucky. "Ours isn't a conventional love story, but I feel like it's a love story nonetheless."

ACCEPTING IT'S REALLY OVER

Eleanor

When Eleanor was obsessing over her ex-husband's new girlfriend, she had little energy left to do much else. She zigzagged between thinking about the mystery woman and trying to win Harold back. What she got in touch with during therapy and by attending Maplewood Divorce Club meetings was that she hadn't been very happy in her marriage, after all. She and Harold had been estranged for years, but she was terrified of change.

She admitted to her psychiatrist how much she had been struggling during the separation, and that she had been upping her meds on her own to help dull the pain. She talked about her outrageous behavior to win Harold back, hijacking mediation sessions and making excuses to be in touch with him, only to realize that she didn't want to go back to the life she had lived with him. It looked good from the outside, and she enjoyed some of their routines and the lifestyle, but they hadn't been close for a long time.

Her daughter, Brie, was scared to tell her mom about her father's plans to marry Eva when the divorce became final. To Eleanor's credit, there were no fireworks. She surprised herself with her calm reaction. "That's when I knew that I was finally accepting the changes," Eleanor says. "It stung, but I knew Harold and I had had our chance together, and it was over."

Eleanor's psychiatrist encouraged her to forgive herself her missteps both during her marriage and afterward, and to do three nice things for herself a day. On the first day, Eleanor allowed herself to linger on the porch with her morning coffee, watching the birds; she prepared her favorite sandwich, a BLT with a tomato from her garden, for lunch; and she got a mani-pedi. These small, simple kindnesses started to have a big impact on Eleanor's self-esteem, helping bring her focus back to her own life.

ACKNOWLEDGING THE PAIN THEY CAUSED THEIR FAMILIES

Pilar

Pilar's young boys couldn't understand why their mom felt she had to move out, and neither could her husband, Justin. Even though he was still feeling upset and shaken by her affair, Justin didn't want her to move out. Justin was left with the role of running their household, with Pilar only showing up for parenting time. Meanwhile, Pilar felt an uncomfortable mix of giddiness that she was free from all the duty and obligation she'd felt and also guilt for leaving the family. "I really felt I had no choice but to leave. I was so unhappy. I was suffocating and needed time for myself," she says. "I needed to find the person I'd left behind when I had kids. I wanted to become a whole human being."

Pilar saw that she had been acting out in destructive ways, like having a fling with the young teacher. Learning that she was in perimenopause added to her pain and worries that her life was slipping by too fast. "I didn't know if

Resources | Finding Forgiveness and Acceptance

Broken Open: How Difficult Times Can Help Us Grow, by Elizabeth Lesser, cofounder of the Omega Institute. Drawing on the world's great spiritual and psychological traditions, Lesser shares tales of ordinary people who have found peace, strength, and wisdom after struggling with illness, divorce, or the loss of a job or a loved one.

The Descendants, directed by Alexander Payne. George Clooney stars in this film as a man at a crossroads. After his wife is badly injured and hospitalized, he is left to raise his two daughters as he struggles with the news that she had cheated on him.

"The Heart of the Matter," by Don Henley. The man knows of what he sings, warning that carrying around anger will "eat you up inside."

Learningtoforgive.com. Dr. Fred Luskin, professor and director of the Stanford Forgiveness Project, discusses the medical benefits of forgiving and offers a nine-step path to help you get there.

I was having a midlife crisis of sorts or what was happening, but I knew I had to take some time for myself to be of any use to my family," Pilar says.

Pilar apologized to Justin for what she was putting him through. She told him she was starting therapy and promised to keep the lines of communication open as she tried to get a handle on what she was feeling and what she wanted. Pilar continued to show up for the boys, staying at the house half the week, preparing their favorite meals and helping them with schoolwork. They were angry at their mom but were still happy to see her when she was there.

Like Pilar, Denise felt that few understood her choices or actions. She, too, was told that her reasons for leaving weren't good enough. But unlike Pilar, Denise didn't feel depressed or confused. She felt clear that she wanted a passionate relationship; this wouldn't be possible with Mitch, and that's why she had to leave him.

For Denise, the most difficult man to leave isn't the man who clearly mistreats you but the good guy who simply doesn't rock your world. Over and over again, she felt like she had to defend her decision to leave Mitch. In conversations with her friends and family, many felt that her choice, which broke up her family, wasn't justified.

It was through the Maplewood Divorce Club and hearing the many stories of her friends and their difficult marriages, dealing with alcoholics, bullies, narcissists, and philanderers, that Denise realized many women would have happily stayed married to a sweet couch potato like Mitch. Here was a man who would take her car to get the tires filled with air, do the laundry, and buy all the groceries she put on the list. She could count on Mitch to sweep the kitchen floor, but he could never sweep her off her feet.

> "I agonized over the fact that here I am, a smart woman, who made such a blunder with one of the most important decisions of my life. I had to forgive myself for marrying the wrong man and then for leaving him." —Denise

Denise knew leaving a kind and loyal husband for the promise of romance was seen as an act of selfishness, but she didn't care how it looked to others. "I felt I had to be true to myself," she says. "It was eating away at me to spend my days and nights with a man who didn't view intimacy the way I did. I was in a state of always wanting a connection with him that he couldn't give me." Denise felt if she stayed, she would miss out on experiencing true love. The price was too great. She was able to accept her choice, and let go of some of the guilt, when she saw Mitch stepping out to date and moving on himself.

WHEN YOU'RE CARRYING AROUND THE HURT

Part of Meghan's training for her massage therapy certificate included seeing clients three days a week. Meghan was taught to begin each session with a quick intake to learn about the client's physical needs or limitations. One particular morning, Meghan began asking her female client, who was complaining of aches and knots in her shoulders, if she was under stress. Without missing a beat, the client said, "I'm in the middle of a divorce."

Meghan worked on the body of her client, loosening the knots of disappointment, the ache of the end of a relationship, and the tight back muscles from all the arguing. Seeing the tension in this woman's body reminded her how important it was to lessen her own stress in any way possible. For Meghan, this meant accepting that Joan was no longer her partner,

> "Around the same time that I started letting go of my attachment to Joan, I started going for body work on myself to help release the tension I was feeling. It made a huge difference in how I felt all day." —Meghan

and that she would survive without her. Meghan truly wanted to move past the failed marriage. She didn't want to carry around the damaging anger and the heavy burden of upset any longer.

Meghan decided that the first baby step toward acceptance was to start imagining a Joan-free future. She would now start each morning with her cup of coffee, a notebook, and a pen, imagining possibilities for herself and what might be next.

Iris knew all too well about the physical ramifications of the stress, anger, and anxiety she had been experiencing over the past few months. In addition to the fifteen pounds she had lost off her already slight frame, she noticed more gray in her jet-black hair, dark circles under her eyes, and a tightness in her chest. Iris barely slept at night. Guzzling coffee to get through each day, she felt run-down all the time. The divorce and fighting with Flint were taking a toll.

Still, Iris was holding tight to her anger at Flint. Though she knew she was paying a heavy price for living with venom coursing through her veins, she just couldn't excuse him for abandoning her and their three young daughters, for ruining her credit, and for being unreliable as a coparent. Iris's parents were worried about their oldest child. Their "little spitfire" seemed to be withering away under the stress. Iris's mother decided to organize an at-home spa night and asked Iris's dad to take the girls to spend the night with their cousins to give Iris a break. Iris's mom let her know that they would have the house to themselves. They put on face masks, soaked their feet, and painted each other's nails.

"How are you picturing your future, Iris?" her mother asked her as they were sipping tea and nibbling cookies. "What future?" Iris snapped. Her mom continued, "The future in which your children grow up day by day and see you as their role model." Iris and her mother had a long talk that evening. Iris knew she was struggling under the weight of the divorce and everything Flint seemed to continually heap onto her already full plate. She also knew that she wanted to live a long, healthy life and be a good role model for her three girls. She would have to find a way to distance herself from Flint and all he had done. "I had to work on releasing him and all the hurt he caused me," Iris said. "I wasn't going to carry it around any longer."

FORGIVING YOURSELF FOR CHOOSING HIM

Jamie

After Jamie moved out and Doug was too busy dating to pick on her anymore, Jamie found herself taking over that role herself. She started beating herself up for marrying the wrong guy and then staying with him for so long. When the dust settled, Jamie's despair centered not so much around his dating other mothers at her boys' school, but on how she wound up choosing such an angry and aggressive man to marry in the first place. When she reread her journals from their dating days, she saw that she was very clear about looking for a man who could provide for her financially, and that's who she found. Doug took her to fancy restaurants, and Broadway plays, and sent her flowers at work.

At the time, she glossed over the fact that he was rude to the waiter, snapped at the usher, and that her friends didn't like how he treated her. Working a low-paying job while living in an apartment with three other women and eating ramen noodles every day, Jamie had ignored the warning signs about Doug's temper. She was focused on the good things about him and the life he could provide. His two-carat diamond proposal seemed like a lifeline.

She had always thought of herself as meek. She was a quiet, gentle, and conflict-averse woman who married a loud, angry man. It took some time for Jamie to accept why she chose Doug in the first place. "It seems sad to say, but the truth is that I didn't think I could take care of myself," Jamie says. "The irony is that now I'm responsible for myself and my two boys, working more hours than ever before, and up for a promotion at work." The act of leaving revealed a courageous side that Jamie didn't know she had and encouraged her to take other steps out of her comfort zone.

AFTER ACCEPTANCE COMES ENERGY AND LIGHT

Jill found her way to acceptance once she became sick and tired of hearing herself talk about her ex. It didn't mean that he no longer upset her. What changed was that she stopped waiting for him to act differently. "I gave up saying, 'If he would just . . . ,'" Jill says. "Instead, I dealt with whatever was happening in a rational, detached way. That gave me a feeling of being on solid ground.

Suzanne was able to accept her ex exactly as he was and have a more peaceful relationship with him when she gave up expecting that they would see things the same way. When differences cropped up, Suzanne no longer tried to cajole, influence, or change her ex. Instead, she accepted him as a unique person who marched to the beat of his own drum. "If there was something that I wanted done in a certain way, I would now do it myself," Suzanne says. "I stopped trying to convince him of anything."

When they accepted their exes for who they were, Suzanne and Jill were surprised how much closer their own friendship grew. They no longer focused every discussion on the men and were able to talk about other interests, their kids, vacation plans, and their hopes for the future.

With more space and energy, they started to explore creative projects. It was during their walk and talks that they realized how much they got out of sharing their challenges and solutions. They started to daydream about how to share this kind of support with other women. They were excited about what they could do to spread a message of optimism around the challenges of divorce. When they formed the Maplewood Divorce Club, their excitement about how women can help one another was contagious. A steady stream of women asked to join the club. Local press got wind of their success and wanted to help spread the word. The response to the club encouraged Suzanne and Jill to explore the possibility of writing a book to reach even more women.

Accepting whatever happened to cause the end of your marriage allows for a powerful shift to feeling energized instead of drained. You're no longer obsessing about how you were cheated of your happily ever after. Instead of focusing on what could have been, you're becoming more interested in what can be. The timeline and the path to acceptance are different for everyone, but the benefits that are waiting for you are the same: peace, serenity, and the ability to move forward.

What I Wish I'd Known

Jamie

"I wish I'd realized earlier that I had reserves of strength within me. Once I stopped thinking of Doug as a monster, and recognized why I chose him in the first place, things started to open up. I'd thought I needed someone to take care of me—I discovered I can take care of myself."

—Jamie

Chapter 9

IT'S AN INSIDE JOB

"The world breaks everyone and
afterward many are strong at the broken places."
—Ernest Hemingway

Mitch's accepting nature was a breath of fresh air to Denise when she first met him. Whatever she wanted, he was on board. You want tacos? Sure, no problem. Want to move to a different neighborhood? That would be cool. Since Denise is quite particular—some would even say difficult—Mitch seemed like the yin to her yang. Denise was sure that after they got married and had a baby, her laid-back, lovable teddy bear would grow up and become the hardworking, ambitious partner she knew he could be.

When Denise would tell her friends in the Maplewood Divorce Club that she and Mitch rarely had sex, they couldn't believe it, because her husky husband had plenty of sex appeal—just not to Denise. What she felt for him after they settled into married life was growing resentment, especially mornings when she would rush out the door to work while Mitch lounged on the couch playing video games after dropping Andre at school, one hand on a Big Gulp and the other on his gaming console. He didn't seem to put many hours into his stereo-installation business. Denise was always tripping over one of his half-completed projects around the house. "What I initially loved about Mitch later on had the opposite effect on me," Denise says. "He started to seem lazy and immature."

For Denise, a go-getter with a to-do list a mile long, Mitch's ambling take-it-easy attitude became a real turnoff. Denise knew Mitch's business could grow exponentially if he just did it her way. She recalled the time when she created a business marketing plan for him, with the hope of landing him more clients. Her efforts backfired. He didn't appreciate her hard work, her flow-charts, and her marketing slogan to "Flip Your Switch with Mitch!" In fact, he resented it. He liked things the way they were with a manageable client base that he felt he could handle.

After her divorce, when she started to look at her relationship patterns, Denise was surprised to realize that she had dated many "Mitches" in her day, men who seemed so affable and breezy only to sorely disappoint her because they didn't live up to her expectations. "I fell in love with their potential, and they never grew into the men I thought they could be," Denise says. "Now I can see how unfair this was to them, and how self-defeating it was for me."

Like Denise, many of us took a look at our relationship patterns so that we would make choices that were better suited to us in the future. We were all reeling from painful emotions—whether we felt let down, regretful, angry, betrayed, scared, or abandoned—and we wanted to do better next time. Some of us turned to old friends to discern relationship patterns, asking them to help us see our history of behaviors and choices. Others turned to psychotherapy to explore stories of their past in order to dismantle old patterns. You may recognize yourself in more than one of the following scenarios. The goal is to become aware of your relationship patterns and of any behavior you want to change. Rather than blame yourself, or him, for what went wrong, we encourage more of a fact-finding mission—the goal is to foster nonjudgmental awareness. Understanding your patterns is the golden key that will help you unlock a more meaningful relationship in the future.

DISCOVER YOUR RELATIONSHIP PATTERNS

Since the split, you've likely spent a lot of time thinking about what he did or didn't do that contributed to the demise of your relationship. In fact, this may have been the subject of most of your conversations, journal entries, and therapy sessions. But as Rob Base and DJ E-Z Rock sang in the late '80s, "It takes two." What about what you did or didn't do? Here's your chance to identify your own patterns, choices, and past actions. Do you jump into relationships quickly, like Suzanne? Do you pick fun-loving nontraditional men, like Jill? Or maybe you kept trying to change someone, like Denise? Were you waiting for a knight in shining armor to rescue you, like Eleanor? Or do you tend to be anxious and sabotage your relationships, like Carlotta? It was only when we took a hard look in the mirror and started examining our own role in the breakup that we got new insight into our patterns.

Our childhood can offer clues. The dynamics of the romantic relationships we witnessed in our parents and close relatives, as well as our relationship with our primary caregivers growing up, can help us understand why we repeat the same behavior again and again with the men we dated and in our marriages.

NEWS FLASH! A RELATIONSHIP DOES NOT GUARANTEE HAPPINESS

Many women in the Maplewood Divorce Club say that their biggest aha was to realize that a romantic relationship won't make you happy if you aren't already happy. Thinking a relationship can fix all your problems is like thinking a new pair of shoes, a promotion, or a fresh haircut will magically make everything okay.

They say that lottery winners are happy when they get the news and then return to their usual emotional state. They're not permanently on cloud nine. And no man is going to keep you there, either.

Instead of looking to outside influences to make her happy, Meghan started looking inside to get in touch with what brings joy and meaning to her life, like spending time outdoors, using her skills as a masseuse to help people heal, and trying new recipes out on her friends.

As a child, you had a front-row view of your parents' relationship that played out for you every day and night. That's why taking a look at your relationship role models can help you recognize your own patterns. Even if we vowed we'd be different, we often play out aspects of our parents' relationship.

We knew that looking at our own behavior was the only way we could identify areas to work on. "We didn't just want to go through our divorces," Suzanne says. "We wanted to grow through them." We were determined to identify mistakes we made in our marriages so that we weren't destined to repeat them in future relationships. "We wanted to be real, but also gentle with ourselves," Jill says.

If something comes up again and again in all your relationships, it's likely worth investigating. Rather than blame yourself for past actions, this is your opportunity to become aware of your patterns so that you can shift to behavior that's more likely to get you what you truly want in a relationship.

Carlotta experiences anxious attachment

Carlotta

When you were dating, did you interpret text messages from a love interest five different ways? Would you imagine the worst when you didn't hear right back from someone you liked? Would you retreat when you didn't get your way in a relationship? Do you tend to be jealous? If you answered "yes" to any of these, you may have an anxious attachment style, like Carlotta.

In her marriage, her efforts to control Bill to manage her own anxiety almost always backfired. She realized a pattern in her relationships: She would act on her unfounded fears, in many cases ultimately causing a boyfriend to break up with her. Her anxiety about people leaving her became a self-fulfilling prophecy because she often acted in ways that caused them to go.

Anxiously attached people often let their romantic relationship consume all of their emotional energy. This was certainly true for Carlotta. She had always been very sensitive to the shifts in her partner's behavior toward her and read into everything—usually as a doomsday prophecy. If a boyfriend said he would call and didn't, Carlotta assumed a breakup was imminent. If a boyfriend canceled plans, she would be tempted to pick a fight and break up with him, just to spare herself the pain of him leaving her. Her anxious energy would often lead to regrettable behavior, like calling and hanging up "to see if he was really home," going to a bar where his friends frequently hung out to flirt with other men to make him jealous, or nosing around his apartment for clues when he was in the shower.

When Carlotta married Bill, this behavior continued. She would over-analyze his every Facebook post, call him many times a day when he was away on a business trip, and pout or sulk when he didn't have time to talk. If she ever saw him talking to an attractive woman at a party, he knew she'd appear in an instant with their coats—and a scowl on her face.

Carlotta's therapist helped her to see how her actions, based often on unfounded fears, led to the end of many relationships and contributed to the end of her marriage. Carlotta by no means saw her anxious attachment style as something that gave Bill a green light to cheat and have an affair with Allyson, but she knew that her anxious behavior drove him crazy and was damaging to the relationship.

> ➡ *Next Time:* With this new awareness, Carlotta decided she would try to stop herself before acting on her anxious feelings. This would prevent her from sabotaging perfectly good relationships, as she had done in the past. She hoped her self-awareness would lead to more self-control. "If someone doesn't call me, I won't make up a story about what it means," Carlotta says. "And if I do, I'll remind myself that it's not the only explanation for what's happening. I don't want to be so quick to assume the worst."

Jamie gives herself away in relationships

Jamie never felt emotionally safe with Doug, but she did feel attracted to him when she met him, and she knew he would be a good provider. She let the pull of the lifestyle he offered overshadow evidence of his temper. "I had no idea what I was signing up for," Jamie says. "After we got married, he didn't hide his temper anymore."

After their sons were born, Jamie found herself keeping her opinions and feelings to herself. She had trouble saying what she really wanted over things large and small. When Doug would get angry, she constantly said she was "sorry" even when it wasn't her fault. It got to the point where she couldn't stand to hear herself apologize anymore. Gender linguist Deborah Tannen notes that men apologize less than women because they're more attuned to the fact that an apology can symbolize defeat, and defeated Jamie was.

Jamie felt that Doug wasn't really looking for a partner but a bellhop to carry his emotional baggage, and a scapegoat. According to him, Jamie should have gone into labor *after* the big game was over; she should have told him what exit to take when he was driving; and why are the kids home with the flu when he has a big presentation the next day? The list of her offenses went on and on. There were many days that Jamie felt she should have her name legally changed to "Doormat."

Jamie didn't realize she'd married a narcissist until a friend suggested she read a book about toxic relationships. Doug was indeed a classic narcissist. The more she gave, the more he took and the more controlling he became. Jamie knows that she doesn't want to pick another narcissist and continue to play the role of the victim. These days, she tries to speak up for herself. "Tiptoeing around doesn't work," she says. "As a wise friend who goes to Al-Anon meetings once told me: 'Say what you mean, mean what you say, but don't say it mean.'"

Jamie also wants to pay close attention to how she feels when she is with a potential romantic partner. She never let herself admit that Doug's angry outbursts when they were dating were actually an essential part of who he was. She doesn't want to be in the position again of explaining away someone's bad behavior. Going forward, she knows she needs to ask herself: Does she feel calm, peaceful, and relaxed with this person? Can she be herself and express her feelings? Does this person make her feel good about herself? When Jamie was with Doug, she noticed that she felt terrible about herself. The reason? "I think he actually feels terrible about who he is, and he projected that onto me," Jamie says.

> ➲ *Next Time:* Jamie knows that her challenge is to steer clear of men who put her down or try to make themselves look or feel better by blaming or shaming her. If she meets another Doug, she vows to put on a hazmat suit and walk away. She wants to feel fully accepted by her next partner—someone who helps her feel confident and calm.

QUIZ: THERE ARE NO VICTIMS, ONLY VOLUNTEERS

True or False? Circle one.

1. I feel like everyone treats me poorly.　　T / F

2. I always give more than I receive.　　T / F

3. People don't appreciate all I do.　　T / F

If you answered "true" to any of these statements, take this opportunity to look at the behavior you allow. You may feel like a victim, but you actually influence how others treat you. You get to choose whether or not you tolerate certain behaviors. We teach others how to treat us. As Eleanor Roosevelt said, "No one can make you feel inferior without your consent."

Jill often chooses Mr. Goodtime

Jill wanted to get over her pattern of choosing Peter Pans when what she really wanted was a responsible adult who could also have fun. She hoped to change her relationship tagline from "Hopeless Romantic Seeks Fun Guy for True Love and No Arguing" to "Romantic Seeks Fun-Loving, Responsible Man to Express Ourselves and Find True Love."

Jill's parents, high school sweethearts, never fought in front of Jill and her brother when they were growing up. Not rarely—never. Jill's relationship blueprint was two people who loved each other, seemed to compromise and get along, and genuinely enjoyed each other most of the time. They presented a united front against the world. Jill felt loved, secure, and safe. She was impish and was gently disciplined, mostly with long "why did you do that?" talks from her dad. Her mom had a steady outpouring of affection for her. She would rouse Jill in the morning with a gentle "Wake up, little rosebud."

This isn't to say that Jill's parents never disagreed, but whatever challenges came up were handled out of view and earshot. This left Jill with little experience of and a very low tolerance for conflict. Jill's mom was the main caretaker and homemaker, even after she returned to work as a speech pathologist when

Jill was in elementary school. "My dad was into sports and his pals—he was in the bowling league, the recreational basketball league, and would often go out with his friends after work," Jill recalls. "My mom didn't seem to mind. I remember sitting at the kitchen table many times when my dad came home from work. My mom would stop cooking dinner, give him a hug and a kiss, and welcome him with a 'Hi, boyfriend.'"

When Jill began dating in high school and college she was drawn to fun-loving athletic types—guys who were happy to let Rock, Paper, Scissors decide the outcome to their problems. It was when she was ready to have a more mature relationship that things went off the rails. Immature men are often more comfortable being *wanted* not *needed*.

> "I want to be able to talk about problems, to work on them, and not just swerve into a ditch to try to avoid them." —Jill

When she married at twenty-six, she chose a man who fit right in to her family dynamic in lots of ways. But after they had children, Jill's priorities shifted to diapers and 3:00 a.m. feedings. "I realized that what I was looking for or needing from a partner changed at different points in my life," she says.

As the years in her marriage ticked on, the "you and me against the world" mind-set she wanted to cultivate wasn't being realized. "Communicating in a constructive way when we had disagreements was something I didn't have a lot of experience with," Jill says. She wanted a relationship like her parents had but didn't know how to create it or sustain it for herself.

➡ *Next Time:* Jill realizes that she can't expect the man she picks to change into anyone else. She also knows that conflict is part of any relationship, and taking the time to truly talk through difficulties is a priority. "Every relationship is going to have bumps in the road," Jill says. "The key is to find ways to get over them. I know that now. Even my parents had their share, even though I didn't witness them."

Meghan shows up insecure and needy

Meghan always felt insecure in her romantic relationships, relying on her partners to bring a sense of security to her life. As relationships progressed, she would usually find herself increasingly needing reassurance and approval. She thought back to how many times Joan told her she was clingy and insecure. Though she didn't want to admit it, Meghan was often on the alert and worried when it came to Joan. When Joan stopped providing that validation, and seemed to be embarking on an affair, Meghan felt an unbearable loss—not only of her partner but of the person who propped her up and helped her feel okay about herself.

As she started to look at her relationship patterns, Meghan traced her insecurity back to her early childhood experiences when she was an army brat who was always the new kid in class. She never had a chance to form lasting childhood friendships. Her family moved around often because her dad's job in the army involved getting transferred to different bases. She never had the chance to feel settled and secure. When she started dating in high school, as soon as she felt attached to someone she would have to move.

When Meghan and Joan started dating, Meghan gave up her friends and interests to focus all her attention on the relationship. They moved because of Joan's career, picked a log cabin because Joan always wanted one, and didn't adopt a baby because Joan didn't want to be tied down. Meghan now knows her goal is to create a life for herself and not give everything up for another person when she falls in love again.

⟳ *Next Time:* Meghan learned that she wants to work on her relationship with herself. "If I don't value myself and treat myself like a prize worth winning, nobody else will," Meghan says. "I need a partner who gives as much as I do and meets me halfway."

Suzanne jumps into relationships too quickly

In love with love, Suzanne almost always had a boyfriend ever since junior high. She dreamed of love that would last, like her parents had. Suzanne's parents met in college, were best friends, and later professional colleagues, like two peas in a pod. Both psychologists, they had their offices on the first floor of their home so that they could see each other during the day, have lunch together, and catch up during breaks. They were so close that after almost fifty years of marriage, it was hard to tell where one ended and the other began. Suzanne marveled that they still held hands when they walked anywhere together.

It wasn't until her divorce that Suzanne looked for patterns in her behavior and choices to try to understand why her marriage and other relationships had ended. What Suzanne saw was that she tended to fall in love quickly, before she really got to know a man. In her excitement over a new relationship, she would rush into it, leaping before she looked into the arms of a starving artist, then a struggling actor, and a would-be wordsmith. It would go something like this: She would meet a man, hit it off, and they would become instantly inseparable. They both would feel like they had known each other for years and were happier than ever before; each new man would become the center of Suzanne's universe.

Suzanne didn't realize that she was often filling in the blanks, projecting qualities onto the men she dated that may not have been theirs. This certainly was true in Suzanne's marriage, where she was swept off her feet and ready to spend her life with a man before she knew whether they wanted the same things or were truly compatible.

> *Next Time:* Suzanne knows that she needs to slow things down in her next relationship, take her time to get to know him, and not be so quick to fall in love and give her heart away. "I see now that I need to use my head, not just my heart, before I start another relationship," Suzanne says. "I need to proceed with cautious optimism instead of only stars in my eyes."

Pilar fears abandonment

When Pilar started to look at her patterns in relationships, she thought back to the desperate longing she felt after her parents died. After losing her mother when she was sixteen and her father five years later, she felt an obsessive need to fill the emotional emptiness. "My desperate goal was to be loved and find someone who would never leave me," she says.

When she fell for Justin in college, it was because of the way his blue eyes crinkled when he smiled, his steady presence, and how happy she felt when they would walk into a room hand in hand. Justin was more reserved than some, had a young Republican haircut, and was solid, loving, and kind. He worshipped her and she felt safe.

> "It's so much easier to focus on how your husband is letting you down than on your own role in the relationship."
>
> —Pilar

As her marriage progressed, and she and Justin had two boys, Pilar was unable to speak truthfully about how bored she was in suburban married life and with her very predictable husband. She appreciated the stability and resented it at the same time. "I felt stifled in my marriage but had trouble telling Justin anything that wasn't positive," she says. "I hated confrontation, which meant I didn't give us a chance to work on anything because I was afraid to speak up." As a result, she stuffed her feelings inside and started acting out, going so far as to have a fling at work. After she left to get some perspective, she realized she had been blaming Justin and her marriage for her unhappiness. "He wasn't in the picture anymore romantically, and I was still unhappy," Pilar says. "I realized I had to take a look at myself."

With the help of a good therapist, Pilar realized that she was so afraid of being abandoned again that she became a people pleaser who never made waves. She saw how unfair it was of her to avoid confronting her fears and frustrations by escaping and having an affair, rather than talking to Justin. She knew that working on expressing herself honestly and rebuilding trust was a crucial next step.

⟶ *Next Time:* Pilar learned that it was worth the risk to let herself be vulnerable. She would rather be honest and give her partner a chance to understand her than continue hiding in fear. "I knew that I would have to feel enough trust to reveal what I was thinking and feeling, even if it wasn't easy to hear."

BOB, MARK, AND GREG—A LOOK AT PAST LOVES

Take a notebook and a pen and make a list of your past boyfriends, including your ex-husband, and the words that come to mind when you think about those relationships. What patterns can you notice in your relationships with them? What appealed to you about them initially? What do you remember was the reason that things didn't work out? This is a first step in recognizing patterns that can help you to be more self-aware. As many of us in the Maplewood Divorce Club discovered, when we become aware of our patterns, we are able to start acting in ways that promoted happier and healthier relationships.

Eleanor wants to be rescued

Growing up, Eleanor got the message that she was expected to marry a man who would take care of her. Throughout college, she lived at home, knowing she would move from her parents' house to the home she would share with her husband. One evening Eleanor's father announced that he was bringing a new associate at the law firm home for dinner the following night. He said his name was Harold and he was "full of promise," winking at Eleanor.

Harold had a lot in common with Eleanor's father and seemed to want the same things Eleanor did. Before the end of the year, the young couple was engaged.

Dashing, attentive, gainfully employed, Harold swooped in and took care of everything like a knight in shining armor. Of course, the catch with the knight is that he doesn't really exist. As Eleanor discovered during her marriage, her man was human. He fell off his horse now and then, forgetting her birthday, not helping out around the house, and putting his work first.

Eleanor never had to worry about how much money was in the bank, didn't pay attention to directions when they drove somewhere, and never turned on the security alarm at night. She loved the prestige of her husband's job and didn't have to think about what she wanted to do with her life because she was happy to be a judge's wife. "It wasn't until I was on my own that I realized how much I acted like a child, leaving Harold to take care of just about everything except the household," Eleanor says. "After we separated, it took me a long time to believe I could take care of myself."

→ *Next Time:* Eleanor discovered that underlying her rescue fantasy was fear. "A man can be my partner, but he can't save me," Eleanor says today. "It took me some time to let go of that idea and develop a life and interests independent of a man."

BE GENTLE WITH YOURSELF

As you have epiphanies about how you behaved during your marriage and what you may wish you had done differently, remind yourself that it's brave and constructive to take a look in the mirror. We urge you not to beat yourself up! Awareness, though it may be painful, is the first step toward positive change.

If you feel disappointed with yourself for ways you acted or for choices you made, you may want to numb those feelings. We learned that it's next to impossible to do that. That means you can't drink away depression. Though Eleanor tried it, she will say today that her Chardonnay habit only made things worse. She would wake up with all the same problems she had the day before, along with a raging hangover. You can't eat away sadness. Carlotta got to the bottom of many bags of Hint of Lime Tostitos, only to find herself gaining weight but no insights. You can't smoke away your anger, like Pilar tried to do. She lapsed back into her college Marlboro Light habit. It didn't calm her down; she felt worse for compromising her health and wasting fifteen dollars a pack.

Trying to numb one feeling actually numbs them all and delays your recovery from your divorce. Feeling your feelings, rather than avoiding them, helps you to heal and move past them—instead of staying stuck with them buried inside you.

THREE STEPS TO HEALTHIER RELATIONSHIPS

No matter what role you tend to play in your relationships, or who you choose to marry or date, or how your parents' relationship and your romantic blueprint shaped you, there are three key actions that can help you improve your relationships going forward—and your relationship with yourself. As the French actress Simone Signoret said, "Chains do not hold a marriage together. It is threads, hundreds of tiny threads, which sew people together through the years." We believe these threads are made up of healthy behavior, everyday kindnesses to yourself and to your partner, a delicate balance of "you" within the "we," and clear communication.

STEP 1: Set boundaries. Do you tend to sacrifice activities you enjoy and responsibilities you need to address and give more than you receive in your relationships? As your relationship progresses, do you find that by giving up so much, you lose your own identity? It's time to draw some boundary lines that distinguish where your partner ends and you begin.

 Meghan was at the beck and call of her ex, Joan, who didn't take Meghan's needs into consideration before, during, or after their marriage. Even after Joan left, if Meghan heard from her at the last minute, she would cancel on her friends to be available for her.

Meghan had an epiphany one cold December morning when she was in the middle of driving her ex to the airport, neglecting her work, her laundry, and her holiday shopping. The airport was a few hours away, and they got stuck in holiday traffic. Joan barely looked up from her phone the entire trip, immersed in texting her new girlfriend, whom it turned out she was on her way to meet up with in Florida.

"This airport trip wound up wasting most of my day, and Joan hardly spoke to me at all," Meghan says. "I was sitting there fuming and wondering why I was doing a huge favor for someone who's not even nice to me. This was a habit for me. I didn't want to admit that she wasn't interested in me anymore and a ride to the airport wasn't going to change that. I needed to accept that it was over and learn to say no to her." Meghan had always let her partners treat her poorly. In return, she treated them kindly, essentially creating a reward system for bad behavior. "When I started considering my own needs instead of jumping through hoops for other people, it set up a whole different dynamic," Meghan says.

STEP 2: Express yourself. The opposite of being self-expressed is being self-contained. Imagine if you never spoke a word during your marriage about your true desires. Instead, you scribbled them on a scrap of paper and threw them into a plastic bag. You stuffed that bag with your desire for a romantic night out, a request for a behavior change, thoughts on how to grow your relationship. When the bag couldn't hold one more scrap of paper, it exploded.

Emotions that you have stuffed inside usually come out in an outburst that starts with something like, "I am sick and tired of your . . ." The problem is, your ex never got to read all those little notes stored in the bag and was denied the clues to your wants and needs. He may never have had a real chance to please you and work on your relationship because you never expressed yourself clearly. For example, if you want a man to take you on a trip, stop leaving his wet towel on your silk duvet, or never ever play "Electric Boogie" on his keyboard again, tell him.

Jamie

The bliss that exists in owning your truth and speaking it, regardless of the outcome, is off-the-charts empowering. Jamie lacked the confidence to speak up in her relationships. It was only after she took a long look at how this behavior affected her serious

> "If I want something and don't ask another person to do it, the answer is always no. If I ask, there's a chance of a yes." —Jamie

relationships over the years that she realized she wanted to do things differently. She had an unsatisfying sex life, men seemed to walk all over her, and she believes not speaking up had an impact at work as well. "I found that small conversations where I spoke clearly about what I wanted made me braver," says Jamie.

STEP 3: Give him your attention. This was an important shift for Pilar, who tended to multitask and rarely look at Justin when he talked to her. When she visited after their separation and he made a bid for her time or attention, she gave it to him. "Look out the window, the Zachman boy is on a unicycle!" Justin said. Pilar stopped what she was doing to join him at the window.

Scientist John Gottman, who once ran what was nicknamed the "Love Lab" at the University of Washington, studied newlyweds and then caught up with them six years later. He found that couples who frequently responded to their partner's request for attention, what he calls the "turn-to" rate (scoring 86 percent or higher), were still married. Couples who repeatedly failed to respond to their partner's bid for attention (scoring 33 percent or lower) had gotten divorced. The lesson for your next relationship? Put down your cell phone, your book, or whatever you're doing, and give your significant other the gift of your attention. This tells your partner: You're important to me. It's a message Pilar wanted to start sending to Justin.

What I Wish I'd Known

"I wish I'd realized earlier that I didn't need Harold or anyone else to be okay. I can actually do all those things—like figure out my taxes and get my car serviced—that I didn't think I could. In fact, taking care of those chores is quite satisfying. And so is spending time on my own. Sometimes it takes only one to tango." —Eleanor

Chapter 10
FINDING PEACE OF MIND

---

*"Holding on to anger is like grasping a hot coal with the intent
of harming another but you end up getting burned."*
—Buddha

f you're like we were during that first postseparation year, you may be caught
up in a swirling vortex of emotions. You zigzag from feeling overwhelmed or
angry to hopeful and excited. We called this phase Limbo Land. "So many
parts of my life were up in the air," Suzanne recalls. "I couldn't imagine how
it was all going to work out, so I stopped trying to. I focused only on the next
right thing I could do."

While traveling through Limbo Land, you may feel as though you're reading an upside-down map, making U-turns, and running out of gas. You also
find yourself asking a lot of questions about what *he* did: *Why did he decide to
stop trying? How can he prefer to be without me? Why isn't he begging me to come
back?* On other days, you may be wondering if *you* made a mistake: *Maybe
he's changing for the better. What if we could still make it work? Maybe I was the*

problem. We've been there, and we know how you can emerge from this loop. It involves realizing what you can control, focusing your energy there, and letting go of thoughts and behaviors that don't serve you.

We reminded ourselves—and each other—many times a day that all we can control is ourselves and our own attitude. We tried to leave our exes out of it and focus instead on what *we* did during our marriages and how we were feeling. We started asking ourselves questions like, *Why did I tiptoe around our problems? Why didn't I talk to him more honestly about how I was feeling? Why didn't I listen when he said he wasn't happy?*

You will learn how meditating helped Suzanne and Gina feel more serene; how Iris and Renée started individual therapy; how Carlotta's depression lessened when she started speaking in a way that energized her rather than discouraged her; and how Jill took on small everyday challenges that in the past she would have relied on a man to do, like figuring out how to fix a tripped circuit breaker when she found herself in the dark.

The good news is this phase is temporary. Your thoughts and emotions are like the weather. They will come and they will go. We're going to show you small changes you can make starting now that will help you let go of the emotions and beliefs that keep you tied to your ex and to "what should have been."

MEDITATING TO QUIET YOUR MIND

Anyone, anywhere can practice meditation; it can be a wonderful tool to help you work through problems as well as relax your mind. Suzanne started meditating after her divorce. She liked the way it taught her that she could choose not to engage with her thoughts but instead let them float by. Meditating helped her feel peaceful. "Even ten minutes a day made a big difference," Suzanne says.

Research now confirms that meditation improves your mood, helps with anxiety and depression, reduces stress, boosts concentration, and aids with sleep. There are multiple styles of meditating but the basic idea is always the same: You focus on something (your breath, counting, repeating a mantra, etc.) and then allow the thoughts that naturally occur to drift by, as though they're traveling on a celestial conveyer belt. You acknowledge the thought but don't engage with it, letting it continue to move along. Nothing to see here, folks.

When Suzanne started meditating, she had to learn to let thoughts go. For example, if she was ten minutes in and realized she was hungry, rather than start thinking about whether she wanted a turkey sandwich or some soup, she acknowledged that she was hungry and chose to figure out what to have for lunch after her meditation session. The discipline of not engaging with every thought that pops into your head can serve you when a negative feeling about your ex arises—you can decide not to dwell on how he picked a fight that morning. Rather than be impacted by the stress of the argument, you can choose to let your ex and his truculence float into the sky like a balloon.

After building to thirty minutes of meditating daily, Suzanne found a new sense of calm and shared what she had learned at a Maplewood Divorce Club meeting. "You sit and focus on your breath only," Suzanne said, "breathing deeply through your nose and counting each inhale and exhale to help you stay present." Jill remembers feeling more relaxed just hearing Suzanne talk about meditation!

Eleanor

Aware that her mind was always racing, Eleanor asked Suzanne if she would stop by sometime to give her a mini meditation lesson. Suzanne was happy to oblige and arranged to come by the following weekend.

As Suzanne approached Eleanor's front door, she could smell the patchouli incense before she even stepped foot on the porch. Eleanor opened the door in a flurry of excitement, as though she were hosting a party and Suzanne was the long-awaited guest of honor. With a bindi dot on her forehead and bangles up to her elbows, Eleanor flung her arms around Suzanne. "Do you know what's playing? I just downloaded it for today," Eleanor said breathlessly. Suzanne couldn't quite place it. "It's the soundtrack to *Slumdog Millionaire*!" Eleanor beamed. "Everyone loved that movie. Did you love it, too?" Suzanne appreciated her enthusiasm but asked if they could finish listening to the music after they meditated because they would need quiet.

Walking into the living room, Suzanne noticed that Eleanor had arranged a dozen pillows on the floor, had purchased a Buddha statue, and had lit at least twenty candles. Eleanor waved a bunch of takeout menus. "I thought I'd order in. Do you like Tikka Masala? Tandoori Chicken? Lamb Khumbwala?"

"How about we start with some basics?" Suzanne said. She encouraged Eleanor to sit comfortably, with her palms up. She suggested that Eleanor leave her eyes open, stare at an object in the distance, and breathe deeply, slowly counting each inhale and exhale. A few minutes later, the quiet was interrupted by Eleanor shifting her position, causing her bangles to jingle. The silence was again broken when she repeatedly spoke in a hushed whisper: "Excuse me, I forgot to offer you a glass of water." "Do you need another pillow?" "Should I turn on the AC?"

> "When I try to meditate, my mind drifts before I have finished counting down from ten! Listening to guided meditation helps because I have another voice to focus on. I just follow what it tells me to do. I like to try different guided meditation apps on my phone." —Jill

It was clear that for Eleanor, quieting her mind and actually sitting with her own thoughts and feelings was a foreign practice. When Suzanne brought this up, Eleanor admitted that when there was quiet, all she thought about was Harold being happy with his new girlfriend and how she was all alone. "What I came to realize was that in allowing my feelings to bubble up and experiencing them, I was able to release them," Suzanne said. "When I felt my feelings instead of trying to distract myself, I could let them go. If I resisted them, they kept coming back and knocking at my door."

Eleanor saw that by trying to keep her feelings at bay by staying busy, she was holding on to her pain. "I spent a lot of time setting the scene for today because it was easier than sitting still and being alone with my thoughts," Eleanor said. "But that's actually what I need to do."

Spreading good energy

Compassion meditation, which also goes by other names, is about sending light, energy, and good thoughts to someone else. Jill stumbled onto this approach because the method Suzanne introduced her to wasn't working for her. Jill's mind kept drifting to thoughts of what to cook for dinner, wondering whether she'd paid her electric bill and if she'd remembered to make an appointment at the vet for her cat. She also liked the idea of sending positive thoughts to someone else. The goal of compassion meditation is to first direct good energy to yourself, and from there to expand it out to loved ones, friends, strangers, and yes—even your ex, like Jill did. You never have to divulge to him that you spend a few minutes of your free time sending him goodwill and positivity, but he might notice the effects, whether you tell him or not. Many devotees of compassion meditation end up with increased empathy for themselves and others.

You can start with a few phrases, first directed at yourself and then others. The phrases can be helpful because they offer a focus. There are different versions of these, but one Jill likes is: "May I be healthy and strong. May I be happy. May I live with ease." Then you repeat the sentence, substituting in a friend. For example, "May Jenny be healthy and strong. May she be happy. May she live with ease."

Gina used compassion meditation to help her sort through her complex feelings toward Clayton, her ex-husband. Sometimes she still wished they were married and raising their daughter together, living under the same roof. As different as her life was now, Gina was thankful that Clayton played an active role in raising Valentina. Clayton was even slowly starting to bring his boyfriend, Gary, around Gina and the baby. Gina didn't want to like Gary on principle alone, but she couldn't help herself. Gary was self-deprecating, smart, and kind, and seemed to adore Valentina. While rearing a child with two dads wasn't what Gina ever imagined, it was actually working out pretty well. She felt supported by two men who each cared for her, respected her, and emotionally supported her in her role as a mother.

Gina started to spend a few minutes every morning mentally bathing Clayton in light and sending good energy his way. She would envision Clayton at his best moments in their relationship: making her tiramisu on her birthday, traveling around Italy on their honeymoon, and surprising her at the salon with a bouquet of flowers. "I felt like practicing the meditation was a safe space for me to act in a loving way to my ex, because even though we aren't together anymore, I still love him," Gina says. "I could appreciate what we shared and focus on what was still positive between us."

Ready to try compassion meditation? Sit down comfortably on a chair or on a pillow on the floor and close your eyes. Picture yourself as happy, in a place you love with the sun shining on you, and begin to generate feelings of kindness and benevolence toward yourself. Bathe yourself in beautiful white light. Feel free to add words if you like—perhaps, "May I be healthy and strong. May I be happy. May I live with ease" or a variation. Try to stay on the images of yourself for a few minutes, then move on to directing this loving energy toward others—first people close to you, then acquaintances, then strangers, then those you feel hostility toward. When you're ready, open your eyes. That's all there is to it.

DEALING WITH DEPRESSION

Caring for your mental health is as important as caring for your physical health. If you're having trouble controlling your thoughts, and meditating or other efforts to quiet your mind aren't working, consider getting professional help. Seeing a psychologist, psychiatrist, social worker, or life coach can help you get back on a positive path. Iris felt immensely helped by her sessions with a psychologist, and Renée got back on track with help from a psychiatrist. Many other women in the Maplewood Divorce Club also reaped the benefits of individual and group therapy, including Eleanor, Carlotta, Jill, and Suzanne.

 With so much of her life up in the air and disturbing thoughts about Flint and the voluptuous Broadway actress he was dating popping into her head all the time, Iris had trouble sleeping, concentrating at her job as a nurse, and completing chores, like putting away laundry and buying groceries. "I just couldn't seem to move past Flint leaving," she says. "I was so angry at him and scared for me and the kids. I was worrying a lot and felt constantly on edge." She knew she needed to function at her job and be able to take care of her daughters. "I felt like hiding under the covers, but I knew I couldn't afford to keep collapsing into tears," Iris says.

Iris made an appointment with a psychiatrist, who suggested she take an anti-anxiety medication when she felt she wanted to take the edge off. He said she also had the option of taking an antidepressant if she felt she needed more than an occasional boost. As a nurse, she knew how addictive anti-anxiety medications could be. She realized she wanted to try talk therapy first.

Iris selected a psychologist in her network so that her health insurance covered most of the cost and started seeing her once a week. She appreciated the supportive environment where she felt safe enough to talk truthfully with someone who was objective and nonjudgmental. "The very first session the psychologist told me we would work together to identify and change the thought and behavior patterns that were hurting me and holding me back," she says.

> "Having a psychologist to talk to who was in no way connected to my life and who could see things dispassionately but was invested in my well-being was incredibly helpful." —Iris

Iris found herself looking forward to her Tuesday sessions, feeling that perhaps for the first time in her life, she had someone she could confide in who would help her develop coping tools that would enable her to feel better.

Renée

Renée was doing a good job of masking her depression to others. Meticulous about how she presented herself to the world, her hair, makeup, and clothes were impeccable. She always came across as gracious and upbeat no matter how she was feeling inside. When her friends would ask her how she was holding up, Renée, a private and reserved person, would say she was just fine. But home alone, she noticed that she had started to get panic attacks. She would feel jittery, with negative thoughts filling her head. At times she wondered if she was making a huge mistake. "I was with Hector most of my adult life," Renée said. "I didn't know what life would be like without him. I was terrified."

Renée felt she needed medication to take the edge off while she explored how to feel purposeful again. A psychiatrist suggested she take Zoloft while also participating in weekly therapy sessions to help her understand what was underlying the panic attacks. For Renée, who kept a lot bottled up inside, sharing her deepest fears and regrets with a stranger took some time. She found the process helpful and took her therapist's suggestion to look for ways to get involved in her community. When she heard that her church was opening up a food pantry with the goal of reducing childhood hunger within their community, she signed up.

TWENTY THINGS THAT WILL MAKE YOU FEEL GOOD

1. Soak in a bath with two cups of Epsom salts. Stay in the tub after you open the stopper. Feel the relaxing pull of the water as some of your troubles, and excess water weight, flow down the drain.

2. Get your hands in your kids' Play-Doh. Squish it, roll it, and flatten it.

3. Make someone else's day by giving back. Hold the door for someone. Help your elderly neighbor by taking her garbage cans back in for her. Leave a potted flowering plant on the doorstep of a friend. Pay for the person behind you at the tollbooth. We found that doing good feels good. Research shows that volunteering reduces depression.

4. Sit on a lawn chair and watch the stars in the night sky. See if you can find any constellations. Your troubles will feel insignificant.

5. Plant something. Get your hands dirty and cultivate life.

6. Read those novels that everyone says "you have to read." Escape into someone else's story. If you feel up to it, start a book club with some local friends who are avid readers.

7. Go for a bike ride or a walk in a park that you haven't explored before: Findyourpark.com.

8. Find an upbeat friend and take a tour of a winery or brewery.

9. Grab a load of towels out of the dryer and dump the full laundry basket on top of you. Relax into the warmth, soothing scent, and softness. Sounds silly; feels good.

10. Visit a fair or a theme park and enjoy some rides. Everything looks different from the top of a Ferris wheel.

11. Focus on what you're grateful for. Start or end your day making a mental list of what you're thankful for. Feeling grateful reduces

As she spent more and more hours driving to pick up donations, stocking the shelves, making lists of needed items, and packing grocery bags of food to give away, Renée felt grateful to be busy doing something that gave her a sense of purpose and had an impact on the greater good. She and other volunteers gave out food early on Saturday mornings at the pantry. Renée liked getting to

many toxic emotions, from envy and resentment to frustration and regret.

12. Sign up for a lesson or a class teaching something you have always wanted to learn. French? Surf lessons? Mambo? No time like the present. It's exhilarating to try something new.

13. Declare a fashion goal and stick to it—like Wild Print Wednesday or Fuchsia Friday—to help you get out of a rut. Ready for a challenge? Try no black clothes for a week.

14. Roll the window all the way down and let your hand dance in the breeze while you drive around town.

15. Schedule a massage. Find a spa that has a reason to linger, like a pool, gym, steam room, or sauna, and make a day of it. Feel like you can't afford the time or expense? Even a ten-minute shoulder massage at a nail salon can do wonders.

16. Write a letter to someone you care about who has fallen out of touch.

17. Wiggle your toes in the sand as you watch the waves go in and out. Not near a beach? Fill up the bottom of a bucket with marbles, warm soapy water, and a few drops of lavender oil. Put your feet in and slosh them around.

18. Hang some musically tuned wind chimes outside your front door.

19. Paint. Don't want to invest in materials? Just pick up a paint-by-numbers kit.

20. Create something. Bake it, knit it, build it—whatever you enjoy—and get lost in the project.

know the families who came in. She personally replenished formula and diapers for families with babies and toddlers and was able to anticipate the needs of the regulars. Renée liked to dream about the possibility of combining her love of travel with her passion for helping others. "It lifted my spirits to feel like I was making a difference," she says.

Renée envisioned herself traveling to Haiti, or even Africa, to help combat hunger. "I was still working on sorting out my own problems, but I felt a lot more peaceful when I was able to do something positive for kids and their families who really needed help," she says.

The opposite of depression, she learned from a TED Talk, isn't happiness but *vitality*. Renée wasn't sure if it was the therapy, the antidepressants, or the volunteer work, but she was feeling more energized. She started cooking again, something she had stopped doing when Hector moved out. She returned phone calls from friends who wanted to know how she was feeling, and she was more ready to share her difficulties and her progress. "For me, therapy and medication were a lifeline," Renée says. "And having more activities in my weekly schedule that brought me joy started to changed my mood in a profound way."

Jamie

Jamie had started talking to a life coach to help her understand why she chose someone as violent and angry as Doug. She was surprised when her coach suggested she attend free Al-Anon meetings. "Since Doug was the one with the drinking problem, I couldn't understand why she wanted me to go to a twelve-step program," Jamie says. She learned that Al-Anon is not for the alcoholic but for the friends and family of problem drinkers.

In her very first meeting, when she heard others describe what they were feeling and experiencing, she felt their stories resonate deeply with her own. She heard them describe how they learned to apply the principles of the Al-Anon program in their lives and felt hopeful for the first time in a long time that she would be able to learn more about why she chose to marry an alcoholic. She felt that she wasn't alone in the problems she was facing. "It's a spiritual program that I found deeply meaningful," Jamie says. "I learned so much from the other members and feel that going to these meetings, sometimes two or three a week, saved my life."

STAY CONNECTED SOCIALLY

You may feel like hiding while going through this difficult time, but maintaining social connections is important for our health and every bit as powerful as getting enough sleep, eating well, and not smoking. Dozens of studies have shown that people who have satisfying relationships with family, friends, and others in their community are happier, have stronger immune systems and fewer health problems, and live longer.

Don't shut the world out just because "How are you?" is a difficult question to answer right now. Sometimes saying, "It's been really hard, but I'm working on it. I appreciate you calling," will help keep friendships alive.

Your friends and family may not know what you need, so if you want check-in calls, ask for them. If you need face-to-face time, let them know that as well. There are people who want to be in your life and help you even when everything isn't sunshine and roses.

USE ENERGIZING LANGUAGE

Carlotta

Our words have power. Our word choices convey our mood and mind-set to others and influence the way we feel. Many of us made changes to the language that we used when we were healing from our divorces. "I didn't think it would work at first, but changing the words I used actually helped to change my mood," Carlotta says. Desperate to feel something besides bitterness and jealousy, she was encouraged by friends to stop using the word *whore* when referring to her ex's girlfriend. "Give it up already," they kept saying. Carlotta used a lot of Debbie Downer language such as: *hate, never, can't, won't*.

Carlotta realized she had morphed into the type of stormy person she used to avoid, and one of the ways she got there was by using negative language. "I still had so much hatred that I just couldn't call Allyson by her name. All she was to me was the person who took my husband away," Carlotta says. "The truth is, every time I called her a whore, I felt the sting of the betrayal all over again. I realized I probably didn't need to talk about her at all. She wasn't thinking about me—and I didn't want to be thinking about her anymore, either."

Carlotta made the connection between speaking in a more positive way and feeling happier overall. She vowed to add energizing and positive words from here on out. Carlotta wasn't going to "try" to go to Spin class, she was "choosing to go to Spin class and be healthy." Carlotta's heavy rotation of positive words now included: *discover, will, am going to, get to, love, awareness, acceptance, growth,* and *choice.*

 Meghan knew she had to stop talking about her ex, Joan. Friends and family, and even Carlos, her new roommate, were starting to grow weary of her endless musings about how Joan made the best omelets on the planet, always had great music playing, and made her life feel exciting. Meghan's friends could all reel off her pet names for Joan, knew Joan's favorite color was royal blue, and had heard the story about how she and Meghan met at a garage sale so many times that they could recite it themselves. Though Meghan knew she wanted to get over Joan, she kept herself connected by talking about her so much.

One day during a break at school, Meghan's new friend, Theresa, told her that she needed to find other topics of conversation. "I can't listen to another story about Joan. No more," Theresa said. "I don't think this is helping you move on."

Meghan could see she was actually keeping her connection to Joan alive by talking about her all the time. This was making the task of getting over their relationship next to impossible. "I hadn't been ready to stop feeling connected to her, but that changed when I decided to stop saying her name for at least one month. I wouldn't ask acquaintances how she was, and I wouldn't relive our glory days by telling stories about us anymore. I didn't know if it would make a difference, but I knew it was worth a shot," Meghan said.

When she forced herself to stop talking about Joan, Meghan noticed that other topics easily came to mind, like what she was reading, something she saw on the news, and different places she wanted to try around town. Plus, she was starting to feel better.

Take Meghan's lesson to heart. If you're having trouble getting over your ex, the less you talk about him the better. Removing him from your conversations will help him fade into the background, where he belongs. This is what we call a "Colin Cleanse," thanks to our friend Janice, who gave up uttering her ex Colin's name for six months. Colin, Brad, Joan—whatever your ex's name is—stop repeating it all the time and see how you feel. You're usually not saying his name in a positive context, are you? Your energy is your power—don't waste it. Remove his name from your vocabulary, at least for a week, and see how that feels. This also includes not using any nickname you've come up with. So you won't be saying, "The InTIMidator wants the boys for Christmas," "Deadbeat Dylan didn't pay alimony again," or "Howard the Coward is still avoiding my calls." It's no longer about him; it's about you.

Like Carlotta, consider dropping watered-down words like *should*, and instead say *choose, want,* or *desire.* Rather than complain, "I should clear out my office," say, "I want to clear out my office so that I can find things."

Words that can weigh us down include *must, try,* and *maybe.* As Yoda himself said in *Star Wars,* "Do. Or do not. There is no try."

Words that make us feel lighter and more hopeful include *choose, intend, aim,* and *yes, I will,* especially to new experiences. For example, Iris decided to replace a sentence like, "I'm confused. I don't even know what I want" with "I'm discovering my priorities and goals." Pepper your sentences with positivity and see how it can make a difference in your life.

CREATE HAPPY HABITS

We noticed dramatic benefits to letting go of behavior that wasn't serving us. For Eleanor, this translated into giving up her morning drive-by of her ex's house to snoop on his new living situation. "What it really meant was that I

SMART SUBSTITUTIONS

It's easier to change a habit by replacing it with a different action, rather than try to simply drop it. The only way Renée was able to stop noticing every silver Mercedes and looking to see whether Hector was driving it was to actively turn her attention to other things. She started listening to podcasts anytime she was in her car, everything from Radiolab, about science, creativity, and innovation, to Loveline, which offers relationship advice. "I filled my mind with subjects that were actually a lot more interesting to me than wondering why Hector was driving down Main Street," Renée said.

had to accept that I was now starting my day alone, not with Harold," Eleanor says. "Somehow, just driving by his house made me feel connected to him." She gave herself a new morning routine of meditating for twenty minutes and then walking to her favorite local café to read the *New York Times* with a cappuccino and a scone. Replacing the habit she was trying to give up, drive-bys, with a new habit gave her a substitution that prevented her from relying on sheer willpower alone to stop her drive-bys.

Amali realized she wanted to stop stalking her ex via social media sleuthing. No surprise, after her prior online shenanigans—encouraging Facebook friends to call Sugi a coward after he left her—Sugi promptly "unfriended" her on Facebook. But she had created a couple of false profiles so she could continue to follow him on Snapchat, Instagram, and Twitter. She recognized that her danger time for online stalking was at night, so she started watching a lot of movies, especially comedies her friends had recommended.

> "I was spending way too much time obsessing over the happy images my ex and his friends posted when they went out. Even though I knew they were only a sliver of what was going on his life, I tried to piece them together like they were clues to a mystery. Weaning myself from that habit was liberating."   —Amali

"I compiled a long list of must-see movies and also binge-watched seasons of hilarious TV shows like *Veep* and *Parks and Recreation*," she says. "Having that to look forward to before bed really saved me." Amali gave herself TV watching as an alternative to the online stalking behavior she was trying to give up.

If there's something you would like to give up, find a new activity to take its place. If you think you need more motivation, create a reward system. It worked for potty-training your three-year-old, and it can work to encourage you now. If you need more than two M&M's to inspire you, then pick something that will: a manicure, new shoes, an extra twenty dollars going into your vacation fund—use your imagination.

CULTIVATING SELF-RELIANCE

Just as letting go of actions that aren't constructive is healing, so is taking on new tasks and challenges that we have never attempted before. Living alone after you separate often means that when there is a jar with a too-tight lid, a shelf that needs to be hung, or a creepy-crawly thing in the bathtub, the person who will need to take that on is . . . you.

For us, the day-to-day tasks we dreaded weren't necessarily the most difficult. They were simply the ones that we had told ourselves for years and years we couldn't do, and we believed that to be true. They're likely the ones your husband used to handle that now you will need to take on or delegate. The first time Suzanne was faced with connecting a new printer to her laptop, she felt ill-prepared. She had always relied on her husband to deal with everything involving her computer. This time, however, she was determined to follow the simple steps in the instructions and have her computer recognize her new printer. Instead, mysterious error messages kept popping up. Her printer and laptop didn't seem to want to enter into a dialogue. Suzanne could have called her ex, but she wanted to prove to herself that she could manage on her own. Eventually she called tech support, which she still counted as a victory because she found a way to get her printer working without relying on her ex. These days, when she has general computer problems, she calls Amali, who happily trades her IT skills for home-cooked meals. Amali has the added advantage of patiently explaining what she's doing so that Suzanne needs to call her less and less.

Jill felt a similar sense of accomplishment when she changed a lightbulb in her kitchen for the first time after her separation. A simple task? Yes, you'd think, especially for the daughter of an electrician, but for whatever reason, Jill had always relied on roommates or men to change the lightbulbs for her. Jill isn't the first woman to worry about getting electrocuted. She got confirmation from her dad that all she had to do was turn off the light switch before screwing in a new lightbulb. Her other fear was using the wrong wattage. He explained that modern fixtures have a maximum wattage rating label that says what that limit is. It's visible inside the fixture. "It sounds so silly, but just having my dad reassure me about what to do made me feel better," Jill recalls. "I stopped wishing I had a handyman around. Now I'm handy. I even changed the brake light on my car. My dad got me a toolbox and is always getting me new tools for it. I am no Bob Vila, but it's a start."

Two years ago, Jill's dad got her a powerful snowblower for her rental home. "It's a real confidence builder to be able to handle clearing out my driveway on my own," she says. Changing that lightbulb led to bigger challenges and helped Jill cultivate an "If somebody else can do it, so can I" attitude. Blown fuse? She now knows where the breaker box is located and how to flip the main switch (the breaker) back and forth when needed; she understands the basics about operating her furnace and even has a power drill. Jill also bought a tire pressure gauge to check the air in her tire after ignoring the low tire pressure light in her car for three weeks. Using the gauge was simple and empowering.

Want to feel like the "can do" person you are? Pick one of the chores that your husband used to handle and do it on your own—it's important to learn to take care of yourself in ways big and small. Car registration about to expire? You, too, can go to the DMV—or renew it online in some states. Oil change? Every three months or three thousand miles. When it comes to clogged sinks and toilets, we suggest investing in a good plunger and mop and using toxic Drano with caution (beware of the splash back and be sure to have a twenty-four/seven plumber on speed dial). Need some man muscle to move heavy furniture or hang cumbersome objects? Hire a handyman. Pests? Get the number of an emergency exterminator.

There are professionals who can handle all the tasks you find intimidating. If money is tight, don't be afraid to ask friends. Gina was the go-to person that her group of divorced friends called whenever they had plumbing, electrical, or fix-it questions. "I actually felt really good that I could give practical advice and help ease the minds of so many of my friends," Gina says.

Resources Get Handy!

Dare to Repair: A Do-It-Herself Guide to Fixing (Almost) Anything in the Home by Julie Sussman. This do-it-herself book is for every woman who wants to be self-reliant. Nobody can escape the home maintenance and repair problems that will crop up, from a clogged toilet to cleaning your gutters.

All American Handyman. Catch an episode online of this HGTV show to inspire you to take on projects in your house—like tiling a kitchen backsplash or installing a new pedestal sink—instead of calling a handyman.

YouTube demos. Before calling a professional, see if there's a YouTube video that someone made to address your very problem, whether it's putting a door back on a hinge or installing weather stripping on your garage door.

What I Wish I'd Known

"I wish I'd known how empowering it would feel to go to the auto parts store, buy a new brake light for three dollars, and learn how to replace it instead of going to a mechanic and paying fifty dollars as I had in the past. There are so many things I take on now that I wouldn't have before, and I know I can figure them out."

—Jill

Chapter 11

YOUR TLC ACTION PLAN

"Love yourself first, and everything else falls in line."
—Lucille Ball

Jamie couldn't remember driving through the stop sign, but she'll never forget the face of the woman whose SUV she crashed into, distraught blue eyes filled with tears. "What the hell's wrong with you?" the woman shouted. "Are you insane? How could you miss that stop sign? You could have killed me!" Jamie recalls two policemen arriving at the scene, and her boys, seemingly unfazed, playing on their iPads in the backseat. All Jamie could muster was "Sorry. I'm so sorry."

After putting her kids to bed that night, Jamie realized that exhaustion was the reason she ran the stop sign. "I must have dozed off," she says now. "I have no memory of seeing the sign or going through it." Since her separation from Doug, Jamie had been unable to quiet her mind at night. She had trouble falling asleep and also found herself waking up around 3:00 a.m., filled with anxious thoughts, unable to fall back asleep. She would worry about unpaid bills, think about the latest "other mom" from school that Doug was dating, wonder if she would be alone forever, and fear that her kids were scarred for life. The next day, she would drag through meetings at the advertising agency, feeling as though she could fall asleep at any moment.

Jamie saw her asleep-at-the-wheel fender bender as an actual wake-up call. "It could have been so much worse," she says. "I was relieved that my kids were okay, I was fine, and so was the other driver. But I was reminded that there are very serious consequences when I let myself get totally run-down."

Many of us found the experience of divorce so consuming and over-whelming that it caused good health habits to fall by the wayside. When you feel discouraged, stressed, or exhausted, setting your alarm an hour earlier to exercise doesn't feel like a priority, especially when your to-do list is a mile long. But we found that taking care of ourselves when we were going through our divorces made a big difference in our ability to handle whatever came our way—the difference between struggling under the weight of all we had to do and facing challenges with energy and optimism.

> "It was all interconnected. If I wasn't sleeping enough, I didn't have the energy to exercise. And when I wasn't exercising, I didn't eat very well. The first step was getting enough sleep."   —Jamie

Our TLC Action Plan is a three-week spotlight on you to help you make self-care a priority. You will hear tips that helped Jamie, Eleanor, Carlotta, and others get enough sleep so they stopped looking like *mombies* from *The Walking Dead*. You'll learn quick, easy ways to swap in foods that impact your mood and make you feel better, and to sneak in exercise each day. Though developing a new habit can take time, our three-week plan aims to help you jump-start your efforts with simple steps you can take even in the middle of upheaval. We encourage you to form new, healthy habits, like exercising when you feel stress instead of indulging in a bag of chips. Embrace these practical strategies to sleep, eat, and sweat like the resilient woman you are.

SLEEP YOUR WAY TO THE TOP

Sleep helps your body recover from stress and repair itself. When you don't sleep enough, your immune system and your digestive system suffer, and every

THE MAGIC OF A TWENTY-SECOND HUG

We're not talking about the half-second hug with air kisses or the quick arm squeeze. Hugging for a full twenty seconds is the magic length of time that your body needs to produce oxytocin, and research shows that the more oxytocin your pituitary gland releases, the easier you can handle life's stressors and the more connected you feel. The University of North Carolina reported that longer hugs reduced the level of the stress hormone cortisol. So hug it out for twenty seconds with your friend, your child, or your pet, and enjoy the sense of calm and well-being that washes over you.

task feels more difficult. Research connects lack of sleep to poor memory, as well as heart disease, high blood pressure, diabetes, depression, and weight gain. Neither Jill nor Suzanne slept through the night for months after their separations. "It's hard to have perspective after you've been tossing and turning all night," Suzanne remembers. Though she would fall asleep easily, she would find herself waking in the middle of the night, feeling unsettled. Our friend Pilar missed having her ex in bed, lying beside her.

Jill recalls feeling as sleep-deprived during her divorce as when she had newborn babies. She would wake in the morning with dark circles under her eyes and puffy eyelids. These she could conceal with makeup. However, she didn't know what to do about how foggy her brain was. She would forget what day it was and was even late with the rent one month. She would often walk to the parking lot after work and wonder, *Where's my car?* and have to wander around looking for her Sebring. Everything from buying groceries and emptying the dishwasher to paying bills and helping her kids with homework felt much more exhausting than usual. Here are our favorite strategies for getting a good night's rest when your divorce is making it difficult to quiet your mind and relax.

HAVE A MORNING ROUTINE. What you do first thing in the morning can impact how well you will sleep that night. We set our alarms for the same time every day, about eight hours after we go to bed. "When you have so much that's unpredictable during your divorce, and kids who also need their sleep, having a predictable sleep routine helped me train my body to get the rest it needs," Jill said. She sets her alarm for 6:30 a.m. and places the clock across the room so she has to get out of bed and walk over to turn it off.

Make your way to the kitchen and pour yourself a glass of water first thing. It has been hours since your body had a drink. Drinking and eating when you first rise signals to your body that it's time to wake up. Suzanne felt best when she started her day with oatmeal that she sweetened by adding chopped apple and cinnamon. Jill felt charged up when she started her day with Greek yogurt with berries and flaxseed. Jamie chose avocado wedges with a squeeze of lime, salt, and pepper on a slice of whole-wheat toast.

DELAY THE CAFFEINE JOLT. It's best to wait to have your first grande latte until after you've eaten, exercised, and taken a shower, according to sleep expert Michael Breus, PhD. This is because the stress hormone cortisol is at its peak in the morning, and it's your body's natural way to wake you up. Eleanor shared what she learned in an article about coffee and our morning routines: "Your cortisol levels are high shortly after waking up. Cortisol is a hormone that makes us feel alert. It's also related to stress. Piling caffeine on top of the cortisol does two things—it interferes with the body's production of cortisol and it increases your tolerance to caffeine, so you won't feel the boost that coffee offers." So, as much as Eleanor loves her morning cup of coffee, she now waits until two hours after she wakes up, when the stress hormone starts to fade. While she used to drink coffee all day long, she also makes it a point to have her last cup of coffee by around 2:00 p.m., since caffeine can stay in your system for eight to ten hours.

GET MOVING. After breakfast is the ideal time to exercise. Doctors report that exercising in the morning lowers your blood pressure throughout the day and will help you sleep better that night. Carlotta always felt better when she took a Spin class in the morning. When she put it off until later in the day, it rarely happened and she would have more trouble falling asleep at night. Can't make it to an exercise class? Try going for a brisk walk.

EAT (AND DRINK!) TO PROMOTE SLEEP. At lunchtime, we include some healthy fats, such as the omega-3 fatty acids—notably DHA—found

COUNT YOUR BLESSINGS, NOT SHEEP

Gina often found herself lying in bed, worrying about being a single mom, her low credit score, and who would take care of Valentina when she returned to the salon full-time. To interrupt the negative spiral, she started making a mental gratitude list. "As I thought about what I appreciated in my life, I started seeing even more things to be grateful for," she said. Her list included Valentina and her successful business, her gorgeous wavy hair, and close friendships.

Research finds that your brain can actually be trained to look on the bright side. Once you start looking for more things to be grateful for, you can create a cycle of gratitude. Try going through the alphabet, letter by letter. Start with A, perhaps for your aunt or for autumn, and B for your best friend or maybe the beach. You just might be asleep before you get to Z, which, of course, is for z's.

in fish like salmon. Jill and Suzanne had many plates of grilled salmon with Montreal steak seasoning and sautéed spinach while writing this very book. New research shows that higher levels of omega-3s are associated with fewer sleep problems. Studies show that DHA helps release melatonin, the elusive hormone that gets you to sleep. Jill also gives her girls a spoonful of lemon-zest-flavored fish oil every day, and they actually like it! Carlotta swears by having two small glasses of tart cherry juice each day. According to the researchers at Louisiana State University, this may help you sleep longer and better at night as the juice boosts the body's melatonin levels.

MAKE HAPPY HOUR EARLY. If you're going to have a cocktail or a glass of wine after work, the earlier, the better (within reason, of course!). Research suggests that alcohol disrupts the body's circadian rhythms and that it takes one hour to metabolize an alcoholic drink. If you're struggling to get a good night's sleep, Dr. Breus recommends no alcohol after 6:00 p.m.

EAT CARBS. The ideal sleep-inducing dinner includes carbs. If you've shunned pasta because of the carb backlash in recent years, consider this: When pasta noodles cool, their molecular structure changes. They become a resistant starch and are passed through the body as a fiber instead of being absorbed as a sugar, according to Janine Higgins, PhD, of the University of Colorado School of Medicine. Jill dug up her favorite summer pasta salad recipes, prepared them in advance so she could refrigerate them, and then enjoyed them for dinner.

HAVE A WIND-DOWN ROUTINE. Pilar found it very helpful to have a routine that she started following each night before bed. She takes a hot bath with soothing bath salts, lights a candle, and meditates for ten minutes while soaking in the tub. After her bath, she dots lavender oil under her nose and on the bottoms of her feet for a relaxing scent that promotes sleep. After her bath, she will often have a cup of herbal tea, such as passionflower, a natural sedative, or Sleepytime or Bedtime tea, available at most grocery stores. Your nighttime ritual doesn't have to be as involved as this, but finding ways to signal to your body that it's time to wind down can make it easier to drift off to dreamland.

UNPLUG. Amali makes sure that all her electronic devices are turned off by 9:30 p.m. The blue light that's emitted by our cell phone, laptop, TV, and e-reader can suppress the body's production of melatonin, delaying the start of the precious REM cycle. So for the sake of a good night's sleep, stop going to bed with your cell phone! In fact, consider getting an old-fashioned alarm clock so that you don't use your smartphone as your alarm.

KEEP YOUR COOL. Denise always liked to sleep in a cool room. Experts agree, advising you to set the temperature to sixty-eight degrees because studies show that a slight drop in room temperature helps us go to sleep and sleep well. If you don't like running air-conditioning in your bedroom while you sleep, open the window or run the AC for an hour before bed to get the room cooled down.

MAKE THE ROOM DARK. A truly dark room enables your body to go into a deeper REM state. Jill's solution to creating cavelike darkness in her bedroom was to buy a sleep mask at the drugstore. "That six-dollar mask was one of the best purchases I made after my separation. Along with the darkness it provided, I also found it really relaxing to have the gentle pressure on my face," Jill says. The very first time she tried it, she slept easily through the night. You can also install room-darkening shades or curtains.

ACCESSORIZE. Iris got a white noise machine from Brookstone and selected the sounds of soothing waves to remind her of the beach. Jamie bought a body pillow at Target and named it Federico. "Hugging Federico at night really helped me fall asleep," Jamie says. "Turns out Federico is a lot cozier than my ex ever was."

If you've worked on your sleep routine and habits and don't notice any improvement, consider reaching out to your doctor for further recommendations, like Renée did. She tried everything her friends suggested and still couldn't sleep through the night. Eventually, her doctor prescribed a sleeping pill. This approach worked for her. Be sure to consult your physician to discuss whether this is an appropriate option for you.

YOUR TLC SLEEP PLAN

GOAL: Sleep seven to nine hours a night.

Week 1: Determine your bedtime based on how early you need to wake up, and start winding down an hour earlier, following the suggestions starting on page 163. Purchase sleep aids you think might be helpful, such as a sleep mask, herbal tea, a white noise machine, lavender oil, or a body pillow.

Week 2: Follow your new routine.

Week 3: Jot down the number of hours you're sleeping each night. As you track your sleeping progress, you will see the benefits of your new routine in action. If you don't see progress, consider talking to your doctor about factors you haven't considered that could be impacting your sleep.

Resources **Sweet Dreams Are Made of This**

Good Night: The Sleep Doctor's 4-Week Program to Better Sleep and Better Health by Michael Breus, PhD. The author, who specializes in sleep disorders, outlines a program that shows you how to identify sleep issues and resolve them. With quizzes and worksheets, this book covers the importance of choosing the best mattress, soundproofing your room, developing good bedtime habits, and understanding your own sleep issues.

The Sleep Revolution by Arianna Huffington. Using her own experience with lack of sleep, the author draws on the latest research in psychology, sleep, and physiology that shows the transformative effects of meditation, mindfulness, unplugging, and giving. Learn about the history of sleep and the consequences of sleep deprivation.

Go the F**k to Sleep by Adam Mansbach and Ricardo Cortés. A funny take on the challenges of getting your child to go to sleep so that you can get some rest yourself. This entertaining bedtime book for parents gives us permission to admit our frustrations and to laugh about them.

NOURISH YOUR BODY AND SOUL

Jamie

It's so easy to revert to comfort foods and takeout when you're feeling depleted from your divorce, but it's actually an especially important time to eat balanced meals. Jamie felt overwhelmed caring for her two boys while working more hours at the ad agency and dealing with all the calls and meetings that her divorce entailed. She knew she was feeding her kids too much fast food but felt she had little energy for meal prep. Jamie found it difficult to find time for trips to the grocery store every few days.

One rare evening when her ex had the kids, she went to a Maplewood Divorce Club meeting and sought advice. "I felt totally tapped out when it came to meal prep," she says. "I asked the group how they were managing meals for their kids during all the upheaval." If you're feeling like the word *cooking* has been replaced by *defrosting* and *takeout*, consider some tips that we shared to help us eat better at mealtime during our divorces.

PLAN AHEAD. What made it easier for Jill to cook meals for her girls on school nights during her divorce was planning out at least three dinners the weekend before and making her grocery list. "I kept it very simple," Jill says. "Sometimes a grilled cheese sandwich with tomato soup and apple slices was dinner. Other go-to meals were cheesy scrambled eggs on whole-wheat toast with fruit salad, and salmon patties with wild rice and baby carrots." When she made stews or pasta dishes, she would prepare extra to use another day.

> "The key for me to avoiding mealtime stress during my divorce was to make sure I wasn't standing in my kitchen at 6:00 p.m. without any groceries or any plan for dinner." —Jill

Iris got very organized about meal prep during her divorce because she worked night shifts and didn't want to burden her parents with feeding her kids night after night. She would carve out a couple of hours on Sundays, which she usually had off, to plan her grocery list and shop for the week. "I discovered that the Crock-Pot was my new best friend. I loved coming in the door after picking up my kids and smelling dinner that had already cooked itself," she said. "It was important to me that my kids ate well despite my low energy and stress."

MAKE YOUR OWN FAST FOOD. Have at least five go-to healthy meals you can whip up with what's usually in your pantry. Suzanne swears by her son's favorite meal: chicken and cheese quesadillas with a side of black beans and salsa. Jill's girls love spaghetti and meatballs. She keeps turkey meatballs in the freezer, sautés garlic and spinach to "healthy it up," and garnishes with parmesan. Iris makes meal after meal in her Crock-Pot: Italian chicken, pork loin, stew, and chili. Denise whips up a tuna white-bean dish with canned tuna, canned cannellini beans, finely diced onion, and minced garlic. Ask your friends for their favorite quick and healthy recipes, and keep them in heavy rotation.

STAY HYDRATED. Even mild dehydration can impact your mood, so be sure that you drink enough liquids and choose beverages that will fortify you during your divorce. If you're guzzling sugar-laden whipped-cream-topped coffee drinks, Red Bulls, and sweet tea, remember that calories count whether you eat them or drink them. Suzanne carries around a thirty-two-ounce thermos filled with water, while Jill downs vanilla seltzer because the bubbles make her happy. Carlotta kicked her diet soda habit, and Meghan gave up her daily seven-dollar latte (that was a whole latte money down the drain) to save hundreds of calories and hundreds of dollars.

If you feel that the stress and worry of your divorce are making it difficult for you to think straight, drink at least four glasses of water a day to get your brain working optimally again. Studies show that drinking enough water helps you focus better, reduces headaches, and improves everything from your complexion to how your kidneys function. Meghan noticed that she felt less hungry between meals and more clearheaded after she started carrying around a thermos of water, usually jazzed up with fresh mint from her garden. If your tap water doesn't taste great, get a Brita filter instead of buying endless bottles of water at the store. Your wallet and our landfills will thank you.

PICK FOODS THAT IMPROVE YOUR MOOD. Can choosing the right foods make you feel better during your divorce? We have experienced the mood-lifting powers of everything from salmon to blueberries. Of course, there are times when two scoops of Häagen-Dazs chocolate chip ice cream or a few nachos are in order, but it's important to remember that chocolate bars, ice

---

Resources Eating Well to Feel Great

You: Staying Young: The Owner's Manual for Looking Good and Feeling Great by Dr. Michael F. Roizen and Mehmet Oz. Grounded in the latest scientific research, the authors present a fourteen-day plan that will help you increase energy and boost vitality.

Robin Takes 5: 500 Recipes, 5 Ingredients or Less, 500 Calories or Less, for 5 Nights/Week at 5:00 PM by Robin Miller. If you would like help getting a healthful meal on the table quickly, this is the book for you. Includes ten different ethnic cuisines, and dishes that range from soups, pizza, and pastas to chicken, beef, and seafood.

Food Rules: An Eater's Manual by Michael Pollan. This slender, easy-to-digest book shows that eating well doesn't have to be complicated. The handbook includes straightforward rules for eating wisely, one per page, accompanied by a concise explanation.

cream, and the like may make you feel better while you're eating them but can leave you feeling bloated, lethargic, and ready to collapse on the couch from your sugar crash. Carlotta kicked her salty chip habit and felt less puffy almost immediately. For us the old adage "You are what you eat" proved to be true. When we ate crap, that's how we felt. When we ate nutritious power food, we just felt better. We call foods that can help us feel better Mood Foods. Our short list of Mood Foods that we love to keep on hand includes:

Oatmeal. If you're feeling too depleted to handle a stressful lunch meeting with your ex and your lawyers, eat a good breakfast including oatmeal. It's rich in soluble fiber, which helps smooth out blood sugar levels by slowing the absorption of sugar into your blood. It's also great for lowering bad cholesterol and keeping you full until lunchtime.

Walnuts. Feeling blue? Have a handful of walnuts. They're an excellent source of omega-3 essential fatty acids, a type of fat that's needed for brain cells and mood-lifting neurotransmitters to function properly.

Wild salmon. Looking for a natural antidepressant at the grocery store? Wild salmon is rich in vitamin D, which research has suggested may increase the levels of serotonin, one of the key neurotransmitters influencing our mood. It's also an excellent source of omega-3 fatty acids. Tip: Going out in the sunlight for ten minutes midday (without sunscreen) is another way to get your daily dose of Vitamin D and boost your mood.

Lentils. Want your brain to be firing on all cylinders before a difficult custody discussion? Eat lentil soup for lunch. Lentils are a great source of folate, a B vitamin that has been linked to proper nerve function in the brain. Low levels of folate have been linked to depression. Spoons up!

Greek yogurt. Look no further if you want a snack that can ease mood swings, depression, and anxiety. Greek yogurt contains whey, an easily digestible protein, and the live cultures are great for your digestive tract. It's also high in calcium. Try plain Greek yogurt in place of mayonnaise or oil in recipes.

Eggs. Eggs are not only rich in protein but they contain zinc, which can help you feel more awake and energetic by regulating your metabolism and blood sugar. Breakfast of champions, indeed.

Peanuts. Want some help keeping anxiety at bay? Peanuts are one of the best ways to elevate your mood because they contain the mineral selenium. Peanut butter works just as well. If your ex is visiting and you want to put out a snack, this may help everyone feel more at ease.

Black beans. You can use black beans to help you stay alert and focused on anything your divorce throws your way, thanks to their mix of protein, fiber, and carbohydrates, all of which help you get what's needed to maintain a healthy state of mind.

YOUR TLC MEAL PLAN

Goal: Eat five fruits and veggies a day, incorporate Mood Foods, cut the crap off your grocery list, get recipes from friends, and learn to shop like a pro.

Week 1: Take a multivitamin, eat five servings of fruits or (non-starchy) vegetables, and drink at least four glasses of water every day. Plan meals in advance to avoid junk food. Ask friends for healthful recipes.

Week 2: Start incorporating Mood Foods into your meal plan to feel better all day.

Week 3: Read food labels, shop like a pro, and cut out highly processed packaged foods that you can live without.

A PEEK IN OUR FRIDGES AND CUPBOARDS

The contents of a person's refrigerator are like a window into their soul—or rather stomach. Here's what we tend to keep on hand.

JILL: Bai5 drinks, seltzer, Greek yogurt, spinach, cheddar cheese, low-fat milk, apples, whole-wheat bread, Mission brand Life Balance tortillas (25 grams of fiber), frozen turkey meatballs, and a good wedge of parmesan cheese.

SUZANNE: Pregrilled lemon chicken from Trader Joe's; hard-boiled eggs for a quick protein snack; Nova smoked salmon; spinach and goddess dressing;

blueberries, strawberries, and raspberries; cantaloupe; hummus and veggies; dark chocolate–covered almonds.

CARLOTTA: Feta cheese, carrots, Amstel Light, kale (hooked on kale chips), cauliflower and root veggies to roast, cashews, spring salad mix, sweet potatoes, and frozen tilapia.

MEGHAN: Almond milk, premade smoothie packets in the freezer, green juice, turkey from the deli, lettuce, fresh herbs (the secret to making anything and everything taste better), natural peanut butter, and coconut oil.

IRIS: Juice boxes, mini water bottles, a pitcher of water with a few cucumbers or lemon (so much more delicious that way), pasta, leftovers, almond butter, yogurt cups, string cheese.

SWEAT THE SMALL STUFF . . . OUT

As we faced frustrations and challenges during our divorces, we realized we needed a way to get the stress out of our bodies. Meghan took up kickboxing to pound it out on a bag. Carlotta got back to Spinning with Suzanne. Jill ran or used workout videos in her home if she had her kids. Finding ways to get your sweat on every day, if you can, or at least three times a week, helps release tension and keeps you strong and healthy. If you have budget concerns, there are plenty of no-cost exercise options, so don't let that discourage you. Make a promise that you will make time to sweat out divorce stressors.

Amali

Amali always knew that she had a Type-A personality. Her friends and colleagues would politely refer to her as "intense," but she had a sinking feeling they meant she was "tense." When she was setting up a home computer for a single mom in her neighborhood, the client invited Amali to try a free yoga class in her studio. Soon Amali found herself hooked on yoga, discovering that the focus on breathing and simple stretches helped her slow down and be in the moment. "I'd leave class feeling an incredible sense of calm," she says. "I put yoga into my schedule, booking classes just as I would a session with a client or a lunch date."

MAKE WORKING OUT WORK FOR YOU

Make it fun. Figure out what kind of exercise you enjoy doing. Do you like to walk, work out with weights, or take dance classes? Are you a grouper who prefers the motivation of a class, a homer who likes to pop in a video, or someone who would rather hike outdoors? Pick something you always wanted to try or always loved to do.

Make it unavoidable. Find ways to remind and motivate yourself to get moving. Suzanne had her workout gear lying out, ready to slip into, to make it easier to head out the door for an early Spin class. Jill would sleep in her workout gear. "It's uncomfortable to sleep in a sports bra but it made it impossible for me to skip a workout," she says. When Jill would run in the morning, having her neighbor waiting outside also helped her stick to her plan.

Make the goal specific. Don't fall into the easy trap of telling yourself you will "exercise more," like Iris initially did. Somehow, "more" never seemed to happen. Gina told Iris that her best tip was to be super-specific about her goal. Gina's goal was walking three mornings a week at a minimum. Iris put a mini whiteboard on her fridge and wrote "Exercise goal: four days a week," and she would jot down when she exercised and for how long. Jill would use a race a few months out as a motivator. "A half marathon needs months of prep and training. It gets me out the door on cold, gray February mornings to run."

Gina had always been proud of her curves, but lately her clothes were uncomfortably snug, and she wasn't able to fit into most of her pants, preferring the stretch of her maternity clothes. "I love to cook, and to eat, and definitely found comfort in lasagna and milkshakes during the pregnancy, since I was eating for two," Gina said. "Once Valentina was born, I realized I was eating that extra serving just to fill the void left by Clayton." Her solution was to start each day going on long walks with Valentina in her stroller as she listened to audio books. Valentina would nap in the fresh air while Gina got moving and enjoyed hearing the latest mystery book read aloud to her.

Carlotta

Carlotta's most successful exercise routine had always been with a buddy. Though she fell out of her habit of going to Spin class with Suzanne when she was at the lowest point of her divorce, she welcomed the chance to drive to class together once she started feeling better. "I looked forward to the few minutes we had in the car to catch up," Carlotta said. "More important, having someone hold me accountable was what I needed. The fact that I felt myself getting stronger and feeling better helped me stick with it." Carlotta also saw her confidence build. "I found myself excited to be able to fit into my regular clothes, instead of loose-fitting sweats," she says. "I bought a few new figure-flattering exercise outfits from Victoria's Secret. Even my daughter, Bailey, started to notice the new, more put-together me."

YOUR TLC EXERCISE PLAN

Goal: Get moving if you're a newbie. Keep moving if you're a seasoned exerciser.

Week 1: Choose your exercise and how you will pursue it (with a buddy, solo, by joining a gym, buying a video, etc.). Start moving at least ten minutes a day.

Week 2: Schedule three twenty-minute exercise sessions for the week, and do them!

Week 3: Fine-tune your exercise plan. As your fitness level increases, continue to challenge yourself.

STEER CLEAR OF ENERGY VAMPIRES

During the stressful and often prolonged divorce process, it's important to spend time with people who support you and help lift you up, rather than drag you down. Identify the energy vampires in your life, anyone who leaves you feeling attacked, drained, or depressed, and decide to limit contact with them until your spirit can handle their negativity. Then pick a few people you enjoy being around and make a conscious effort to spend more time with them. Make no mistake about it, we are affected by one another's mood.

Like attracts like—and energy is no different. The energy we put out attracts people with similar energy. If you've been feeling badly about yourself during your divorce, you may draw negative people and experiences to you. To attract more positive people, focus on the positive changes you are making in your new life as it's developing. "I spend time with people who are warm and loving, people who are finding ways to enjoy themselves and grow," Suzanne says. "You get to choose what you want to focus on and who you want to surround yourself with."

Amali had heard that "like attracts like," and also knew she was oozing with negative energy. "I was blindsided when Sugi left," Amali says. "I didn't know how to feel like myself again." She started getting into a more positive mind-set when she decided to join her colleagues at a dinner celebrating a coworker's promotion. "I could actually feel my mood shift from negative to positive when I was out with them, and I didn't bring my ex up once," she says. "I'm so lucky to have a job I enjoy where I'm around smart, cool people all day."

Amali suggested a weekly Friday happy hour with her IT colleagues, which gave her something to look forward to and helped her ease back into socializing. When negative thoughts popped into her head, Amali also started making it a daily practice to consciously let them go. "Power yoga really helps me feel centered," she said.

Finding ways to lighten your mood even when you're home alone is sure to give you a positive energy boost. Some of our favorite pick-me-ups include YouTube videos. We're partial to "Carpool Karaoke" with James Corden. We also enjoy stand-up comedy specials by Louis C.K., Sarah Silverman, and Mitch Hedberg.

When they could get together, Jill, Suzanne, and members of the Maplewood Divorce Club found that singing karaoke, dancing like crazy, and having picnics in the park with their kids left them feeling connected and joyful. Who are you spending time with whom you enjoy and who leaves you feeling lighter and more hopeful?

YOUR HEALTHY HABITS COUNTDOWN

Here are ten simple actions you can take every day to feel better right away.

10 minutes every hour: Walk, stand, or move to give your body and your mind a break, especially if you have a desk job.

9 minutes a day: Watch funny videos like those by Key and Peele or Amy Schumer. A little laughter goes a long way toward improving your mood.

8 hours a night: Sleep. It's totally essential.

7 days a week: Mentally list a couple of things you are thankful for.

6 days a week: Connect with a friend, loved one, or family member via phone, email, FaceTime, or in-person visit.

5 times a day: Consume a serving of a fruit or vegetable.

4 times a day: Drink a tall glass of water.

3 days a week: Get your sweat on with some exercise (do it more often if you can).

2 times a day: Compliment someone or do something nice for them.

1 time a day: Take a multivitamin.

What I Wish I'd Known

Jamie

"I wish I knew what a huge difference getting a good night's sleep would make. When I started sleeping through the night, I felt like a new person. I was even able to give my ex a genuine, wide smile and a cheerful, 'Thanks, see you later,' when he dropped off the kids. His confused expression said it all. I was no longer cranky and sleepwalking through my life. I had more energy and goodwill to spare."

—Jamie

Chapter 12

WRITE YOUR OWN HAPPY ENDING

"Be the heroine of your life, not the victim."
—Nora Ephron

D o you see your divorce as the worst thing that's ever happened to you? Or did it teach you lessons you needed to learn to cultivate more meaningful relationships in the future? Was it a disappointment so great you will never get over it? Or did it crack you open and help you grow into a better person? How we recount the story of our divorce matters because the stories we tell ourselves have power. They influence our actions and our self-image. To see two very different tales that women told themselves after they were abandoned and in pain, we offer up stories that will be familiar to many: Hollywood actress Jennifer Aniston, who made headlines for years after her husband left her for his costar, and Miss Havisham, the unforgettable jilted bride from Charles Dickens's novel *Great Expectations*.

For years during and after her divorce, Jennifer Aniston was cast by the media as the spurned woman who couldn't make a romantic relationship work.

She spoke openly about the challenges of having her divorce play out in front of the world and struggled to rise above the fray. Rather than criticize her ex publicly, she spoke of wanting to grow and said she was grateful for the chance to rediscover herself. She was also determined to make a different choice from her mother, who had been angry and bitter after her own divorce. In time, the actress moved gracefully past the press's unflattering portrayal. She gave her divorce story a happy ending by learning about herself, seemingly keeping a positive attitude, and making peace with the experience.

Miss Havisham, the jilted heroine in *Great Expectations*, tells herself a very different story. Heartbroken and humiliated after she is left at the altar and defrauded of her fortune, she never again ventures outside her home. She leaves the wedding breakfast and wedding cake rotting on the table. Even the clocks in the mansion are stopped at the exact time she received the letter from her fiancé calling things off. She stays stuck in a bitter place, never again making herself vulnerable to another relationship, or even taking off her wedding dress. That one disappointing man who left her shapes the rest of her life . . . because she lets him.

You're the author of your tale. You decide how you want to view your divorce—and whether you might want to reframe the story you've been telling yourself and others. Many women in the Maplewood Divorce Club stopped telling woe-is-me divorce stories in which they were the victims. Instead, they recast their tales using what we call the Reframe/Reclaim Technique so that they emphasized their personal growth and accentuated the positive. And you can, too.

REFRAMING YOUR DIVORCE STORY

We found inspiration in public figures who have discovered opportunity within their divorces and in doing so, reframed their stories of personal challenges into success stories. One of our favorite performers, Tina Turner, could have let her story of abuse at the hands of a man she loved define her life. Instead, she found a way to move past it. When she left her husband, she was not only emotionally and physically bruised but also financially destitute. One of our greatest singers, who by then had several No. 1 hits, cleaned houses for a period of time to pay her rent as she rebuilt her career and her credit. Tina Turner's story of abuse became just one chapter in the life of a survivor.

REFRAME/RECLAIM TECHNIQUE: GIVE IT A TRY!

1. Write down the bare-bones facts of your divorce, not your opinions, including who left whom and what that has meant for you emotionally and financially.

2. Write down the "story" you currently tell others. Is it positive? Negative? How does it make you feel? Is it going to make the person you're speaking with want to jump out a window to get away from you?

3. Act like your own PR spin doctor to retell your story accentuating the positive, especially how you have grown from the experience and the opportunities you have as a result.

4. Think it's pretty good? Test-drive your reframed divorce story on a friend and get some feedback.

Lawyer and politician Wendy Davis was just twenty-one, with a young daughter, when she went through her divorce. To make ends meet, she worked at a doctor's office and as a waitress while she attended community college. She didn't let go of her dreams even though things weren't working out as she planned. Later accepted to Harvard Law School and elected to the Texas State Senate, she credits her success to hard work and optimism.

Arianna Huffington could have shunned the public eye after her divorce from her husband, who came out as gay. Instead, she reframed her divorce as a great business opportunity to create the wildly successful Huffington Post. She could have taken her hefty divorce settlement and moved to Turks and Caicos but chose to follow her passion for journalism and do what she loves, all the while enjoying the spotlight.

Carlotta

There are countless ways to tell the same story. As any PR guru knows, you choose which facts you lead with and want to highlight in your story. The basic facts of Carlotta's story are: She was married to Bill. They have a daughter named Bailey. Bill had an affair and left. The version of the story Carlotta would tell about her divorce: "Bill gave up on me. He lost interest and fell in love with someone else. He cheated on me and ruined my life. He broke up our marriage and destroyed our family." Carlotta also *believed* her story wholeheartedly and saw it as proof that she was undesirable and unlovable.

Carlotta used the Reframe/Reclaim Technique to retell her story in a positive way. These days, she no longer clings to Bill's rejection like a life raft. When she thinks about her divorce, or tells the story, it's not a tale of betrayal. She notes she was married for seventeen years, has a beautiful daughter, and has been able to rekindle her love of gardening since the split. "I've been embracing living on my own and doing whatever I want," she says. "I paint the front door a new color every spring; this is the year of aqua." The facts of her divorce haven't changed, but her attitude and the way she talks about it certainly have.

Carlotta isn't our only friend who needed some help viewing her divorce in a more positive light. "I'm such an idiot," Gina moaned when she was trimming Carlotta's hair one day. "Who would believe that a man who never misses an episode of *Real Housewives of Atlanta* and asks you to give him highlights was actually straight? How did I miss the signs? What's wrong with me?"

As Gina styled Carlotta's hair, Carlotta told her about how she had reframed her own story and felt better as a result. Gina gave it a try. "Okay, just the facts," Gina began. "I really loved Clayton and married him. I thought he really loved me, too. Clayton realized he prefers men. He left me when I was pregnant with his daughter." Gina burst into tears and said, "I'm going to need to put down the scissors and take a breather."

Carlotta thought for a moment and suggested: "What if your story is that you met a great guy and fell in love. He wanted you to be the mother of his child. He loved you so much he tried to go against his desire for men but ultimately had to be honest with himself, and you." Gina breathed a sigh of relief when she heard this. This version of her story made her feel like someone who fell in love and was deeply loved in return—even though the marriage didn't last.

When Amali went to visit Gina in her townhouse to meet the new baby, she found it hard to hide her surprise that there were still framed pictures of Clayton everywhere she turned. There was even one of Gina's ex holding baby Valentina in a photo magnet on the fridge. "So, it seems like Clayton is gone . . . but he's not really gone," Amali said, as she gestured to the fridge. Gina fixed her gaze on her friend as she rocked her baby. "I'm just saying,"

Amali continued, "he left you high and dry when you were pregnant with his baby. Clayton doesn't deserve a spot on your fridge or in your house."

Gina sighed. "I know you're saying that because you're my friend, and you're mad at him. He did leave me when I was pregnant, but that's not the only truth. He also loves me and is always there for me when I need him. Clayton was there for Valentina's birth, he's helping me take care of her, sharing all expenses, and that's what I'm focusing on. And he's also being really sweet. He gave me those flowers," she said, pointing to a vase full of tulips. "I could be outraged, but I'd rather find ways to stay positive and focus on learning how to be a good mom, and figuring out how to swaddle this baby."

Amali went home that night and looked at the empty picture hooks in her two-story entryway. She ran her finger over one of the hooks, which was now covered with dust. You could still see the faint outline of where her wedding pictures used to hang on the wall. When Sugi left, Amali immediately tossed all traces of him and their life together into garbage bags that she heaved into the dumpster. As she sat on her couch nursing a Coors Light and thinking about her visit at Gina's, she called her sister, Seema, and mulled over the facts: Sugi and I had an okay time together and shared a love for all things IT, but maybe not each other. We got married because my parents wanted us to. He left me with a sloppy good-bye note. I miss saying hi to someone when I walk in the door, but I actually don't miss *him*.

AVOIDING THE D WORD

Eleanor didn't like to describe herself as divorced. "I won't say it— there's a stigma of failure attached to that word," she lamented at a Maplewood Divorce Club meeting in her home. "I don't want to check that box on my medical forms. Even filling out a magazine subscription card and checking Ms. instead of Mrs. was hard to do."

Eleanor preferred to describe herself as "currently unspoken for." Here are some alternative descriptions you can try on for size. Feel free to cross out *divorced* on the next form you see and replace it with one of the following: *Resingled, Untethered, Unhitched, Split but Not Broken, Legally Single Again, Back by Popular Demand, Duo to Solo.*

Seema listened, letting out a laugh now and then. Amali told her that their parents, some of her friends, and maybe even her nosy neighbor, Dot,

> "When I took the part about being left out of the story and simply looked at where I was now, I realized that things were actually pretty good."
> —Amali

seemed to expect that when Sugi fled to Chicago, Amali would have fallen into a funk. "But guess what? It's months later and I'm feeling pretty okay," she said. "Here's my new story: Sugi and I got married because we thought it would make our families happy. Sugi made everybody very unhappy by leaving me." Seema chimed in, "And Sugi is a horrific speller. Don't leave that out of your story." Amali continued, "Sugi did leave a poor excuse for a good-bye note. I've found many sources of happiness since he left, including my new puppy, Grep."

Regardless of how your divorce story is unfolding, you can still give it a happy ending. We agree with social researcher Brené Brown, who says that when we deny the story, it defines us. When we own the story, "we can write our own brave new ending."

LOVE LOST . . . AND FOUND (AGAIN)

One of the biggest heartbreaks in life is when someone you truly love leaves you. At the time, whether you're sixteen or sixty, almost everyone thinks, *I will never love again.* However, this event doesn't need to be the end of your love story. You *can* go on to love again. You have likely seen brokenhearted friends fall in love again. Jill fell in love with the second person she went on a date with after her separation. Suzanne, Iris, and Renée all fell in love after their divorces.

You may even have read about actress Sandra Bullock thanking the man she loved when she accepted an Academy Award, only to learn shortly after that he had been cheating on her. Beauty, wealth, and fame didn't protect her from a broken heart. She has admitted the split left her "on the floor and . . . heartbroken." But five years later, she found love again with a photographer. She described the betrayal in her marriage not as a personal failure but as something that wasn't supposed to work out because "something better is supposed to come along."

Iris was determined to make sure her heartache wouldn't define her or turn her into a bitter person. "I used to be a romantic, but I must admit that after Flint left me, I had a really hard time watching happy couples in real life and on TV," she says. "It made me so jealous, and I secretly hoped it wouldn't work out for them. I didn't want to be so spiteful, but I was." When she saw older couples holding hands, she would wonder if she would ever find someone to love and grow old with.

There were days that Iris felt weighed down by the facts of her life and melted into a puddle of tears: Her ex had an affair and left her; she was the main parent to three kids age eight and under; and she was currently living back home with her parents. Other days, she watched her sheer force of will kick in. "I knew I would find a way out of this mess," she says. Going back to school to renew her nursing accreditation and then returning to work as a nurse was the beginning of her new chapter. She was also saving to buy a house as she waited for her share of the proceeds from the sale of her marital home and was happy that the school social worker said that her daughter Jiang was doing much better in school. "I'm working really hard to build a new life for my girls and me," she says. "And hopefully one day that will include a new love."

LEARNING FROM THE PAST

We've all done it: latched on to a fantasy (marriage, baby, white picket fence) and insisted it come to fruition, overlooking any warning signs (drinking, spotty employment, lack of chemistry) that stood in the way of our goal. "We can want something so badly that our dream overrides reality," Jill says. "I've done it many times myself."

As you're creating your next chapter, keep in mind that one of the traps we can fall into is wishful thinking. Many of our friends remember deciding to get married despite seeing red flags. They made excuses for concerns they had, because they didn't want to admit that there were problems. Denial looks something like this: He has a scary temper? *He's just under stress right now.* He seems to be drinking an awful lot? *He's just a social guy.* He's unreliable? *He'll step up once he becomes a dad.* Don't feel the passion? *He's kind and loving, and that's what matters.*

Take off those rose-colored glasses before you write your next chapter. Jamie had ignored her internal warning that Doug was behaving like a bully at times because she had decided she'd found her husband. "I didn't want to believe that he was troubled," Jamie says. "By the time I noticed he was drinking four drinks to my one, I really liked him." She later realized that she had let her desire for a husband override what she knew was reality.

Like all our friends in the Maplewood Divorce Club, Suzanne was determined to learn from her experiences. "I didn't want to spend my life repeating the same relationship patterns that weren't working," Suzanne says. She had a tendency to ignore warning signs in relationships that she *really, really* wanted to work out. This is where wishful thinking took a front seat. "I realized that I let the momentum of exciting relationships carry me along even if I had flashing neon warning signs blinking before my eyes," she says.

> "I realized that if I wanted the story to turn out differently, I would need to make different choices. Seeing things as they are instead of as I wished they were was a big part of this." —Suzanne

Suzanne got better at seeing the signs and paying attention to them. She recalls one man she dated after her divorce who was thoughtful, funny, smart, and who loved the beach as much as she did. They seemed incredibly compatible, and at first Suzanne had high hopes for their relationship. But she listened when he said that he had been unable to sustain long-term romantic relationships, had strained relationships with family, and had very few friends. Though Suzanne enjoyed his company, she noticed how much difficulty he had communicating his emotions and how his many fears limited how much he enjoyed life. It can take some time to determine whether a relationship is right for the long haul. When Suzanne started to see warning signs, instead of ignoring them as she may have in the past, she gently parted ways with the man because she knew the relationship wasn't sustainable.

These days, Jill makes sure she finds out what the people she is dating are looking for. She knows she wants a serious relationship, and seeks a partner looking for the same thing. When a man she was dating didn't seem to want to take their relationship to the next level and still hadn't filed for divorce even though he had been separated for years, she moved on. "I realized that I had to be willing to acknowledge the feeling of 'this isn't right' for me," Jill says. "I have a tendency to ignore unpleasant aspects, to zero in on the good parts and let the romantic in me take over. It was a red flag that he never filed for divorce."

A red flag means stop and reassess. "Now I try to be more like the bull warily looking at the red flag, instead of getting lost in the sparkly blue eyes of the toreador who is holding it," Jill says. "He may be handsome, smart, and fun," she says, "but if he's also unwilling to commit and then follow through with actions, I pay attention instead of just just sweeping my misgivings under the rug."

 Another trap to avoid when creating your next chapter is allowing unhealthy relationship patterns to continue to repeat in your life. Meghan started dating shortly after Joan left her because she couldn't stand to be alone with herself. She found a new app that pairs you with lesbians within miles of where you are. "I didn't want to post a profile and wait weeks for someone to find me," Meghan says. This was instant. I wouldn't have to sit at home with my dark thoughts, feeling like a loser."

Carlos, the graduate student who was renting out the spare room in her cabin, thought this app was risky and dubbed it drive-by dating. Though he was five years younger than Meghan, he seemed to be an old soul with loads of common sense. "Do you really think you're going to find someone compatible based on the fact that they happen to be driving through the neighborhood in their Subaru?" he teased her. It turned out Carlos was right: Meghan was meeting women with whom she had little in common.

Carlos usually got home late at night—he was either working as a bartender or out with his friends. One rare night that he happened to get home early, he found Meghan collapsed on the couch in a funk. "My date asked me to lend her money," Meghan said. "She seemed so nice, and everyone I've been meeting has been so disappointing, that I wound up going with her to the ATM and giving her $200. Do you think she'll pay me back?"

"I don't know," Carlos said. "I'd never lend money to a stranger."

A few weeks later, Carlos came into the kitchen to find Meghan slumped over a cup of tea. "You okay?" he asked.

"I've been texting the woman I lent the money to about getting together and she hasn't written back," Meghan said. "I didn't even mention the money. I'd just like to see her."

Carlos saw that some tough love was needed. "You're a great catch, but you're acting desperate," he said. "This makes you someone people think they can take advantage of and mistreat. You need to vet these women and value yourself. It will save you disappointment—and gas money."

Carlos told her that he always found that when you want something too much, everybody feels how badly you want it and they don't want to give it to you. "I don't know why, but when I've let go of wanting something really badly, like a relationship, that's when it's always appeared."

Meghan knew he was right. She was afraid that if Joan didn't want her, no other woman would, either. Her desperation was palpable. "It was the hardest thing I've ever done, but I started spending more time doing things that I enjoyed," Meghan says today. "I started reading, watching movies, kickboxing, and joined a hiking group." She also realized that if she expected every woman to reject her, like Joan had, her focus was in the wrong place. "I started to remember what's great about me and fall in 'like' with myself."

Meghan then observed an amazing alchemy: Once she thought more highly of herself and valued her time, this new energy seemed contagious, and women she dated started to treat her better. "I realized that if I don't think I'm great, why would a stranger who just met me think so?" Meghan said. "Learning to enjoy my own company was a totally new way of living for me."

EXPLORING NEW POSSIBILITIES

There's a very good reason why we try to control parts of our lives. We want to feel less anxious. The reality is, though we may attempt to orchestrate our future so that we don't face the terrifying uncertainty of what tomorrow may bring, we simply can't. We learned that it can be powerful to embrace the mysteries that follow a divorce as a time to explore different possibilities. "I literally felt like just about anything was possible," Jill says. "I felt that the impossible had happened—getting divorced—and it strangely opened up a lot of other doors."

Jill and Suzanne didn't know what was ahead. "We just knew we were taking steps that made sense, trusting our intuition, and seeing new possibilities," Suzanne says. "We decided to give ourselves free rein to blossom."

Suzanne

Suzanne realized that during her marriage, she often felt she had little free time to try anything new. Now, when she didn't have her son with her, she decided to do things she had never done before, including rock climbing and surfing. "When I went climbing the

BE INSPIRED BY PEOPLE WHO OVERCAME HARDSHIP

Going through a divorce, it's easy to get wrapped up in your daily challenges and to need mental pep talks now and again. One quick, effective way to get perspective on the difficulties in your life is to look for heroes around you who overcame their own hardships. Who do you know who inspires you with their tenacity and spirit? Who pushes forward and doesn't lose sight of their dream? Whether your heroes are people who show great compassion and generosity, who are courageous, or who quietly persevere facing a challenge, look to them to lift you up. When Sheryl Sandberg, the COO of Facebook, lost the love of her life, she offered advice that had been given to her, "Option A is not available, so let's just kick the shit out of option B." Put your boots on and find your option B.

first time, I was afraid of how I'd feel once I reached the top and looked down, but I wound up feeling safe, and it was fun," she says. "It was the same with surfing. I was at the beach with my family and decided to take my first lesson. I always loved the ocean and wanted to experience standing up on my board and riding a wave." Suzanne surprised herself by riding a wave by the end of her first lesson. She signed up for six more on the spot. "Surfing felt intimidating," Suzanne says, "but being a little scared and trying it anyway felt exhilarating. I loved it."

This new energy and confidence helped Suzanne tackle the many challenges her divorce presented and gave her faith that new and exciting things she couldn't even imagine were around the corner. "I've always had a plan, and taken deliberate steps to reach my goals," Suzanne says. "After my divorce, I learned to loosen my grip."

Though Denise left her marriage in search of passion, it was her ex who found it first. It actually relieved some of her guilt to see him happy and not destroyed by her ending the marriage. Still, she felt selfish for leaving a good man and breaking up the family because she desperately wanted a mind-body-soul connection. "I was really dead inside for so long," Denise says. "I couldn't go on that way. I know it took a lot of courage for me to realize I wasn't going to settle for a platonic marriage, but I faced a lot of anger from my family and friends for my choice. I felt like everyone was always asking, 'Who are you dating?' The implication was if I didn't have a great new guy in the picture, then why did I bother to leave Mitch?"

Denise went on many dates but found men who weren't available or who didn't have that spark she was seeking. She focused on working on herself and encouraging the universe to bring her an amazing man. She started cutting out tiny paper hearts in various sparkly hues, giving them to friends, and leaving them everywhere she went. She was literally leaving a shiny trail for Cupid to follow and putting love out into the world.

Another new habit for Denise was getting dressed up and going out by herself if a friend couldn't join her. "I'd sit at the bar, have a glass of wine and an appetizer," she says. "I wouldn't allow myself to stare at my cell phone. I'd chat with the bartender or anyone who was nearby just to see if I might meet someone interesting." Taking these small steps helped Denise feel that "he" was out there somewhere and it was just a matter of time before she bumped into him.

What I Wish I'd Known

"I wish I'd known sooner that I get to decide how much my disappointment over Flint and our failed marriage shapes the rest of my life."

—Iris

Part Three
REVEAL

As you start to socialize again, we help you switch up your look, boost your confidence, and share easy conversation starters to break the ice with someone new. Get the scoop on online dating, from creating an irresistible profile to handling the bad dates . . . and the good ones. We also show you how to launch a divorce club in your own community, so you can share what you've learned with other women as your new life continues to take shape.

Chapter 13
GUIDE TO GORGEOUS

"Beauty is about being comfortable in your own skin.
It's about knowing and accepting who you are."
—Ellen DeGeneres

A mali wasn't used to men on the street giving her double takes. She had always worked with a mostly male IT crew who saw her as one of the guys. She thought it was frivolous to spend a lot of time thinking about her hair, clothes, and makeup. Her go-to outfit? Jeans and a T-shirt, her long hair pulled back in a waist-length shiny ponytail, no makeup, gaze turned downward, lost in thought.

For Amali, deciding to cut her nearly waist-length hair after her husband left for Chicago was a way to reclaim her identity and get a fresh start. She had gotten married because her parents thought it was time, to a man who seemed like the "right" choice because he fit her family's criteria, but he wasn't some-one she truly connected with. Similarly, her long, traditional hairstyle that so many women from India wear was not a style she had ever actively chosen. "I realized I had just accepted the long hair that I'd always had as a child, and that most of the women in my family had, but it wasn't really me, just as being married wasn't me," she says. "I was done just going along with what everyone in my family wanted me to do and how they expected me to look. I was ready to make my own choices."

Gina had given her a few shoulder-length wigs to try on to make sure she would feel comfortable with a shorter hairstyle. "The last thing you want to do when you're going through your divorce is get a haircut that is drastic and doesn't feel like you," Gina says. "I spent a session with Amali discussing options and showing her how they'd look." With Gina's input and several soul-searching talks, Amali decided on a cute, choppy new bob. She was not only giving herself an updated hairstyle, she had also decided to donate her hair to Locks of Love, a group that provides hairpieces to financially disadvantaged children suffering from long-term medical hair loss. This way she would be giving someone else a fresh start, too.

Gina had an assistant videotape the dramatic chopping of Amali's pony-tail, so she could post it online. The result? "I absolutely loved it," Amali says. "I felt like I was cutting ties with the past. My long hair was weighing me down. I felt lighter and free."

Like Amali, we encourage you to begin to think about any style updates you may want to make. You're not the same woman you were when you got married, or when your divorce began, and this can be a good time to think about evolving your look, either a little or a lot. Though hair and makeup may feel like they belong on the bottom of your to-do list, they do make a differ-ence. Image consultants know that when you look good, you feel better and perform at a much higher level in your personal and professional lives. Of course, there are still challenging days, and life can be chaotic, but it's worth thinking about whether you're projecting that chaos out to the world. If you wake up and don't feel good, dress *as if* you do. This can impact your self-esteem and help you shift to a positive perspective.

You may find, as we did, that while a great shade of lipstick, choppy new bangs, or a sleek three-quarter-sleeved top with a deep V-neck can do a lot to put pep in our step, there is more to a good "breakover"—your makeover after a breakup. A woman who is at peace with herself, content with what she has, grateful for her many blessings, and living in the moment is the kind of lovely

DRESSING TO FLATTER

Choosing clothing that flatters is both an art and a science. The goal is to figure out which shapes and colors highlight your figure.

Proportion. What you put on your body tells the eye where to go. Jill learned that with her average height and straight body lines, she looks best in shapes that create the illusion of a nipped-in waist. Suzanne, petite and athletic, found that she looks best in fitted styles. Gina is more zaftig and now knows to choose looks that skim her curves and define her waist. She also wears three-quarter-length sleeves (a slimming look for everyone). Iris is a bit pear-shaped, so she adds volume on top with boatneck necklines, boxy jackets, and full sleeves to balance out her hips.

Color. Dark colors make your body recede. Light colors will draw the eye first. Think of a color-blocked sheath dress. If you're small-busted and pear-shaped like Iris, you would want white on top and black on the bottom. If you're busty yet slim-hipped like Meghan, you would want the reverse palette. Here are two rules on color to keep in mind.

1. Wearing beiges, khakis, and browns can make you look washed-out. Most women look better with color by their face. Add a bright scarf or jewelry to make neutrals more flattering.

2. Figure out whether you're a "cool" or a "warm" and buy clothing that is in your color family. Suzanne is cool-toned and looks best in bright jewel-toned colors like blue, emerald green, bright purple, and red. Jill is warm-toned and looks best in orange, violet, turquoise, and cream. "A simple test to figure out if you're cool or warm," shares Jill, "is to pull all your hair away from your face and with no makeup, hold something hot pink under your chin. Then do the same with something bright orange. One of these will make shadows on your face less visible and give you a healthier look while the other will make you look wan." If hot pink works for you, you're cool-toned. Choose cool colors such as berry, brick red, white, purple, evergreen, gray, and powder blue, and silver jewelry. If orange worked for you, you're warm-toned. Choose colors such as peach, orange, tomato red, raspberry, teal, and moss green, and gold jewelry. Navy and turquoise tend to be flattering to all.

and joyful person that everyone wants to be around—and be. In fact, what truly draws people to you and makes them want to stay near you is a positive attitude and good energy. How do you show up in the world? Regardless of what you do to your hair, your makeup, or your clothes, if your attitude remains angry and resentful because of the divorce, it will show. Continue to take the time, and keep doing the work, to find more peace in your life. When you show up feeling calm, happy, and in the moment, you don't just look better, you make everyone around you feel better, too. To feel better inside and out, consider some style tips that worked for us.

UPDATING YOUR LOOK

If you're like most of the women in the Maplewood Divorce Club, you may have gotten into some fashion ruts while you were married. Perhaps you found some looks that worked as a mom or a working woman and simply stuck with them. Now that you're starting to think about socializing and putting your best pedicured foot forward, it's time to reconsider your clothing choices. If you're ready to add a little oomph to your wardrobe, we're here to provide you with shopping and shop-your-closet tips to help you reinvigorate your style.

Carlotta

Take Carlotta, who was making great strides. She was back to spinning and starting to shop a bit again. She wanted to feel and look better, but she was having trouble pulling it all together. One day on their way home from class, Carlotta told Suzanne that she was buying new clothes but she didn't really know what looked good on her, so most of the new purchases hung in her closet with the tags still on them. "I'm afraid I'm wasting my money," Carlotta said. "I was in my room trying on these khakis, and Bailey walked by, and she was so dramatic about how ugly they were: 'Are you trying to repel men, Mom? Not even Grandma wears pleated khakis.' Isn't that so mean?" Carlotta lamented.

The women put their heads together and decided to do a "Sip and Swap" with friends from the Maplewood Divorce Club at Carlotta's house. Each woman was asked to bring items to exchange for something another woman brought. A $0 shopping spree. "While we're there, you could model any of the outfits that you bought that you are unsure of and we can all give you our opinions, too," Suzanne suggested.

NEW SEASON, NEW SCENT

Anyone who has read Marcel Proust's *Remembrance of Things Past* understands that smells or scents awaken memories. In that book, the author recalled how having tea with a madeleine biscuit flooded him with memories of his childhood.

Rachel Herz, PhD, a recognized expert on the psychology of smell, says that scents have direct access to your hippocampus, the area of your brain that can recall specific memories. This means if your ex always showered with Irish Spring and used Right Guard deodorant, the smell of these will trigger your memory and have the potential to upset you.

If you had one signature scent that you wore when you were married, we encourage you to snuff out the Poison of your past, and sniff out a new perfume that calls to you.

There are different fragrance families: oriental, floral, woodsy, citrus, marine, and unisex. Take your nose to the perfume counter and try potential new scents on your pulse points before making a purchase. Perfume reacts with our body chemistry and can smell different on you than it does on someone else.

On the night of the Sip and Swap, Iris, Jill, Suzanne, Pilar, Eleanor, and Gina gathered in Carlotta's living room. Even though the group was made up of such different shapes, sizes, and styles, each woman brought clothing or accessories to trade to ensure everyone would be able to select something that would work for them. The first one to pick was Gina. She got up and flipped through a few shirts, and halfheartedly eyed a blazer. "Nothing is going to fit me while I'm breastfeeding," Gina said as she gestured to her ample chest. Gina was curvaceous before having her baby, but now she was positively voluptuous. "Try the brown belt," Jill offered. "I don't really wear belts, but okay," Gina said. She cinched the waist of the stretchy brown belt over her trapeze-style top, and voilà, an hourglass figure was born. "It helps define your waist and highlight your curves," Jill said. Gina just stared at the mirror. "I look . . . great! Why haven't I been wearing belts my whole life?!" Gina practically shouted. All the women laughed and fussed over how amazing she looked. Gina sat down (without taking her belt off), a happy camper.

Eleanor was next. She went straight for a miniskirt that belonged to Carlotta's daughter, Bailey. When Eleanor tried it on, the group fell silent. Eleanor tugged at the hem and asked, "What do you think? Does this show off my legs?" Pilar jumped up and grabbed a knee-length pencil skirt she had brought. "I think you have great legs, but that style isn't as sophisticated as you are," Pilar said. "Try this." Eleanor emerged a few moments later looking pleased. "This looks great, right?" The group agreed that this was a much more becoming look. "I'm still trying to find a happy medium between the sweater twinsets I used to wear and the more recent tank tops," Eleanor admitted sheepishly. Pilar offered to go shopping with Eleanor to help her find clothes to reflect this new sweet spot. "This is so much fun," Eleanor said. "I would be happy to host the next one so that we can also go through my closet." The group agreed.

Everyone got a turn. Purses, scarves, belts, dresses, pants, and tops were divvied up until almost nothing was left. The women chose items that clearly suited them as well as items that ventured out of their comfort zone—a new shape or brighter color than their usual. It was an easy, low-risk opportunity for testing new boundaries. What no one wanted, Carlotta bagged up to donate to charity. They took their wine and adjourned their fashion party upstairs to Carlotta's room for her to show off new purchases and get a style intervention from her friends. The pleated khaki pants got a resounding thumbs-down, but a peacock-blue cashmere V-neck sweater made the cut, as did a straight-legged berry-hued dress pant. Three pairs of stained, well-worn yoga pants went to the rag pile. The women helped Carlotta put together a few outfits, and she decided on a new fashion rule to live by: *Don't go out in yoga pants unless you're actually going to yoga.*

> "It's amazing how something as simple as a great new pair of boots can give me a boost and put a spring in my step." —Denise

The impact of clothes on mood has been scientifically proven. A group of researchers from the University of Queensland in Australia are currently looking at how we use clothes to improve or mask emotion. The researchers report that the clothes women select have the power to change their mood: If they get up and aren't feeling great, they will put on something to brighten their mood, and it works.

What image do I project?

As you begin to refine the clothing in your closet, this is the perfect time to check in with your girlfriends about the image you're projecting. Ask them what words they think of when they see you. When Denise, Jill, and Suzanne were together one night at a pub, they did this exercise. The words Jill and Suzanne came up with for Denise were: *elegant and professional, with a hint of sparkle.* This is exactly what Denise, a director at a pharma company, was going for. Her look was working for her. The words for Suzanne were *simple silhouette, fitted,* and *classics with a twist.* Jill's words were *current, colorful,* and *approachable.* Jill and Suzanne were also pleased to hear that each of their descriptions matched the images they hoped to project. This wasn't the case for Meghan.

When Meghan was out for trivia night with her roommate, Carlos; her new masseuse friend, Nancy; and Carlos's buddy, Dean, the subject of fashion came up. Meghan couldn't believe that Carlos, who was studying forestry, was able to answer so many trivia questions about designers. "How did you come up with Calvin Klein so clutch like that?" she asked him on their ride home. "I've read some *GQ*s and *Vanity Fair*s in my day," Carlos shared. "Guys can like fashion, too." "You . . . like fashion? All you wear is one boring T-shirt or one flannel after another," Meghan said. "Your look is 'bored lumberjack,'" she teased him. "Yeah, well, your look is 'boobs on display,'" Carlos retorted. Meghan was speechless. She thought her look was sexy and would help her meet someone new. The rest of their ride home was in silence.

The next afternoon, Meghan approached Carlos. "I'm sorry if I touched a nerve last night. You always look great," she said. Carlos smiled sheepishly. "Well, thanks, and listen, I didn't mean to hurt your feelings but seriously, every time I look at you there are inches of cleavage on display. It's just . . . a little too much."

Abashed, Meghan went back to her room and tried on her low-cut top from the night before, but this time she added a camisole underneath. This little tweak to her look still highlighted her assets but left a little bit to the

INDULGENT ME-TIME BEAUTY RITUALS

Everyone knows that French women have the ability to eat sticks of butter for breakfast and swipe on a red lip and manage to look effortlessly gorgeous and radiate health. While American women tend to wear their busyness like a badge of honor, French women insist on time for themselves. Take a page from their book and dedicate one hour a week to pamper and nurture your body.

Hang a "Do Not Disturb" sign on the bathroom door and retreat. Light candles and play relaxing music to help set the mood. Dry-brush your skin (upward strokes, please!); soak in a bath with essential oils such as lavender, chamomile, or vanilla; and apply a face mask and hair mask to work while you relax. After your bath, massage your body with grape-seed or almond oil and give yourself a mani-pedi. Do not rush through your hour—enjoy it. Soon it will become a part of your week that you can't imagine living without.

imagination. Meghan had a nice figure, but with the wrong neckline all anyone could notice was cleavage.

Meghan experimented with a few other outfits and applied what we call the foolproof Conceal/Reveal Technique. This helped to draw attention to one feature, like her nice bustline, while keeping, say, her shapely calves covered in a skinny jean. When she wants to show off her legs, she makes sure she is more covered up on top. Now, Meghan feels like she's getting more double takes—for all the right reasons. Meghan knew she was really onto something and called Amali to tell her to check out her Pinterest board of outfits. Amali, who was a bit more urban-techie in her look, noticed a difference in Meghan's appearance and told her she would share it with the group to inspire others.

DRESS WITHOUT STRESS

Suzanne often teases Jill for including "the ability to put together great outfits" as one of her skills, but no one would dispute the fact that Jill has a special flair. She always looks great and never looks the same. But when Jill started dating, she felt pressure to constantly come up with new outfits, which started to stress her out. Suzanne had the same problem. While Suzanne and Jill had different styles and wardrobes, they both had the same challenge: putting together great outfits for dates without stress.

Jill's solution is that for each season she creates five date looks that make her feel confident and beautiful, going so far as to plan out which accessories she will wear. She loves a flirty sundress or a floaty top with a skinny jean and a heel in the summer months. In the winter, she wants to look sleek (yet not freeze her bum off!), so she will usually wear either her pleather leggings with a high black boot and a silky top, coated denim jeans and an interesting sweater with an open neckline, or a fitted sweater dress and tights.

Suzanne took Jill's cue and decided to come up with her own preplanned date looks. Now they have go-to date outfits that they love and can get ready quickly without leaving their bedrooms in shambles. "I'm no longer tearing apart my closet trying to find something to wear," Suzanne says. "It's such a relief to have outfits for my first few dates all ready—and I feel great in them. With that part taken care of, I'm showing up more relaxed and having more fun."

Dating outfits

What you select to wear will of course depend on your personal style and your dating activity. It's important to remember that choosing the wrong shoes or a dress that's too tight, for example, can ruin an evening. Here are some suggestions to consider based on particular dates.

1. SITTING DATE (COFFEE/CASUAL DINNER/MOVIE/DRINKS OUT). Since you won't have to do much walking or standing, feel free to wear your high heels (as long as you can actually walk in them without tripping). This can also be an opportunity to wear bangle bracelets, longer earrings, and pieces that will showcase your personality.

2. ACTIVITY DATE (BOWLING/STROLLING/SPORTS EVENT/OUT-DOOR ACTIVITY). If you will be doing a lot of walking or standing, please do yourself a favor and wear flats. High heels on a wine-tasting tour or at a stadium are going to inhibit you from actually having any fun, which is the whole point of your outing! Denise learned this painful lesson the hard way after wearing four-inch heels to a concert that had her standing all night. Don't

WHOSE STYLE INSPIRES YOU?

When you're thinking of buying a few new items for your wardrobe, it can help to look at celebrities as well as women you encounter every day whose style you admire.

Jill loves Jessica Alba, a mom on the go, business owner, and activist/actress, who brings a creative flair to every occasion. "She always looks put together and stylish, whether she's on the playground with her kids or heading to a meeting," says Jill. Suzanne likes fellow native New Yorker Jennifer Aniston's unfussy, classic style, favoring jeans and black tops, which she accessorizes with jewelry and fun scarves and bags.

You might feel inspired by a woman you see at the mall, during your commute, or in your office. Be sure to take note of what you like about her style—and by all means, pay her a compliment if you get the chance.

wear anything too fussy or precious. Check the weather forecast to make sure you won't be shivering through a walk in the park or sweating through a baseball game.

3. SOPHISTICATED EVENING (DINNER/COCKTAIL PARTY). A timeless dress that fits you beautifully is something every woman should own. Select your footwear carefully if you will be doing a lot of standing or dancing and bring a clutch-style purse that you can easily place between your upper arm and body so that your hands are free to hold a drink, shake hands, and eat hors d'oeuvres. Add some sparkly jewelry and you will be ready to wow.

FAKE IT TILL YOU MAKE IT (WITH MAKEUP)

Say what? You didn't just get back from a week at Ten Thousand Waves Spa in Santa Fe? Well, neither did we. We are all too busy working, running after kids, unloading the dishwasher, or returning phone calls to spend time at a spa, but we still want to look great. Luckily, we learned some makeup tips that helped our group of girlfriends look like a million bucks.

The goal here is to look fresh, healthy, and lit from within all day long, despite the challenges. Jamie was making rest a priority but would still occasionally have trouble getting a good night's sleep. The result? Puffy eyes and dark circles. Iris was working hard to move her life forward, but sometimes Flint still got to her and she would find herself in tears. She discovered the best ways to hide red-rimmed and bloodshot eyes when she had to leave the house after she had been crying. Carlotta had kept up with her highlights, was exercising regularly, and had some new outfits but felt unsure how to update her makeup routine now that she was thinking about dating again.

The telltale signs of too little sleep

Try as we might, there are still times when we don't get enough sleep at night, either because we stayed up too late or just had trouble dozing off to begin with. Both Jamie and Renée had ongoing sleep problems to overcome during their divorces that resulted in puffy eyes for Renée and dark circles that plagued Jamie. Renée discovered a relaxing treatment for her eyes that generates results and takes about thirty minutes. Jamie, who was always pressed for time, came up with a speedy solution to hide her dark circles so she could get out the door in the morning looking well rested. In addition, both women employ the "ounce of prevention is worth a pound of cure" adage. Renée doubles up on her pillows in bed to prevent any extra fluid from pooling in her eye area. Jamie always passes on the margaritas with salt, chips and salsa, and any other salty snack in the evenings to prevent water retention.

Renée's Relaxing Tea Treatment for Puffy Eyes

- Brew two bags of black tea and steep them for three to five minutes, then place them on a plate and into the fridge for at least fifteen minutes.
- Squeeze out the excess liquid from the tea bag. Lie down on the couch with your feet up and put the tea bags on your eyes for at least fifteen minutes. The tannins and the caffeine in the tea work their magic to stimulate and tighten the skin.
- Remove tea bags.

Jamie's "Adios to Dark Circles" Routine

- Splash cold water on your face. Apply your color-correcting cream (like tinted moisturizer, only better) with SPF 30 or higher to moisturize your face.
- Place a roll-on under-eye concealer into the fridge for a few minutes prior to use. Once cold, use this to help massage out any fluid and conceal the dark circles under your eyes.
- Pat on the peach-toned concealer from your concealer quad to camouflage the dark circles.
- Smudge on some navy eyeliner as close to the eyelash line as possible. Curl eyelashes and add mascara.

Banishing all evidence of tears

Things were going better for Iris. The closing on her marital home was approaching, she was enjoying her new job at the hospital, her girls were doing well, and she was saving a lot of money. Even so, every now and then, if she thought Flint was acting like a jerk or if she was having a bad day, she would still have a good cry. She couldn't let crying derail her day. Iris needed to be able to quickly face the world, whether it was the other moms at the bus stop or her coworkers, without everyone knowing she had been crying.

Iris's Tips to Hide the Tracks of Your Tears

- Splash cool water on your face and into your eyes (contact lens wearers beware).
- Apply redness-relief eye drops ASAP to get rid of the redness. If your nose is red apply some on your skin there as well to constrict blood vessels.
- Drink a full glass of water and take ibuprofen to fight the inflammation if your eyes are puffy.
- Apply eye cream and color-correcting cream, and then see if there is still discoloration or redness around your eyes. If there is, use a green-tinted concealer from your concealer quad (green counteracts redness), line eyes with navy liner, curl lashes, and apply waterproof mascara.

Iris noticed that if she applied pink blush, or red, berry, or pink lipstick, it made redness in her eyes more visible. "I chose a peachy-pink blush or bronzer and neutral lip gloss," shared Iris. "I noticed that any pink-toned makeup would draw attention to any redness on my face." When you have to leave the house and don't have time to counteract the redness, put on some fierce sunglasses for a quick disguise.

Ready, set, gorgeous!

Carlotta had always been more of a wash-'n'-go girl than a multistep beauty routine follower. But ever since the FedEx guy had started flirting with her and she'd begun to think about dating again, she'd been putting a little more effort into looking polished and pretty when she went out the door. After some trial and error, purchasing some unflattering makeup, and asking everyone she knew for their best tips, Carlotta came up with a quick routine anyone can do (or adapt) to look and feel their best.

> "When I took the extra ten minutes in the a.m. to choose accessories and added blush and eyeliner to my routine, I began getting compliments everywhere I went, which made me feel great."   —Carlotta

Carlotta's Quick, Confidence-Boosting Morning Routine

- Wash your face or splash it with cool water to wake up the skin and tighten your pores. Apply eye cream (with your ring finger; it's the most gentle) and color-correcting cream. Dust translucent powder on your forehead, nose, and chin.
- Pat (do not rub) concealer where needed. Add some gel blush to the apples of your cheeks for a healthy flush.
- Brush your eyebrows up and out with clear mascara or brow gel to frame your face. Apply navy eyeliner (to make the whites of your eyes whiter) and "flick" it out and up at the corners of your eyes.
- Curl your eyelashes to help fake your wide-awake look. Apply waterproof mascara in a gentle *S* motion from the roots of your lashes to the tips.
- Trace your lips and fill them in with a neutral lip liner, then top with a creamy long-lasting lip gloss.

Resources Expert Beauty and Fashion Guidance

The 5-Minute Face: The Quick & Easy Makeup Guide for Every Woman by Carmindy. The makeup artist from TLC's popular show *What Not to Wear* shares her positive beauty philosophy. She offers a practical, easy, fast, and mistake-proof makeup routine that works for all ages and skin types.

Vlogger Michelle Phan's Beauty Basics series. Log on to YouTube to check out Phan's easy-to-follow beauty tutorials.

Color Me Confident: Change Your Look—Change Your Life by Veronique Henderson and Pat Henshaw. Learn what shades work best with your skin, hair, and eye tone. The confidence-building plans feature ideal outfits for any shape; tricks for adapting your wardrobe to different lifestyles; and ideas for developing a creative approach to dress.

The Cool Factor: A Guide to Achieving Effortless Style, with Secrets from the Women Who Have It by Andrea Linett. Renowned personal stylist and founding creative director of *Lucky* magazine, Linett offers easy-to-implement, actionable tips and well-illustrated advice to help women develop a distinctive personal style.

When you want to really add a wow factor, Carlotta swears by Whitestrips to bleach her pearly whites a few days before an event. "A great smile is an immediate eye-catcher," she says.

ADVICE FROM THE PROS

Going for a free makeover can be a fun way to get some ideas about what colors look best and how to enhance your features, as well as tips on applying makeup. Denise convinced Pilar to join her one Saturday afternoon and headed to Sephora. Pilar was very budget-conscious since her split. Still, she felt she never applied her makeup properly and wanted to learn some tricks. Denise was ready to splurge on a few new products.

Pilar learned how to contour to bring out her amazing cheekbones and discovered the shade of blush that would warm up her olive complexion. Denise didn't want Pilar to feel pressured to buy, so she let the makeup artists know that she would be the one buying that day. However, Pilar couldn't resist the twelve-dollar peachy blush that made her look lit from within and years younger, while Denise filled her basket with plummy lipstick, shea body butter, and a hair mask to restore the sheen to her relaxed hair. Denise also purchased some of the products her consultant used during her makeover.

> "I thought I knew what I was doing with my makeup, but I learned a few key tips from the pros at my makeover that have made a huge difference. It's fun to add new elements to my makeup routine." —Pilar

She added a long-wearing eye shadow to play up her brown eyes and a gentle illuminating powder she could dust on her cheekbones as well as on her décolletage, bringing out her inner sparkle and sass.

Suzanne and Jill learned that the eye makeup colors that will bring out your eyes are the exact opposite of your eye color on the color wheel. Suzanne brings out her golden brown eyes with navy blue mascara and eyeliner, Jill plays up her green eyes with purple liner, and Jamie draws attention to her blue eyes with a sweep of golden tan shadow.

REBOUND HAIR BEYOND COMPARE

Reese Witherspoon's first triumphant red carpet moment post–Ryan Phillippe split (amid rumors he'd cheated on her with another actress) was in a canary yellow Nina Ricci dress, debuting new, edgier side-swept bangs. She appeared to be telling the world that she had the energy to start again, that she was in control of her image . . . and her life. "She seemed to be saying, 'Who needs him? I don't,'" Carlotta says. "I cut out that photo of Reese with her layered hair and her face-framing bangs to remind myself that changing your look and feeling good about it can give you a boost even if you're still working through stuff."

After a big breakup or a divorce, it's not unusual for a woman to get a new hairstyle to show the world—and herself—that she's let go of the past and is bouncing back. This is the phenomenon known as Rebound Hair. Of course, a hair makeover isn't a time for a DIY approach, so put down the scissors and that box of hair color and go see a professional you trust!

Carlotta

Carlotta brought the photo of Reese to Gina, who had already helped Amali with her Rebound Hair. Gina believes that before you go under the scissors, you should talk with your stylist and be sure you know what you're doing. "You want to avoid getting an impulsive cut that you'll regret," says Gina. "I never encourage women to make a drastic change in a fragile state. I talk with them extensively about how they see themselves, what they're hoping for, and how much time they have for their hair each day."

Carlotta and Gina discussed the pros and cons of bangs, the work they'd involve, and whether Carlotta would be comfortable with the fact that they'd take a few months to grow out when she got tired of them. Carlotta was ready to commit to bangs and encouraged Gina to pick up the scissors and start her transformation. "I loved my new bangs, and we also did a keratin treatment," Carlotta says. "I felt great and got tons of compliments on my new look."

Denise had been relaxing her hair for as long as she could remember. She felt her hair looked sleek and professional but lacked personality. After her separation, she chose to switch up her hairdo and made an appointment to get a weave. She loved having swingy shoulder-length hair and the new 'do made her feel gorgeous.

Though it may be tempting to change your hair color or style dramatically, it's important to be aware that going too far can take years to fix. As a rule of thumb, after talking with your hairstylist, continue to pay close attention

SIDE EFFECTS MAY INCLUDE UNWANTED ADVANCES

Jamie had been taking better care of herself, and it showed. Her skin glowed with health, her eyes sparkled, and she seemed to exude happiness. Her ex, Doug, noticed the difference when he was invited over for their younger son's birthday party.

Jamie was in the kitchen preparing snacks when he wrapped his arms around her and whispered in her ear, "Jamie, you have never looked more beautiful." Jamie elbowed him in the gut with all her strength. "You don't get to touch me anymore," she snapped. With that, she picked up the tray of snacks and made her way to the waiting children in the living room. Doug never made another move on her again.

Your ex will notice the new and improved you, and he will likely have something to say about it. Remember who your new look is for—you!

WHAT MAKES YOU FEEL YOUR BEST?

Think about what makes you feel great—and do more of that! One woman's snake-print heels are another's favorite scent. Here are a few things that work for us.

"When I want to feel put-together and stylish, I throw on an A-line dress and a chunky necklace." —Iris

"I don't go out the door without perfume. My favorite scent these days reminds me of the smell of honeysuckle." —Jill

"I like to start my day with a workout. It helps me feel energized all day." —Suzanne

"I don't overdo it, but I love the feeling of being a little sun-kissed and using bronzer. Catching a few rays makes me feel great." —Pilar

"I always feel great in my skinny jeans. I can dress them up or down with different tops and I'm always comfortable." —Amali

"I wear my grandma's charm bracelet on special occasions—it reminds me of her and makes me happy." —Renée

"High heels make me feel irresistible and in control, like I can conquer the world." —Denise

"Listening to '80s music and dancing around before I go out always puts me in the mood to have fun." —Jamie

"I know how massaging out tension makes a huge difference in how I feel in my body. It's lucky for me I am surrounded by other therapists to barter with. I get a massage at least once a week." —Meghan

"I started investing in lingerie after my divorce. It makes me feel sexy no matter what I'm wearing over it." —Carlotta

"It's a real treat to have someone style my hair and give me a bouncy blowout." —Gina

"A crisp white shirt with colorful jewelry always boosts my mood." —Eleanor

when he starts to cut your hair so he doesn't get scissor happy. Sometimes two inches turns into six inches, and suddenly your long hair is, well, not long at all. The best choice is a stylist you've worked with for a long time so he understands your taste and what makes you feel comfortable and confident.

As a professional hairdresser, Gina has seen many women come in with hair that they colored themselves that ended in disaster. "You really don't want to go more than two shades from your natural color if you are coloring it yourself," she advises, "and definitely see a professional if you're looking for a dramatic color change. I've seen too many horror stories where the cost of fixing the red that turned brassy orange or the blond that turned green is far more than the single-process color would have been in the first place."

What I Wish I'd Known

"I wish I'd had a better sense of what image I was projecting. I was surprised to learn I was wearing clothes that came off as too revealing—I thought I was just being sexy. It was all tied up in my lack of confidence—when I felt better about who I was, it was easier to dress more conservatively, but still make an impact."

—Meghan

Chapter 14
HAPPILY EVER AFTER . . . WITH YOURSELF

"It is only possible to live happily ever after on a daily basis."
—Margaret Wander Bonanno

I f you're like us, you may sometimes succumb to "if I just had a man" thinking. It goes something like this: *If I just had a new man in my life, everything would be so much easier. I'd be so much happier. I wouldn't feel lonely, sad, or like I'm missing out.* Well, you already had a man in your life, and that didn't solve everything. Trying to replace him likely won't solve everything, either. We took time after our divorces to figure out what we wanted our lives to look like and how we could take steps to make that happen. A man wasn't part of the initial plan. It was up to us to create the lives we wanted for ourselves.

Nora Ephron noted that "marriages come and go, but divorce is forever." Similarly, people will come and go in your life, but there's only one person who is guaranteed to be with you from the day you're born till the day you take your last breath—and that's you. Accept this fact and do everything in your power to create the experiences, friendships, opportunities, and outlook you desire.

We've learned that when you wait for the perfect time to do anything, you can miss out on so much because there's no such time. We put off buying homes after our divorces because we were waiting for the right man to do this with us. Gina put off dating until she lost those last twenty pounds. Amali put off applying for her dream job fearing she didn't have the right experience. All of us realized that our joy is there for the taking and ours for the making. Today.

THE BENEFITS OF BEING SINGLE

You never know how long this period of being single will last, so why not enjoy it? When you're on your own, you decide how you want to spend your time and your money, and what you want to eat for dinner, watch on TV, or do this weekend. During this period, you don't need to consider a partner's wants, needs, or desires. For Jill, that meant never again listening to another World Cup soccer game at 3 a.m. For Denise, it meant not having to clean smashed Fritos from the carpet. Gina was finally able to decorate her home exactly as she liked. Suzanne got the car she always wanted because she picked it out. Whether you plan to plant roots in Singleville, USA, for a while, like Amali, or you're just passing through and plan to start dating again, like Jamie, Iris, and others, make sure you take the time to enjoy being single while you can. Here are reminders of the upside to single life.

You're Living a Life with More Choices

Maybe you ended up in Albany because that's where his sister lives. Perhaps you ate steak and potatoes more often than you liked, or you never went on a beach vacation because he hates the sand. Those days are over. Want to watch three episodes of your favorite show back-to-back and eat almonds in bed? Go right ahead. Feel like salad for dinner again? Why not? Want to take the kids to your parents for a week? Do it. You can now spend your holidays traveling to new places, with your family, or however you want. Savor this period when you're the center of your world.

Being Single Doesn't Mean Being Lonely

Though you're single, you can still have lots of people in your life and an active social calendar, if that's what you want. There's a difference between being alone and lonely. Being alone means you're enjoying your time by yourself and doing the things that you want to do. Being lonely is akin to sitting in a dark room wishing anyone would call and ask you to do something. Alone is "active" and lonely is "passive." Alone is finding contentment in whatever you're doing yourself, while being lonely has a "woe is me" flavor as you wait for someone else to change your circumstances. If you live in a town, city, or thriving community, there is always something to do. You can volunteer, go to a lecture series, sign up for a class, campaign for someone running for office, fund-raise for something you believe in, join a meet-up, go to a play, take an exercise class, or attend a service at your house of worship. There are countless opportunities to join groups and mini communities. If you're in a more rural location, you will likely have to travel a bit farther but don't discount message boards, Facebook groups, and other online communities to connect with people interested in the same hobbies and passions you have. Be sure to connect with our community at optimistsguidetodivorce.com.

> "Between my husband, our son, and my job, I didn't have much time for my girlfriends when I was married. Since the split, one of the things I value most has been reconnecting with my girlfriends in a deeper way. They've offered so much support— and so much fun." —Denise

You Can Immerse Yourself in Girlfriend Land

Schedule a boozy brunch with your besties, stat. Plan that girls' trip you always talked about to Mexico. Eat dinner with your pals on a Tuesday for no reason at all. Reconnect with the friends you might not have given enough attention to when you were married. Enjoy this rare time when you get to see your friends a lot more often.

You Get to Date Yourself

This is the part of the story where you fall in love and can't wait to spend time . . . with yourself. You give yourself thoughtful gifts, like those earrings that caught your eye last week. If you want to see the new Tina Fey movie, then you get tickets and go on opening night. You take yourself to that modern art exhibit you've wanted to check out. That's right, you're dating yourself. You're a lot of fun, and you've never been happier.

You're whole and complete just as you are

One night Amali and Pilar were catching up and eating popcorn, sitting on Amali's couch with the movie *Jerry Maguire* playing in the background. The end scene came, where Jerry (Tom Cruise) bursts into Dorothy's (Renée Zellweger) living room to proclaim the oft-repeated line, "You complete me." Onscreen, Dorothy bawls because she is so happy and relieved to be rescued by a man. The scene at Amali's was quite different: "I complete me, Tom!" Amali shouted, as both women threw popcorn at the TV.

Amali had been analyzing all the choices she had made so far in her life, taking the time to see where she had made the decision or where her family and their expectations were the deciding factor. She realized that unlike a lot of women who dream of their wedding day, of starting a family and growing old with someone, she was pretty sure she preferred being by herself. Amali knew that she loved working with computers, and that she enjoyed being alone, and she was okay with that. A few weeks later, when Amali got home in the evening she found on her stoop a five-by-seven-inch

KNOW YOUR BEST QUALITIES

Getting in touch with what you really want will happen gradually as your sense of self gets stronger. Since your divorce, you may have started to second-guess just about everything, including what's special and wonderful about you. On those days when you need a pick-me-up, try this self-esteem booster that worked for us. Let the people closest to you remind you of your most lovable qualities. We asked some friends and family to text us five adjectives that described what they love about us.

Suzanne was reminded that others think of her as creative, smart, thoughtful, fun, and open-minded. Jill's list included caring, talented, wise, entertaining, and funny. Denise's list? Optimistic, ambitious, successful, considerate, and hardworking. Ask your friends and family to help you compile a master list of your positive attributes and paste it on the mirror in your bedroom. It will be a great emotional boost when you need it and a constant reminder of how wonderful you truly are.

tage wrapped in brown paper. Amali carefully opened it to find a hand-painted mini canvas from Pilar. The painting was in beautiful sunset colors and written across the sky were Amali's words, "I complete me." The accompanying note read, "Never forget it!" Amali smiled and hung the painting in the entry foyer to her condo where one of her wedding photos used to be. This was a note (unlike the one she received from Sugi), and a message, worth saving.

DON'T PUT YOUR LIFE ON HOLD

Are you waiting to live out certain dreams until you get another partner who will ride shotgun on your escapades? If so, consider that you might be denying yourself the experiences you long for while you wait for a person you don't even know. If that isn't enough to put you in motion, keep in mind that it may be in the very act of living out your dreams volunteering at the Humane Society, going on that cycling tour, taking that photography class, or signing up for a salsa session that you will meet a partner who shares your passions. Even if you don't meet someone, you will be empowered by the fact that you're boldly living life.

Eleanor had always wanted to travel far more than her ex-husband. She'd managed to convince him to go to Europe only once during their long marriage. Postdivorce, she treated herself to a solo trip to Greece with a tour group. She didn't want to wait for a willing travel companion anymore. Eleanor fell in love with the vibrant country, enjoyed sightseeing and shopping with different members of her travel group, and even had an alfresco meal solo one evening by the ocean.

Suzanne knew she wanted to buy a house but put it off for a few years after her divorce, moving into a rental apartment instead. In the back of her mind, she didn't want to pick a new home until she met the man she wanted to live with. Then it dawned on her that during this waiting game, she and her son weren't enjoying the additional space, the kitchen with all the windows, the porch with the rocking chair, or the yard with the hammock and trampoline that they both dreamed about. "I didn't want to put off our happiness today for an uncertain dream in the future," Suzanne says. "The right partner for me would be a creative thinker who would want to figure out how to share a home together."

Gina

Gina had given up on men after her husband, Clayton, left her. She'd drag herself into work, often not even bothering to put on makeup. After she started exercising again, and dressing to flatter her curves, she started feeling better about herself, despite the baby weight she hadn't lost yet. "My sense of self and my self-esteem were coming out of hiding," she says. "I enjoyed my work and I wanted to show up with a smile." Working late one Wednesday night, Gina spread the shiny black cape around Bobby, an attractive man who needed a trim for an important meeting the next day. He told Gina that he found his way to her salon because his usual barber was sick. Gina moved more slowly than usual as she cut Bobby's hair because she didn't want the conversation to end. It turns out Gina wasn't the only one who was smitten. Bobby scribbled a note on the tip envelope, leaving his number and asking her to please give him a call. She did a few days later.

Goals vs. dreams

Dreams can inspire, motivate, and fill you with hope. But your wildest dreams will never come true if you don't attach attainable goals to them and take actionable steps to turn them into reality. The easiest way to figure out how to make your dreams come true is to put a time stamp on them and then work backward to plan how you're going to get there. We all have dreams, some financial, some personal, some far-fetched, and some too private to share with others. Make your dreams a reality like we did through goal setting. If a dream is the *what*, then the goal is the *how*.

> "I knew for a long time that I wanted to move out of my parents' house, but only when I took the time to get out a calendar and a calculator and set specific goals did I start to make that dream come true." —Iris

Iris dreamed of moving herself and her girls out of her parents' home and into a home of their own within two years. Her goal was to spend the next year and a half taking steps to improve her credit score and save a minimum of $15,000 for a down payment. Gina's dream was to lose all her baby weight by the end of the year. Her goal was to lose a few pounds a month, to nurse Valentina until she was nine months old, and to power walk for forty-five minutes at least five days a week. Jamie's dream was to save enough money

CREATING YOUR VISION BOARD

A vision board is a blank space (for example, a piece of poster board or a bulletin board) that will serve as a life map of your hopes and dreams. The theory is that first you have to see it and believe it to eventually get it.

To get started, be quiet and allow yourself to dream. Then go through old magazines and books, and cut out or copy down words, images, and anything else that inspires you. The sky's the limit! A beautiful sunset on the beach, a dream house, a Disney vacation with your kids, a goal for your marathon personal-record time—anything that calls to you deserves a spot on your board.

Look for ideas big and small, from the exotic to the mundane. Think about things you'd like to do, for example, hosting a theme party, bottlefeeding baby animals, running a 5K, or taking a trip to Iceland. Get a glue stick, tape, and pushpins and assemble your poster board.

When the board looks complete to you, hang it in a prominent spot in your bedroom or in your home office. And of course you can always add and remove things as your goals and dreams evolve.

Another idea is to open a Notes page in your cell phone or get a dedicated pocket-size notebook to keep track of your amazing ideas—something you can keep in your purse, so you have it at the ready. The purpose of the list is to gather all those "someday" ideas you have into one place and challenge yourself to actually do them.

to take her two boys to Disney World before her oldest was ten years old. She did some careful planning and calculated that she would need to save at least $7,000 over the next three years. She realized if she gave up buying lunch and brown-bagged it for three years she would save enough money.

When you're coming up with goals, keep in mind:

• Goals have deadlines (this month, next year, per week, etc.).

• Goals are based in reality (attainable with dedication and effort).

• Goals require work (taking consistent steps).

WHAT WILL YOUR NEXT RELATIONSHIP LOOK LIKE?

Before you jump into the dating scene, you may want to do some soul searching so you know what you're looking for (and what you want to stay away from). Eleanor knew she was more interested in an activity partner than a romantic one. She wanted someone to go out with, but she also needed her space. "For most of my adult life, I catered to my husband and daughter when I was home," she says. "I was finally at the point where I felt like my home was my sanctuary, and I really didn't want to share it with anyone just yet."

Denise wanted a wild and passionate romance. She had a drawer in her dresser that she left empty for her future partner. However, she didn't imagine him moving in with her. "I was attached to the idea of him being around and accessible, but I wasn't going to move out of my new place," she says. "I saw him staying over a couple of nights a week, but I wanted to have some days free each week for my son and my friends."

Jill was open to getting married again. She wanted a man to share her life with, but she couldn't imagine changing the dynamic in her household made up of all girls. "It doesn't matter if he has kids of his own or not," she says. "I see the man I will settle down with as someone ready for a real partnership where we take on everything life throws at us, together."

Who do you want to invite into your life? Mr. Right or Mr. Right Now? Mr. Fling or Mr. Ring or no man at all? Realize that the choice is yours. As you start to think about the person you will date after yourself, make a list of the qualities you're looking for in a partner. Read it over. Be the kind of partner you want to attract. You like men who are active? Tie on your own sneakers and make breaking a sweat a regular part of your life. Prefer men who are confident? Guess what—they prefer women who are confident, too. Do you enjoy being with someone who gets out in the world and engages in interesting activities, like hiking, photography, travel, or wine tasting? When is the last time you tried something new?

"The shift for me was to stop looking for someone else to make everything okay," says Suzanne. "That was my job. Another person is someone to enjoy, not someone to make me whole, because I already am." Suzanne likes to remember the words of a friend who told her that a relationship with a man

> ### *Resources* — Enjoying Time Alone
>
> *How to Be Alone: The School of Life* by Sara Maitland. The author gives some tips on how to overcome the fear of being alone so we can embrace this time. She proposes using your alone time to develop skills and hobbies that will enrich your life. In this thoughtful and practical book, she asks deeper questions such as how we have arrived in a culture that values individualism but at the same time is terrified of solitude.
>
> *Going Solo: The Extraordinary Rise and Surprising Appeal of Living Alone* by Eric Klinenberg.
> A sociologist upends conventional wisdom by offering up portraits of single people, ages eighteen to eighty, who are connected to social groups, civically active, and happy with their choice to live alone.
>
> *How to Be Single* (movie, 2016). Need a laugh? This occasionally raunchy, often hilarious comedy set against the backdrop of NYC features an eclectic group of women and men who are all single for different reasons and follows them as they look for fun and new relationships.

is the icing on the cake—but you're the cake. You bring your best self to the party and don't need him to rescue you. He's extra sweetness in your already happy life.

LESSONS AND LIGHT

As the poet Rumi said, "The wound is the place where light enters you." If you look for them, the lessons from your divorce, and the enlightenment that follows, are there for you. Each one of the women in our circle can name things they are thankful for that are a direct result of their separation or divorce process. What can you name as benefits of your relationship with your ex and your divorce?

- Jill made a community of familylike support for herself and other women in her town by forming the Maplewood Divorce Club with Suzanne.
- Suzanne channeled her feelings and learning into a creative collaboration with Jill—the very book you are reading.
- Iris fulfilled her dream of becoming a nurse so she could heal children and help families.

- Denise stood up for a chance at true love and kept her heart open.
- Jamie got to show her boys an example of a strong and courageous woman who puts her children first and advocates for herself.
- Eleanor seized the opportunity to develop her own identity beyond being a wife and mother.
- Carlotta made a difference in her community by volunteering in the community food gardens. She showed her daughter that she could weather heartache and grow through it.
- Pilar gained a new understanding and appreciation of her husband, Justin.
- Meghan gained a feeling of self-worth when she started acting like a prize worth winning instead of a free gift with purchase.
- Renée was able to recapture her dream of seeing the world and traveling through her humanitarian work.
- Amali applied for a higher-level job at her company and landed it. She also launched her side business setting up home computers.
- Gina became more responsible with her finances and her business.

What I Wish I'd Known

"I wish I'd known how powerful repeating positive affirmations would be. All through the day, I would say, 'You are doing a great job, Gina. Keep it up.' When I felt overwhelmed, I reminded myself that I am grateful to have my thriving business, a house to take care of, friends to call back, and a healthy new baby." —Gina

Chapter 15

SOCIALIZING AGAIN: THE SCARLET *D*

"A lot of what is most beautiful about the world arises from struggle."
—Malcolm Gladwell

Y ou have likely discovered that there's a direct correlation between the speed at which word spreads around town about your split and the rate at which your social currency drops from dollars to pennies. Our friends and neighbors didn't quite know what to do with us. Some kept a safe distance, in case what we had was contagious. Others stopped inviting us into their homes, imagining that we were desperately seeking a new man, any man, even their man. We found married men came out of the woodwork thinking we would be interested; we weren't. Iris remembers one cookout where a married female friend, upon walking into the kitchen and seeing Iris and the friend's hubby getting items out of the refrigerator, chided, "Oh no! Stay outside where I can keep an eye on you." Ouch.

Much like Hester Prynne in *The Scarlet Letter*, who is forced to wear a scarlet *A* for adulteress, you may find yourself marked by a scarlet *D* for divorcée.

Gossip has momentum, and as a result the first thing some people in town will think when they see you is "divorced." Suzanne recalls being approached by a mom acquaintance while waiting to pick up her son at school. "Tell me how you did it," the woman said in hushed tones. "I've been miserable for so long. I need to get a divorce. I don't know where to begin. Can you help me?"

For us, navigating our changing social status in a couples-only scene of intact family units felt isolating and lonely. We developed strategies for showing up solo to social events and defusing tension, and found much-needed comfort spending time with our friends in the Maplewood Divorce Club. You will want to keep some easy phrases on hand, such as, "It's awkward because you know us both, but we don't have to talk about the separation. I was just looking forward to having a fun evening together." This can do wonders for deflating the pink elephant in the room with your ex-husband's face on it. Socializing, whether with friends, acquaintances, or our extended families, brought its share of challenges. We learned how to adapt to the changing landscape, and you can, too.

STRATEGIES FOR REJOINING THE SOCIAL SCENE

When you were first going through your divorce, your instinct was likely to circle the wagons—to communicate only with your nearest and dearest, perhaps your sister, mom, and best friends, and otherwise retreat. You will likely find that the world has been waiting for you to come back. Many people would love to hear from you, and a lot of people have missed seeing you around.

As you start stepping out into the social scene and doing things alone that you used to do as a couple—attending block parties, dinners, holiday cocktails, weddings, and school events—you may find yourself having to act outside your comfort zone. You may want to make some adjustments to ease your transition. Approaches that worked for us and our friends include letting the host of the party know that you're separated, practicing conversation starters, and even bringing another separated or divorced friend as your "date." Be sure to have your stock answer for questions about your divorce in place to sidestep any uncomfortable queries.

Learn from our stories about how we found a balance between socializing with other divorced women and everyone else, made face-to-face connections versus relying on social media, and ventured out even when we felt brokenhearted.

Getting out of your comfort zone . . . in heels

If going out alone isn't generally your cup of tea, you may want to consider adopting a new mind-set to become a star at *solocializing* (solo socializing). Start with going out for breakfast. Take a newspaper or a book for company, which can help you feel less self-conscious. A few bites into your bran muffin, you may be thinking, *This is fantastic. I'm great company.* Next, you can venture out to a movie by yourself. Start with a matinee. No need to share your Milk Duds or sit through another smash-'em-up car chase film. *The Notebook 2* (dare to dream) might be just the ticket.

With those experiences under your belt, why not aim for the bleachers? You're going to a party alone! It will help you project an air of confidence if you can muster up the mind-set *I am secure and content, and I am going to take myself out on the town because I want to.* This kind of boldness can add an air of excitement to your evening.

Jamie

Jamie hadn't gone out alone yet, but after hearing about impending layoffs at her job, she was motivated to attend a local Media Networking Night. She fiddled with the straps of her new dress, smoothed down her hemline, and walked into the restaurant. She saw small crowds of people—all strangers. *Who am I going to talk to?* Jamie picked up a marker and wrote out a name tag, *Advertising, Jamie,* and put it on her chest. She walked to the bar and ordered a drink. Feeling embarrassed that nobody had come up to talk to her, a few minutes later she escaped to the ladies' room. She soon ventured back out and did a lap around the room but wasn't feeling brave enough to join a conversation midstream. Back to the ladies' room she went.

> "I felt less uncomfortable out alone if I set a concrete goal—whether it was to introduce myself to a specific person or to say hi to a set number of new people." —Jamie

Jamie felt relieved to be ensconced in the only room where she didn't have to make small talk, when the bathroom attendant, the first person who spoke to her all night, started asking her questions. "Honey, who are you hiding from?" "Everyone," Jamie answered. Jamie told the friendly woman that she'd recently separated and hadn't gone out alone in more than a decade. The attendant handed her a mint and some good advice. "You have a gorgeous dress on. Don't come back until you've introduced yourself to three new people and smiled at five," she told her. "It's not hard," she said, extending her hand. "I'm Colleen." Jamie shook her hand and introduced herself.

"Introduce myself to *three* people?" Jamie asked, as she reapplied her lipstick. "Three," Colleen confirmed. "I've been doing this a long time, and you're not the first shy woman I've kicked out of the bathroom. Three is the magic number. Let me know how it goes."

Jamie gathered her courage and left the loo. She spied an older woman alone, figured she was safe, and introduced herself. After some chitchat about a new shop that had just opened, the older woman excused herself because she was meeting her son for dinner downstairs. Jamie decided to order another drink and wondered if introducing herself to the bartender would count. While she was waiting for her wine, another woman ordered a drink. "Having a nice time?" the woman asked. "It's all right," Jamie said, shrugging. "Let's play a game," her new friend said. "Scan the room—pick the man that you would date, murder, or marry." Jamie dutifully did a 360 and carefully considered the candidates. She caught one man with navy blue glasses looking at her. "I'd date him, then marry him, then murder him when he leaves me," Jamie said with a laugh. "Hear, hear, good choice," the woman said as she picked up her fresh drink and clinked glasses with Jamie. "I think he works at the History Channel. Good luck." And with that she was gone before Jamie had a chance to introduce herself.

When Jamie turned around, Navy Blue Glasses was standing directly in front of her, smiling. "You're doing a great job," he said with a smirk. "Excuse me?" Jamie said. "I'll take six cases," he continued as he gestured to her name tag. "You are 'advertising Jamie,' and I want to buy one." Jamie couldn't help but laugh. "I work in advertising," she explained. He extended his hand, "History Channel. Paul." As the two shook hands, Jamie realized the party and the potential were most definitely outside the bathroom. Jamie and Paul exchanged phone numbers. Jamie and Colleen exchanged emails. Jamie went home that night warmed by the kindness of strangers and truly excited about her single life for the first time since her separation.

The Takeaway: Though you may dread going out alone, you can find ways to feel more comfortable and even enjoy yourself, like we did. It helped us to buy or borrow a new dress to feel confident and attractive, and to set achievable goals, like talking to three new people and smiling at five, as Jamie did. We gave ourselves an out—if we took these actions and weren't having fun, we could go home. Nine times out of ten, we wound up staying and having fun.

Brawl at the book club

When you start going out again, even seemingly safe gatherings may trigger an unexpected emotional reaction. Eleanor was thrilled when her neighbor Cindy invited her to the Read Hot Mamas' Book Club. Eleanor arrived right on time, clutching her dog-eared copy of *The Kite Runner* in one hand and a bottle of Chardonnay in the other. She loved the book, finishing it in just a few days, and eagerly joined the handful of women already gathered in the living room. "I bet I'm not the only one who's dying to discuss this book!" she said as she poured herself some wine. "Oh, I haven't even bought it yet," Alice, the host, said, laughing dismissively. The women introduced themselves and let Eleanor know that they didn't talk about the book until everyone has arrived. About forty-five minutes later, they were still waiting for a straggler. Eleanor was on her third glass of wine as she listened to Alice continue to complain about her job. The topic then shifted to parent-teacher conferences. By the time the women were exchanging stories about how many nights a week they were having sex with their husbands, Eleanor was fed up. She'd also finished her entire bottle of Chardonnay herself.

When Juliette, the last member, finally arrived, the women were enjoying themselves and the easy congeniality of the group—except for Eleanor. She felt irritated and left out, listening to the women chat on and on about their husbands, kids, and jobs. Her husband was gone, she had never worked outside of the home, and her daughter was grown up and off living on her own. "I would apologize for being late, but you will not believe where I just came from," Juliette said with a knowing smile and a wink. Eleanor interrupted her

QUICK CONVERSATION STARTERS TO GET THINGS MOVING WITH ANYONE

Try wearing something colorful or eye-catching that could be a topic of conversation. We're not recommending that you prop a stuffed bird on your head—just something that's somewhat unique or unusual that would be easy to comment on. Suzanne's pendant charm necklace with a heart, saw, and hammer never fails to get noticed by men and women alike and spark a conversation.

Start chatting with everyone—the guy on the bakery line, the man sitting next to you on the commuter train, or even a shop owner. Practicing in less scary situations, like in an elevator or a movie line, can help you build up confidence for events like parties.

Try these opening lines:

1. Pay a compliment, such as, "I love your shoes. Where'd you get them?"

2. Ask open-ended questions that can't be answered with a yes or no. "Hi, I'm Suzanne. Nice to meet you. How do you know the host?"

3. Approach a boisterous group and say: "Sounds like you guys are having a great conversation. What are you talking about?"

4. Approach a man and say: "I made myself a new promise that I'd talk to the most handsome man I saw . . . So, hi."

5. Use your surroundings for conversation starters—you might comment on the artwork, the music that's playing, the food, or the cocktails.

before she could finish. "Afghanistan is my guess based on how long you kept us waiting. Please tell me you traveled there and back to research some of the locations from the book."

"No, I was not in Afghanistan . . . but it was hot," Juliette continued, nonplussed by Eleanor's outburst. The group let out an appreciative *oooh* . . . "Mark took me to the Crystal Springs Day Spa yesterday. We stayed overnight

WHEN YOUR DIVORCE IS THE TALK OF THE TOWN

Did your husband sleep with your neighbor while you were at work? Did you parade your new boyfriend all over town? Are your ears burning at school events because you think everyone knows your business and is talking about your divorce? While your breakup may be the hot topic in town this week, by next month it will be old news.

When you walk outside, throw your shoulders back and, just like a movie star, have a brief statement prepared in case anyone you don't know well is uncouth enough to bring up your split. Something pithy usually works best, such as, "Thanks for your concern. It's been a tough time. I'm putting it behind me." You're letting them know that the subject is closed. In other words, shovels down—no further digging is welcome.

---

and he packed a magic blue pill, so let's just say I needed that massage today because, boy, was I sore!" The women all laughed and talked over each other. No one noticed that Eleanor was positively fuming. She stood up and yelled, "That's it. That is absolutely it. I came here to talk about *The Kite Runner* and hoped for a stimulating discussion about the situation in the Middle East, and instead all you've done is whine about your boss, and your kids, and go into sordid details about your sex lives. . . ."

"Why are you so cranky?" Alice asked. "Can't you just relax and have some fun? Who invited you again?"

"I can assure you I was invited by Cindy," she said, pointing to her friend, who was sinking in her seat, trying to become invisible. "If I wanted to hear tawdry bedroom tales," Eleanor continued, glaring at Juliette, "then I would be reading Harlequin romance novels—not *New York Times* bestsellers."

Alice got up. "I think it's time for you to leave."

"Excuse me? You are asking *me* to leave? I'm the only one who read the book!"

"Then you and your book need to leave," Alice said sternly.

"Let's go," Cindy said, taking Eleanor's arm and leading her out.

The next morning, as Eleanor reflected on the book club, she felt regretful over causing a scene and quickly penned a note of apology to the hostess and a separate note to her neighbor. Eleanor sat at her writing desk and was disappointed that the evening out among potential new friends had been a bust. The women and their conversation topics left her feeling excluded and vulnerable. Eleanor didn't get to discuss Afghanistan, but she realized that there was a place closer to home that was filled with emotional land mines, and for her, that was a room filled with happy women talking about things she didn't have anymore. She knew she had to get a handle on all her loss to prevent flying off the handle again. She had grown accustomed to the safety of the Maplewood Divorce Club, where she was among women who were going through the same challenges she was.

The Takeaway: Socializing again means you will be exposed to conversations about husbands, intact families, and other topics that may make you feel envious, angry, left out—or just sad. Balance your time spent with other divorced women and the time you spend with everyone else in your life so that you can ease back into the social scene with the support of those who really get what you're going through. Like so many things in your life right now, this will get easier.

Hiding out from nosy neighbors

Renée

Renée preferred to lie low after she and Hector decided to take a break in their thirty-year marriage. She felt that everyone would be whispering about her if she showed her face around town. It seemed easier to stay home. It was during this period that her online emotional affair with Larry, whom she met as a fellow volunteer at a charity that helps feed children, really took off. "Texting with Larry was so much more comforting than going out and having all these people feel sorry for me," Renée says. "Everybody knew my business."

It got to the point that Renée even started ordering groceries online so she could relax on her couch, writing back and forth with Larry, who always had a kind word, a joke, and a compliment for her. She always felt better after communicating with him. Though he lived fourteen hundred miles away, she already felt close to him. Her friends, however, were growing suspicious because Larry rarely wanted to talk on the phone and didn't seem to want her to visit him. "If he's really available and so in love with you, why isn't he jumping on a plane to meet you?" her friends would ask. Meanwhile, Renée was turning down real invitations in order to give herself more time to stay home and correspond with her cyber boyfriend. "What's wrong with him?" her friends would ask. "There has to be a reason he doesn't want to meet you. Maybe he's eighty-eight and not sixty." Renée wasn't worried. "I'm not going to push it," she'd say, realizing that she wasn't sure she was ready to meet a new romantic partner in the flesh.

The Takeaway: Though socializing online can be a safe way to initially fill an emotional void, it can't replace in-person connections. Posting on Facebook and Instagram or texting with a potential love interest aren't the same as reaching out to a friend to set up a coffee date and really talking to him or her. If you find yourself getting attached to a man you've never met, like Renée did, realize that you only know what he is telling you—you don't actually know him. The only way to have a real relationship is in real time, in real life. Meet him and take it from there.

Empty seat at the head table

Jill's divorce was finalized a few days before her brother's wedding. At that point, Jill had been dating Yoga Guy for over a year and a half during her separation and their relationship had already had its share of ups and downs. Though very much in love, Jill and Yoga Guy were not on the same page about building a life together. Jill was ready. Yoga Guy was not. He wasn't excited to go home with Jill for the wedding. In fact, he seemed hesitant and wasn't getting back to her about finalizing plans.

When she didn't hear back from him for a full day, she realized she didn't have the energy to coax him into joining her. She was disappointed and hurt when she texted that she would go home alone and needed a break from the relationship.

Jill texted her mom the update, "Broke up with Yoga Guy. Just girls and I coming home for the weekend." In the flurry of wedding prep, Jill's mom never read the text. The message was never received nor spread to her aunts, uncles, and cousins, who all asked over the course of the first hour of the reception, "Where is he? At the buffet? Dance floor? Bathroom? We have been looking forward to meeting him."

Jill had to retell the story of her day-old breakup all evening. She sat at the head table with an empty seat beside her almost as big as the hole in her heart. "Of course the first slow song the DJ played was our song, 'I Won't Give Up.' I wanted to put my head down and cry. But I bit my lip and forced a smile, and I focused on how happy my brother and his new wife were." Jill took a picture of the empty chair beside her and sent it to Yoga Guy. She made her point loud and clear. Jill got through the night and made the best of it dancing with her mom, aunts, and cousins. She even slow-danced with her dad, which she hadn't done since her own wedding.

The Takeaway: You may find yourself attending family celebrations or other important events, like weddings, engagement parties, and anniversary celebrations, with a broken heart. These events may be very challenging. The approach that worked for us was to remember who we were attending the event for, whether it was a favorite niece, a brother, or a close friend. Let their love and happiness carry you through the night, their night. If you feel overcome with emotion, excuse yourself for some fresh air so you can collect yourself. If you truly can't compose yourself, go home early and follow up with an email the next day apologizing for your early exit—whether you blame a migraine or your separation is up to you.

POSTSPLIT SOCIAL ETIQUETTE

When the invitations start showing up again, it will feel different to be socializing as a divorced or an almost single/technically still married adult rather than as part of a couple. With some planning ahead, you can sidestep awkward social minefields with relative ease.

Large Family Function (Reunion, BBQ)

CHALLENGE: Your family wishes you were still married and wants to harp on about how you made a big mistake.

SOLUTION: Explain to your family that you would appreciate their support. Remind them that even though they're still attached to your ex, you're trying to move on; that you can't judge a relationship unless you are in its arms; and that you're getting through this difficult time the best you can.

Wedding, Bar or Bat Mitzvah

CHALLENGE: It's a long stretch of slow songs, and you came solo.

SOLUTION: If you feel like dancing, grab a no-threat male relative and hit the dance floor. If you would rather ignore the Adele lyrics that will make you tear up, consider this a great opportunity to catch up with the elders in your family who hold court at a table seated near the coffeepots, or volunteer to take your cousin's rambunctious four-year-old on a walk around the building playing I Spy.

Your Kids' Recital, Play, Sports Event

CHALLENGE: To sit together with you ex or not sit together? Will either of you be bringing a new love interest?

SOLUTION: Keep the focus on your child's best interest. If you were six years old and onstage, you would want your parents sitting together, united in cheering for you. If that isn't possible, at least sit in the same section so it's easy for your child to spot you both. Do not blindside your ex by bringing someone to the event and not giving him a courtesy advance warning. If you're not serious about someone, do not bring him around your children, especially when they're performing and this new person's presence could negatively impact them.

Your Child's Birthday Party

CHALLENGE: Your kids don't want to feel different or embarrassed by the divorce.

SOLUTION: Make sure the party setting will be in a place where your child is comfortable. If you have hosted parties in the marital home in the past and this isn't possible, consider a neutral setting that you and your ex agree on, like a park, Chuck E. Cheese, or a roller rink. Don't get so involved quibbling over minutiae that you forget why you're planning a party to begin with. Most children would prefer to have one birthday party with both of their parents there. If that's not possible, having two parties may be twice the fun. It's often best not to include a new love interest unless they have met the child many times and your child has requested that they attend.

Work Holiday Parties with Colleagues

CHALLENGE: You're seated between Nosy Nancy from HR and your nemesis; both brought their husbands.

SOLUTION: Keep up the small talk and the safe work talk. If your solo status comes up, answer clearly and quickly: "Frank didn't join me tonight because we have separated." Even though you're in a social setting, these are still your work colleagues. Mind your alcohol intake (always make sure your boss and nemesis are at least one drink ahead) and refrain from oversharing.

Dinner Party

CHALLENGE: You're the fifth wheel while the other couples are feeding each other crudités and holding hands under the table.

SOLUTION: If the dinner party is hosted by close personal friends, go! They invited you because they want to be in your company. Let them know you will be coming alone, except for the herb-crusted cheese ball and the Pinot you'll have in hand. If the invite is from someone you don't know as well and you truly aren't feeling up for it, politely decline but keep the window open for future socializing. "I am sorry to miss it, but I hope to get together with you both very soon."

A Local House Party

CHALLENGE: Bringing a date and introducing a new man to previously "shared" couples, who feel unsure of how to handle your divorce.

SOLUTION: Let the host know in advance that you will be bringing a date and that your ex will or will not be attending the event. This way they know that your attendance will not bring unwanted drama. Clueing the host in may also help diffuse lots of whispering about who you're with and where your ex is. When introducing your date, it helps not to label the person as "my boyfriend," but to simply use his name and give a fact about him. For example, "This is Mark, and he's an investment banker."

TRADITIONS OLD AND NEW

A mix of flexibility and a willingness to be creative helped us keep family traditions alive and dream up new ones. Suzanne and her husband took their son apple picking each October. The first fall she was separated, she took her son without his dad but with some friends. "He was just glad to go," she says. "It wasn't an issue to him that his father wasn't along with us. As long as one parent attends, I think the kids are good."

Sometimes it's not the activity you miss but your children, and your intact family. Vacations were difficult for Iris, who cried when she waved good-bye to her girls when they left for Legoland with their dad. "I was filled with sadness and regret that we weren't all taking this great vacation together," she says. "For years I imagined us traveling as a family. I had to let that go and focus on them having a fantastic time."

The fourth Thursday of every November is Thanksgiving—or is it? Sometimes some creative calendaring is in order. Pilar and her boys decided when, where, and how to celebrate if they wouldn't be together for a holiday. Since she didn't have them her first Thanksgiving after the split, they had a turkey feast on Sunday. "We loved ThanksSunday," she says. "I made the turkey, all the trimmings, the pumpkin pie, and let them know how very thankful I am for them." Get creative and have the holidays whenever you can. There's no reason to miss out on the experience just because the calendar isn't cooperating. Children will likely enjoy the novelty of extra holiday celebrations. You're also giving them a handy lesson in solving challenges in a way that's fun and proactive.

Misfit Thanksgiving

At a Maplewood Divorce Club meeting in early November, women were discussing their Thanksgiving plans, or lack thereof, when Amali was struck with an idea. She texted Gina after the meeting: "I am thinking of hosting a 'Misfit

Thanksgiving' for any of the women who don't have plans—will you help me?" Amali knew that Gina was having mixed emotions about her first big holiday with Valentina but without Clayton. Gina replied, "Turkey time—yes! I will send you a grocery list." Jamie was relieved to be invited to Amali's as she wasn't going to have the boys for Thanksgiving. Iris, who would not have her girls, Pilar, and Eleanor said that they would be there as well. Thanksgiving eve, Gina dropped off two homemade pies and told Amali she would be back in the morning. Amali was thankful to be able to lose herself in preparing the meal, even when she was elbow deep in a turkey. Eleanor was there by 8:30 a.m. and set up a Bloody Mary bar. The women put

> "I sort of panicked thinking about that first postsplit Thanksgiving. I had no idea what I'd do. Having it with friends in my same boat was a huge relief—and a lot of fun." —Eleanor

Macy's Thanksgiving Day Parade on and took turns cooing over Valentina. When the friends sat down to their turkey feast, they all felt thankful for many things, but most of all, for each other.

If you won't have your children or if you need somewhere to go to celebrate a holiday, why not take a page from Amali's book and host a potluck dinner with friends who are in the same boat? Sometimes a Misfit Holiday Dinner can be the absolutely perfect fit and can remind you that you haven't missed out on a thing.

Blue Christmas

The year she separated, Jill had to figure out how to make it through the six-hour drive home to her parents for her first Christmas without her girls. Normally, she would listen to classic Christmas songs by the Carpenters and sing with her girls, over the river, through the woods, and on the better part of Route 80. This year, Jill knew that listening to the music would make her cry. She was left no choice but to listen to heavy metal because that was the only station that wasn't playing holiday music or talking about holiday memories.

With a pounding headache, she looked for a 7-Eleven to buy aspirin, but wanted to find one that wasn't decorated. When she arrived at her parents' home, her mom and dad fussed over her and practically fought over who was going to make her an omelet for breakfast or a sandwich at lunchtime. Jill could imagine them making a game plan to treat her with kid gloves before she arrived. On Christmas night, when Jill spoke to the girls, she put the phone on speaker and she and her parents sang the girls some of their favorite songs.

You will be faced with holidays and events that you won't be able to share with your kids. Having a game plan can help. The next time Jill made the drive without her girls, she brought extra CDs and her phone charger for the car so she had more music options. She found that she appreciated and cherished the holidays she did spend with her children even more.

Surprise under the mistletoe

 Pilar really wanted to continue the tradition of hosting her annual Christmas carols sing-along party at her family home, currently her ex's home. She and Justin had been getting along fairly well over the past few months, so she decided to ask him how he would feel about not skipping the party just because they were separated. Justin was initially reluctant, but Pilar's holiday enthusiasm and their boys' general excitement were infectious. He agreed to cohost the party. Justin and Pilar both got a lot of interesting comments on their RSVPs—from "this should be interesting" to "hope the eggnog is spiked!" Most of their friends had assumed there would be no Christmas party this year. Pilar promised to buy and prepare all the food and drinks and asked her ex to hang Christmas lights outside.

The night before the party, in the living room, Pilar and the boys were decorating the Christmas tree, the fire was roaring, and the house was aglow with holiday sparkle. She fell asleep on the couch feeling very nostalgic, looking at the twinkling lights and thinking about their past holidays together and their good times as a couple.

At the party, Pilar was overcome with poignant longing for the husband she was so ready to leave less than a year ago. The house was filled with their friends, neighbors, and families, and Pilar could barely stand to think about leaving at the end of the night to go back to her apartment.

"I remember getting a glass of wine and looking around the first floor of the house like I was in a trance," Pilar said. "I saw Justin talking, and I just walked over and took his hand, leading him under the mistletoe in the dining room." Pilar told Justin she had done a lot of thinking, and a lot of growing, since she left. "It's not just the music, or the candlelight, or the holidays,

ASK FOR THE HOLIDAYS YOU WANT

If there is one holiday that is more important to you than others, consider working out a deal with your ex. Our friend Linda refused to sign her divorce agreement until her ex agreed to give her the kids every Christmas Eve for a traditional dinner that included her large Italian family, along with attending a midnight Mass at her church. She had to spend extra money in lawyer fees and wait out her ex for more than a month, but he finally agreed. She didn't mind alternating Christmas Day with her ex, but to her, Christmas Eve with her children was her favorite day of the year, filled with happy memories from her own childhood.

If you love going to the beach for the Fourth of July every year, but your ex lives for Halloween, try to accommodate each other and make it part of your parenting separation agreement.

but I don't want to leave here tonight—or ever again," she said, looking into his eyes. "If you forgive me and take me back, I promise to be a better wife and mother and to never run away from my problems again." Pilar had been doing a lot of self-reflection and realized what her priorities truly were. Through her separation, she finally got the space she needed to see what she had more clearly and why she had acted so impulsively. She didn't want to lose her family and her husband. She knew they could find ways to compromise and be happy together.

Pilar pointed up at the mistletoe and wiggled her eyebrows. Justin kissed her and whispered in her ear, "I've missed you, too." That night Pilar and Justin talked about getting back together. Justin said he needed some time to think about it.

Pilar and Justin sat down to talk the next afternoon. Pilar apologized. She admitted that she had unfairly blamed him for every dissatisfaction she had, instead of talking to him. She cried when she confessed that the affair was a misguided and extremely hurtful thing to do, something she would never do again. Pilar told Justin that she wasn't aware until she actually left that she had been making him into a scapegoat for everything that went wrong in her life. What she realized sitting alone in her new apartment was that the initial excitement over the freedom she thought she wanted quickly waned. When she dug deep, she realized she wanted Justin back.

Justin, for his part, had hoped Pilar would come back, but he worried that he wouldn't be able to change enough to make Pilar happy. Pilar said she was ready to accept him just as he was. Justin knew it would take time to rebuild trust and their relationship, but he saw Pilar as the love of his life, and he knew she was worth it. They decided to get back together and tell the boys on Christmas morning.

While most of us won't be cohosting cookie swaps with our exes (or getting back together), it can be helpful for your first holiday season after your separation to keep the traditions that you can alive. Perhaps you always buy your turkey from a certain farm, get your Christmas tree the day after Thanksgiving, attend your neighbor's New Year's Eve party, or host Yom Kippur for your siblings and their families. Look for ways to ease into new traditions while preserving things you've enjoyed in years past.

Knowing the holidays would be hard for us and other members of the Maplewood Divorce Club, we planned a cocktail party and a holiday gift swap. The holidays are a time to reflect on the people who mean the most to us. We all felt that we had formed a sisterhood of sorts, and we wanted to celebrate our friendship.

CREATING NEW TRADITIONS

Suzanne

Building a familylike community with other divorced moms helped many of us find new sources of fun. We did our best to come up with new traditions for our kids and new ways of coping and socializing that worked for us and for our friends. "We missed our family vacation at the beach over the summer," says Suzanne. "That's how we came up with a way to cap off the summer with a glamping (aka glamour camping) trip in the woods." Suzanne, Jill, and a couple of other moms and their kids started a tradition of going away to the Poconos for Labor Day weekend. "This gave my son and I something to look forward to at the end of the summer that gathered our friends and was a lot of fun," Suzanne says.

Four women, six kids around the same age, two cabins, one lake, one beach, lots of bug spray. "We packed groceries, divvying up a long list, and kept meals simple, including pancakes, sandwiches, and burgers," Suzanne says. Special activities were planned, from catching fireflies and making s'mores over an open fire to Wiffle Ball and racing with floaties in the lake. The moms loved the chance to relax on the beach and catch up. The kids enjoyed the woodsy setting and being in nature. This tradition is still going strong.

Mother's Day also changes postsplit. Jamie knew that her sons, five and seven, wouldn't be able to prepare breakfast in bed for her without the help of their dad, who was no longer living in the same house. This day, like so many others, was going to take on a new incarnation postdivorce. It was from the uncertainty of how to mark this day that Jamie came up with the idea of inviting twelve recently divorced moms from the Maplewood Divorce Club and their kids for a picnic in the park. Each mom brought some food and games for the kids, who ran around, happy for the excuse for a big playdate outdoors. "I felt pure joy as I watched my kids playing with their new extended family," Jamie says. "I was so happy to be sharing the day with other women who were forging ahead in unexpected ways, just like me."

Divorce party

If marriages start with a party and a toast, can they finish with one, as well? Though some may raise their eyebrows, celebrities, rock stars, and even women you know are opting to mark the end of one chapter of their life with a celebration. Back in 2011, rocker Jack White and his model wife, Karen Elson, threw a postdivorce party. "We feel so fortunate for the time we have shared and the time we will continue to spend both separately and together watching our children grow. In honor of that time shared, we are throwing a divorce party," the couple said in a statement. Singer Katy Perry hosted a large fete celebrating her independence on what would have been her second wedding anniversary with ex-husband, comedian Russell Brand.

Carlotta

Our friend Carlotta, who was enjoying a major uptick in her mood and self-esteem, chose to do the same. She hosted a party on the Saturday after her divorce became final. The guest list included Bailey and everyone she hoped would be a part of their new life, including the friendly FedEx deliveryman, Bill's sister Chloe, with whom she remained close, and the members of her gardening and divorce clubs. She invited her friends to wear ugly bridesmaid dresses from the back of

I'LL DRINK TO THAT!

There will be many times during your separation and divorce when you will think, "I need a drink!" We would like to offer up some of our original libations, because if you can't beat 'em, clink 'em.

Oh No He Didn't

6 ice cubes, 2 ounces coconut rum, 6 ounces Fresca

When your ex drives you batty and you want to pick up the phone and berate him, pick up your cocktail glass and toast to your freedom instead.

Libertyni

4 ounces chilled champagne, 1 ounce cherry juice, 1 maraschino cherry for garnish

Look down at your empty ring finger on your left hand. Toast your freedom.

Girl Talk

2 ounces whipped-cream-flavored vodka, 3 ounces club soda, 2 ounces pineapple juice

Do you know what you have more time for now? Yourself, and your amazing friends. Pour a drink and pour your heart out to some girlfriends.

their closets, old wedding dresses, or even a stray veil or garter, and decorated her home with peonies, candlelight, and white paper lanterns. She gave a brief speech thanking everyone for their love, support, and encouragement over what had been a difficult year and a half, and then read vows she wrote for herself and her daughter, Bailey.

"I promise to honor and cherish every day of my life, to never waste another day in stained yoga pants, to be the best example of a woman that I can for Bailey, and to spread kindness and beauty in our community gardens and my backyard." Carlotta also showed off her new "divorce ring" that she bought to replace her wedding bling. She chose her favorite stone, an aquamarine gem. When she looked at her left hand, she had a reason to be happy again. "Remember when you first got engaged and you could barely take your eyes off your sparkly engagement ring? It's like that again for me!" she exclaimed. Carlotta served a signature cocktail, the "Oh No He Didn't," and had a playlist of upbeat girl power songs.

We've heard of women hosting a "registry" as part of their divorce party for women to swap out rarely used appliances (for example, that never-used juicer) for items they've always wanted (waffle maker), and of others holding a letting-go ceremony where they wrote all their negative emotions and thoughts on paper that they then burned. Some women opt to get together with a few friends over drinks or dinner to toast their new life. Finding a way to mark the finalization of your divorce and the start of something new can feel hopeful and exciting.

What I Wish I'd Known

Eleanor

"Having a new group of friends and a new social circle as a result of the Maplewood Divorce Club meetings allowed me to feel like I had a place where I always fit in. It was such a relief to just be myself and feel accepted."　　—Eleanor

Chapter 16
DRINKS @ 8—TIME TO DATE

"A busy, vibrant, goal-oriented woman is so much more attractive than a woman who waits around for a man to validate her existence."
—Mandy Hale

There's nothing wrong with cobwebs on your doorbell. Some women take many months or even a year or more to start dating again. Suzanne took more than six months to feel that she had some insight into why things didn't work out in her marriage, could recognize her own patterns, and knew what was important to her in a relationship. Jamie went out for a drink with the History Channel guy, only to realize that she wasn't ready to start dating anyone seriously yet. Other girlfriends can't wait to meet someone new. Jill began dating right away and initially even multidated to increase her odds of finding a keeper and distract herself from her divorce drama.

If you wonder whether there's anyone out there for you, consider that 44 percent of adult Americans are single, according to US Census figures. That means there are more than one hundred million unattached people out there.

One of the most popular ways to meet a mate these days is through online dating. We'll help you write your profile and navigate online communication leading up to that first date. We'll also tell you some of our dating stories from the trenches—both the romantic rendezvous and the scary tales from the crypt.

When jumping back into the dating pool, it's important to remember that things have changed—you don't know who the person you're communicating with online is until you meet him. Don't assume that a person you meet online is single, interested in a long-term commitment, employed, or is even who he says he is until you meet him face-to-face and get to know him. With some caution and common sense, along with our tips, you will find that dating can be a lot of fun. And when you meet the man who makes you tingle and get butterflies in your stomach, your dates with Mr. Overtalker, Mr. Forgot to Shower, and Mr. Very Angry won't matter. They will have been nothing more than stepping-stones that led you to Mr. Great Date.

Our friend Denise likes to say that for every pot, there's a lid. There will be days after you start dating again when you wonder, *Where is my lid?* We promise that if you follow our guidelines, you'll stay energized and hopeful while you're looking for your "lid" and enjoying your life.

DATING AGAIN

Answer the following question: *Have you looked at old happy photos of you and your ex or heard sad music and cried over him within the last month?* If you answer yes, you're not ready to date yet. That's it, the quiz is over. It's pass/fail. Come back in a month for a retest.

If you answer no, move on to the next question: *If you have a good first date and the guy never calls again, will you be devastated?* If you answer, "Hell no, his loss," you're ready. If you answer, "I'd be upset, but I'd get over it in a few days," you're ready to date, but make an effort not to get overly invested in anyone too soon.

When you begin dating, remember that the ups and downs can be emotionally challenging during an ongoing divorce experience. There will be good dates and probably some bad ones, too. There will be some crossed signals, some disappointments, and some boredom. There will also be laughter, fun, romance, and excitement. Learning to find joy in the dating journey, by staying

DATING WHEN YOU HAVE KIDS

When you start to date, you may wonder how to share the news with your kids. While some women date only on the days that their kids are with their father—shielding their kids from it—others introduce the idea of dating early. The information you share with your kids about dating will depend on their age, their emotional well-being, and their comfort level with the changes brought on by the divorce. Here are some tips to keep in mind.

1. Wait to introduce your children to a new partner until the relationship is serious. We didn't want our kids to become attached to someone we were dating while we were still getting to know him.

2. Let your ex know ahead of time that you will be introducing your kids to a new partner.

3. For the first meeting between your new boyfriend and your kids, plan a fun activity that's only a few hours long—keeping it brief and active lessens the pressure on everyone.

4. Accept that your kids may be slow to warm up to your new partner. Don't push the new relationship on them and make sure your boyfriend isn't around all the time so that they don't have to share you before they're ready.

5. Realize that your kids may be disappointed that you found a new relationship if they had been holding out hope that their parents would get back together.

open, choosing places and activities that interest you, and keeping your sense of humor, will help to smooth your ride on the road to your next love.

You may be craving intimacy and connection after feeling lonely in your marriage, which can make you more vulnerable to the charms of strangers before you actually get to know them—or even meet them in person. You may hear from men who want engagement without risk; they will text you, "Good morning, sunshine," when you awake and "How was your day?" before you go to sleep, creating a fake sense of intimacy. It's important to keep reminding yourself that he isn't real until you meet him.

PREPPING YOUR PROFILE AND PICS

Since dating is a numbers game, online dating is a way to increase your odds of meeting someone great. If you're new to this approach, it can be helpful to note that there's no stigma and that people of all ages are online. It may feel strange at first to decide whether you want to meet someone based on a couple of photos, a short profile, and a few email exchanges. Yes, you're taking a leap of faith. We'll help make it fun.

Your profile will include a few photos and a lively description of yourself, much like an ad. When you're writing your profile, tell the truth while also presenting yourself in the most appealing way possible. An old saying from Jill's copywriting days that she always shares with her friends is, "Say it straight, then say it great."

Gina was at a loss with writing her profile, so she enlisted Jill and Suzanne to help her. "What do you like to do?" Suzanne asked her. "Cook, do hair, play with the baby," Gina said. The women took notes about Gina's straightforward likes and hopes and then added some creative flourish. Gina's username, "CutieInTheKitchen," hinted at her personality and hobbies. Pick a username that is unique to you and memorable. They described Gina's figure as "Kardashian Kurvy" and kept the tone light and fun throughout. When it came time for her profile photos, Gina arranged for another stylist to give her a sleek blowout and asked Amali to come by in the early evening light (the most flattering) to take a few shots of her in some different outfits outside.

Denise wanted to get started dating ASAP after her separation. She sat at her laptop and decided she wanted her profile to convey her optimistic attitude and the fact that she likes to try new things. She started with, "I like to say yes." She already had a few decent photos and figured she would start with them and post better ones as she got them. Over the next few days, her in-box was flooded with messages proposing sexual encounters of every sort imaginable. When Denise talked to Jill about the site, complaining that it attracted a lot of sex-crazed men, Jill asked to see Denise's profile. She immediately spotted the "like to say yes" as an unintended invitation to sex. Denise deleted that sentence and replaced it with, "Optimistic and upbeat, with an adventurous spirit." Be sure to have a friend read your profile to let you know if it sounds like you and whether you

FROM FIRST CLICK TO FIRST DATE

Our best practices for quickly moving from connecting over email to meeting in person for the first time:

1. Exchange a few messages via the site/app, but don't get stuck in a long text exchange.

2. If he proposes progressing from communicating via the dating website to texting you directly, and you feel comfortable giving him your cell number, by all means do so. If he becomes a problem, you can always block him from your phone.

3. Have a phone chat to get a hint of his personality, who he is, and what his voice sounds like.

4. Arrange a first meeting ASAP. We suggest one to two hours maximum, over coffee or drinks—not dinner. You want to have a time limit if it's clearly a no go.

5. If you had a nice time and would like to see him again, feel free to give him a kiss on the cheek when you say good-bye and to let him know you enjoyed the date.

may be sending unintentional messages. Here's a roundup from our friends of dating profile strategies that worked:

START WITH SOMETHING MEMORABLE, rather than a wishy-washy "I don't know what to say" or "I hate to talk about myself." This is your full-page ad; make it sizzle! Jill opened her profile with, "I'm a little bit country; a little bit rock and roll," which is corny and kind of funny—and totally Jill.

BE DETAILED AND SPECIFIC. Rather than say, "I like to have fun," elaborate. For example, "I love to salsa, sing karaoke, watch comedy movies, and I have always wanted to go on a hot air balloon ride." This will also give men easy openers when they write to you.

FLATTERING PHOTOS MATTER. We are all visual creatures: The first thing anyone does is look at the photo. Your main photo should be a close-up because it will run very small. Also include one medium shot and one full-length body

Loving Again

Meeting Your Half-Orange by Amy Spencer. A unique and upbeat dating guide written by a relationship guru, this book focuses on the power of optimism and the belief that your ideal mate exists and is waiting for you. Call him forth from the universe in six simple steps.

The Real Thing: Lessons on Love and Life from a Wedding Reporter's Notebook by Ellen McCarthy. Feel inspired to fall in love again. The wisdom and insight that comes from interviewing more than two hundred couples on how they met, the moment they knew, and their big day will restore your faith in marriage and the importance of love in our lives.

How to Make Someone Fall in Love With You in 90 Minutes or Less by Nicholas Boothman. This book promises to help you meet the love of your life. Self-assessment tests show you how to find what the author calls your Matched Opposite (a person who complements you). You will also find opening lines, conversation tips, and the 1-2-3 mantra of never hesitating.

shot. Opt for natural light. Easy on the kids, cats, drinks, and giant group photos where you get lost in the crowd.

BE UPBEAT. Your profile should convey your positive energy rather than sounding sad or desperate. You may not be aware of the tone, so ask a close friend to read it over. It's okay to be a little flirty, too.

BE CAREFUL ABOUT HUMOR. It's hard to convey sarcasm, dry wit, and biting humor in a profile read by people who don't know you. Keep in mind that what you intend as a darkly humorous tone may not translate the way you think to a stranger.

GET A SECOND OR THIRD OPINION. Have a trusted friend or two read your profile to confirm it reads well and is ready to go "live."

A SITE FOR EVERYONE

Whether you want to mingle with a **broad and varied online** population or limit your search to a more targeted group, **there's a site or an app** for you. One case in point: Gluten Free Singles. Demographically focused online match-making sites are indeed growing in popularity, from Single Parent Meet and

Dating for Seniors to Black People Meet, Christian Singles, and JDate (an online dating service aimed at Jewish singles). New sites and apps are cropping up all the time. Below we list the most frequented options. You may want to start with one site and build from there, since the process of looking at prospects and responding to messages across several sites can be time-consuming.

Top online dating websites

MATCH boasts one of the largest dating pools, with seventeen million active monthly users. Browse for free, but to chat with someone you need a paid subscription.

CHEMISTRY, part of Match, is a paid service for people who want to get to know someone online before meeting them for the first time. It has more than eight million users.

OKCUPID is a fast-growing, free site that is very proud of its matching algorithm. Many swear by the "Quick Match" feature to simplify the sorting process.

EHARMONY links people with complementary personalities and lifestyles. The paid service has worked with millions of users over the past fifteen years.

PLENTY OF FISH is a free site that matches people based on mutual likes. The speed feature, Meet Me, makes it easy to find local singles with similar interests.

MEETUP. While not technically an online dating site, Meetup can help you meet interesting people in your community while engaging in activities you enjoy.

Top mobile apps

TINDER. Swipe or tap the images of potential dates to dismiss or add them to your "like" list. You only message people who like you back. Log in via Facebook.

BUMBLE, known as Tinder for women. You must initiate the conversation with a potential match or else they disappear after twenty-four hours. Guys can't initiate contact.

HINGE introduces you to a group of people with mutual Facebook friends. Each day at noon, the app supplies you with a field of potential matches.

COFFEE MEETS BAGEL brings you one "bagel" daily, with mutual Facebook friends, lessening the overload factor. If you both express interest, you're connected.

HOWABOUTWE. You are matched based on the kind of date you want to go on. You check out other people's date ideas and then head off to meet them face-to-face.

Fakers, felons . . . and fun prospects

Online dating works. You can meet your next love. You can meet the next person you marry. You can also meet an ex-con. However, what came as a surprise to us was the percentage of men online who seem available for a relationship but actually are not—they are married, living with someone, engaged, interested in an online connection but not ready to meet in person, or just looking for a hookup.

Keep in mind that many men cast a very wide net. They may be writing the same message to twenty other women. That's why, though they reached

BRAVE ENOUGH TO BE VULNERABLE

If you're afraid of dating again because you don't want to risk getting hurt, consider the wisdom of researcher and author Brené Brown. Her big idea is that vulnerability is good for you even if it doesn't always feel good initially. Making yourself vulnerable—exposing your fears and taking emotional risks—is something most of us want to run away from. But Brown's research shows that it's precisely when we reveal ourselves—often in a relationship—that "we have experiences that bring purpose and meaning to our lives." In other words, sharing our true selves when we're vulnerable allows us to have more meaningful connections.

If you want to feel inspired to give love another try, spend some time on her website (brenebrown.com) or listen to one of her TED talks.

out first, they may disappear. It's not worth dwelling on ghost men who vanish without a word when you're looking for a man who will stick around. Don't consider anyone a real prospect until you've met them and have gotten to know them. Jill likes to say, "Assume you're emailing with Freddy Krueger, who actually lives in the Ukraine, until you meet the man in person."

Renée

Renée didn't follow this advice. She found tremendous solace in her online communication with Larry, who lived in another state, and continued to communicate with him without meeting in person. He would greet her each morning and say good night every evening, leading her to feel a false sense of intimacy. He expressed how wonderful she was in a way that Hector never had. However, his lack of interest in meeting her in person caused her friends to question whether he was who he claimed to be. Feeling pressured and curious, she told him that she couldn't continue their online correspondence. "It was a tough call, because I was really emotionally attached to him and looked forward to his messages," Renée said. "But a part of me also knew that it wasn't real."

Larry didn't answer Renée for three long days, during which she thought she scared him off. When he did write back, he suggested FaceTime as a way to talk and see each other until the day they could meet in person. The first time he called her, she realized the small screen really distorted her face, and was not the most flattering, but she found him very attractive and they talked for hours. Renée learned that he had gone through a difficult breakup of a long-term relationship just a few months earlier. He really liked Renée but wanted to take things slowly. "He didn't close the door on a future together," Renée says. "But it was clear that if things were to develop, it wouldn't be on my timetable. I would need to give him space." Though the outcome was uncertain, Renée was happy to be dealing with a real man.

Jill

Sometimes you may feel like you're in Vegas and the odds are against you. Since online dating is indeed a numbers game, the more dates you go on, the better your odds of hitting the jackpot. Dating can also be the source of many hilarious stories—and it's important to keep a light perspective. For example, Jamie had to laugh when she got a 98 percent match . . . with a drag queen. Jill still tells the story of the guy who after dinner together proclaimed that she must have gained four pounds after eating a roll and steak fajitas, and proceeded to squeeze her waist, using his fingers as fat calipers. "I wasn't the least bit surprised that he said his ex had an eating disorder," Jill says. "Since I don't want to develop one, I didn't go out with him again."

Amali went on a first (and last) date with a man who showed up sporting tattoos on one side of his face. It suddenly made sense why all his photos showed him in profile! Pilar recalls waiting at the bar for a first date with Brad, an athletic fortysomething George Clooney dead ringer whom she'd met online, when she was approached by a seventy-year-old man with a cane. He extended his hand and introduced himself. "I'm Brad. I hope you don't mind, but I used my son's photos for my profile pictures." Pilar did mind. She minded quite a bit. Date over.

Iris recalls Googling a man after a promising date. The first thing that came up was his mug shot. He was arrested for attempted murder. The next time he contacted her, she wrote, "Felon?" He responded, "Yeah, I was wondering when I should tell you about that." She responded, "I think I know all I need to know."

WHO DO YOU REALLY WANT TO MEET?

Are you seeking a companion? A *man*sition, your rebound guy who won't last longer than a menstrual cycle? True love? A partner to have a family with? A Latin lover to warm your cold nights? Regardless of what you are looking for, with millions of people online it's extremely likely that someone compatible is looking for the same thing! Creating your personal dating *man*tra, the five must-have qualities you will look for in a new man, will help you to screen your would-be suitors and stay on track. Your *man*tra should have no more than two physical attributes out of the five. Jill's *man*tra: Attractive, operates with integrity, kind, funny, easygoing. Suzanne's *man*tra: Good communicator, thoughtful, handsome, active, positive outlook.

But what are men looking for? Men and women alike generally start by looking at the photographs and then read the profiles after being drawn to someone physically. According to our guy friends Marcus and Gerry, the least appealing women are typecast as the Drama Queen, the Damsel in Distress, and the Compulsive Complainer. You will find that most men don't want to play the role of your Prince Charming: They want you to have already rescued yourself. Just like you, they want to come into your life and enjoy you, not save you. Men will

> "I know in the first five minutes if the guy is for me or not, but even if he's clearly not, I still try to have fun on the dates. It's a chance to get to know a new person and connect. I've had a lot of great conversations with men I knew I wouldn't go out with again." —Denise

be most drawn to you when you have your life in order and are happy.

Remember that you don't have to wait for the men to find you. You can surf around and write to guys who interest you. Usually a short but specific message, showing that you read their profile, works best. To make it easier for them to reply, it's a good idea to ask an open-ended question. For example, a tame opener to a man who talked about hiking in his profile would be, "Hi! I enjoyed reading your profile. Have you ever hiked in the South Mountain Reservation? There's a great trail that leads to a waterfall." Prefer something more flirty? Flattery is always welcome. "Loved your profile. Body-surfing pro, huh?! Do you give private lessons ;-)" It's good to include an exclamation mark, as it conveys energy. We've heard from many men that they love it when women make the first move and contact them.

MEETING PEOPLE IRL (IN REAL LIFE)

Denise

Eligible men aren't exclusively found online. You can meet them anywhere: walking down the street, at an event with your kids, at the gym, on the train commuting to work, or out with your dog. Are your eyes open to everyone you pass by during your day? Denise made an effort to meet men in her real life. She would go to the martini bar on Thursdays when many men meet for happy hour. She met more than one date that way. When she traveled for work, she always got a drink at the hotel bar. While chatting up a man on a business flight to Dallas, she met a future boyfriend. She still dated online, but found the real-life encounters preferable.

If you're not as bold as Denise, consider bringing along a WingWoman. That's a girlfriend who will play matchmaker for you and someone you want to meet but don't have the courage to approach. Don't discount your married girlfriends, who might consider this big fun. Jill's best WingWoman line, which helped land Iris a few dates, was to walk up to a man Iris liked the look of and say, "Hi. I'd like to change your life tonight." What man isn't going to be curious? "Come with me. I'm going to introduce you to my beautiful friend." This approach has always worked for Jill and the friend she was setting up.

Carlotta

Carlotta's self-esteem took a hit after her husband left her. The first man to pay attention to her after her divorce made a big impact with just a few words. Carlotta had ordered some cute new workout clothes from Victoria's Secret for her Spinning classes. Her regular FedEx guy, who was always very friendly, raised his eyebrows when he handed her the package and said sweetly, "Lucky guy!"

"That made my day," Carlotta says. "It gave my ego a little boost."

Carlotta was feeling ready to date when she realized that the FedEx guy she would joke with at least once a week when her packages showed up was a potential date already on her doorstep. "It was so unlike me to ask him out, but I knew the worst he could say was no," she says. "And if it didn't work out, I'd have to switch to UPS. Before I even finished asking him to go out for coffee, he said yes. He was really sweet about it."

Meghan

When Meghan wanted to come up with ways to expand her social circle, she enlisted her roommate, Carlos, to help brainstorm. The day she finally became a certified therapeutic massage specialist, Carlos took her picture posed with her diploma and a bottle of massage oil. "So," Carlos began after he sat down beside her on the porch swing, "now that you're a big-time graduate, what are you going to do?" Meghan shrugged. "That's the million-dollar question. I want to do something different, meet new people. Not just be in a dark eight-by-ten room all day with naked strangers." The two were tossing some ideas back and forth when Meghan had a lightbulb moment. "You know how the owners of the restaurant where you work are always trying to drum up business midweek?" Carlos nodded. "What if we did a theme night?" Meghan said. "Rub 'n' Grub or something. I could offer ten-dollar neck and shoulder massages with the purchase of an entrée!" Carlos grinned. "That's a great idea. And you can give out your business cards to everyone." Carlos handed her a small wrapped gift. "And here they are. It's your graduation present. I had my buddy who's a design major do them."

Carlos's boss loved the idea. The following Wednesday was the first Rub 'n' Grub. The cash register count at 1:00 a.m. told the story of a night that was a success with double the usual amount of receipts. Word spread, and new customers started showing up on Wednesdays. An unexpected perk was that in addition to meeting new clients, Meghan was meeting potential dates as well. Meghan found a unique way to grow her business and her dating pool at the same time.

DATING DO'S

You may wind up sitting across from someone incredibly attractive and interesting and smiling a lot as a result. On other dates, you may have to work a little harder to find something to smile about. He may appear to be shorter, heavier, older, or to have less hair than in his photo. Be open, and see what's inside. Make the best of the hour in front of you. Though there may not be a second date in your future, looking at him as a potential business contact, the right match for a friend, or someone you become friends with can take the pressure off wanting him to be The One. Give the person a chance. Let him reveal himself. Ask questions not to hear the "right" answer but to get to know him.

Here are our best first-date tips from our experiences:

BE KIND. Treat your dates with the consideration you would want them to show you.

BE IN THE MOMENT. Listen and respond to the person sitting across from you rather than reciting the history of your life. If you need something to talk about, note something funny happening right around you that you can both comment on.

KEEP EXPLANATIONS SHORT AND SWEET. Have your trusty two-sentence statement about why you got divorced ready. You don't want to weigh down a first date with a long tale of woe. For example, "I never thought I would get divorced, but we grew apart, and even though we worked on our marriage, we were unable to repair things."

EMBRACE NEWNESS. Make a list of places you want to try out—a drink at the new Thai restaurant or coffee at a popular spot that always has live music. That way, even if the date is a bust, you've done something new and interesting. Meeting strangers is also a time of discovery, so be open to places he suggests, too.

MAKE EYE CONTACT AND SMILE. Give him your full attention, and keep your iPhone tucked away. If you need to check your phone to see if the baby-sitter contacted you, let him know.

FIND SOMETHING TO ENJOY ABOUT THE DATE. It may not be the man himself, but the wine you discovered, the joke you heard, or depending on where he's from or what he does, learning about a new place or profession.

PACE YOURSELF. When you click with someone you may feel tempted to tell him everything right away, down to the retainer you wear at night, but slow down. According to *Millionaire Matchmaker* Patti Stanger, "Intrigue is to men what romance is to women."

DATING DON'TS

Gina

The two days before Gina's date with Bobby, the handsome stranger she met at the hair salon, she had barely been able to eat. This was partly the result of nerves and also wanting to look her best in the binding waist trainer she'd bought at Macy's. When she arrived at the restaurant, bound and bouncy, Gina saw that Bobby was already waiting for her at a candlelit table in the corner. Cast in the glow of the amber candle, he was even more attractive than Gina remembered. She thought she did a great job with his haircut. They kissed hello awkwardly, but in only a few minutes the conversation was flowing easily. The delicious aroma coming from the bread basket was almost too much for Gina to handle. She kept steal-ing glances at it. Bobby noticed. He had already devoured a warm roll smoth-ered in butter, so he picked up the basket and offered it to Gina. "Have a roll! They're delicious." Gina couldn't imagine eating a roll in front of him. "I can't. I have too many rolls already," she said nervously, as she laughed self-deprecat-ingly. Bobby didn't get it. "Oh, you already ate?" he asked. "No—it's just that I'm still trying to lose a few pounds since having the baby," Gina said. Now Bobby got it. "Gina, you're a gorgeous woman. Just as you are." He smiled warmly at her. "You can eat all the rolls you want with me." And just like that, Gina started to relax. Well, as much as the waist trainer would let her.

Gina's body bashing is just one of many behaviors you'll want to avoid on dates. Here are our top dating don'ts:

DON'T EX-TALK. In addition to not speaking poorly about yourself, you don't want to spend your date speaking ill of your ex, either. And while we're at it, how about trying not to talk about him at all? You can have a one- or two-sentence response if you're asked about your ex, such as, "We weren't a good fit," and save the details for later.

DON'T COMPARE YOUR DATE TO YOUR EX. Realize that a comment like "My ex never wanted to try Indian food. What a nice change of pace you are!" is not a compliment. It shows you're still hung up on your ex. Let the new guy have the spotlight and leave your ex out of it.

CHECK YOUR BAGS. A man doesn't want to hear about all your problems or the bad things in your life. We all have baggage; leave yours at home. Refrain from saying things like: "Being separated is the worst. It's time to do our taxes and he won't help me at all. Ugh! I can't stand it." This doesn't mean you should never tell him about your ex or that you had to cash in your 401(k) to pay for your divorce lawyer, but not on the first few dates—please! Accentuate the positive.

AVOID ROMANCE SQUASHERS. On a first date with a stranger, these include talking about money, politics, your divorce, and how it's going on the online dating websites. If he brings up money or politics, change the subject. If he asks about your divorce, trot out your one- or two-sentence response. If you like him, you can say how your online dating experience just got a lot better. Whatever you do, don't launch into a diatribe of all the bad dates you had and how exhausted you are by the process.

DON'T COMPLAIN OR MAKE EXCUSES ABOUT YOUR APPEARANCE. There's no man on earth who knows what to say when a woman criticizes her appearance or asks for feedback and reassurance. "Would you like me more if I lost weight?" is not a question for a first date. Own your body type, whatever it is, and be confident.

DON'T CHASE HIM LIKE HE'S THE LAST BUS OF THE DAY. Today's man may wear crisp button-downs, use hair products, and be able to read binary code, but make no mistake, underneath it all, many are still cavemen, hardwired to hunt and compete for their women. When you text him nonstop

LET'S TALK ABOUT SEX

Whether you're dating one guy or more, please respect your body and your health, and protect yourself. Get tested for STDs (sexually transmitted diseases) yourself and ask potential partners questions including: When was the last time you were tested for an STD or STI (sexually transmitted infection)? Do you always use protection? Are you sleeping with anyone else?

What came as a surprise to us was that when you ask to get tested for all the STDs, herpes will not be included. It's a separate blood test you need to request. Not one woman we asked realized that herpes is not automatically included in the STD testing. Information is power.

Of course, there's no right or wrong time to have sex. Though the dating sites may ask whether you'd have sex after the third date, sixth date, or after six months, set your own timetable that makes you feel comfortable. Remember that it takes men longer to feel emotionally attached than it takes women. Don't assume that sex equals an emotional connection. If you want to know how he's feeling, ask him.

Being intimate with a new person after years or decades of marriage can feel quite surreal. It's an adjustment. Getting over the initial newness of sex with someone other than your ex is something you only need to go through once. After you get back in the saddle, you may find, like many of our girlfriends, that this is an area of your life that's reawakened with a whole new level of passion.

and ask him out, you could be taking the fun of the chase away from him. The more you conduct yourself like you're a prize worth winning, the more likely he will treat you that way.

DON'T SHOW UP AS A VICTIM. You may feel that you had an especially painful marriage, an awful divorce, financial losses that still impact you, or unusual health challenges. These are only topics for a first date if you want him to run for the hills.

WHAT TO DO AFTER THE FIRST DATE

You thought you had a great first date—now what? There are no hard and fast rules to follow, but based on our personal dating experiences, we've come up with some guidelines for navigating next steps. Did he mention a second date on the first date? Did he linger after he kissed you on the cheek? Sometimes it's just plain obvious when you're both into each other. Other times, the signals are harder to read and you're left wondering, *Does he like me? Will I hear from him again?*

We've found that if a man likes you and wants to pursue you, you will know by his actions. He calls or texts you within two or three days after the date. He asks you open-ended questions to learn more about you and then sets up another date. If you haven't heard from him a week after your date and you thought the date went well, you can write to him, something along the lines of, "Hi, Josh, I hope you're having a great day. If you're up for it, I'd like to go out again. There's a new dim sum place I'd love to try." Sometimes

PROCEED WITH CAUTION

Though you may feel a sense of familiarity with someone you've been writing to online, the truth is that he is a stranger. Get his full name before going out with him and Google him. You may find out before the first date that the handsome high school teacher on the screen was arrested for sleeping with his underage students.

Choose a well-lit public place for the first date—certainly not his home or yours. The news stories of men drugging women aren't limited to Bill Cosby allegedly slipping pills to up-and-coming starlets. Though someone could slip something into your drink in public, it's still the safest place to meet.

Park your car under a light, as close to the restaurant as possible. Tell at least one friend the name of the person you're meeting, where you're meeting, and when you expect to be home. Don't have more than two drinks. And always listen to your instincts. If something doesn't feel right, if he seems overly pushy or aggressive, trust your gut. Ask a manager from the restaurant to walk you to your car if you're feeling unsafe.

he will be thrilled: "I'm so happy to hear from you. I wasn't sure you liked me." Other times he will be vague in his response and the communication will fizzle out. Sometimes you might even hear, "Thanks but I don't think we are a fit." If he doesn't respond, then that will be your answer. Move on!

If you don't think you clicked but have a hunch he thinks you did, you may want to communicate that you're not interested before he asks you out again, as a courtesy. A statement that he cannot argue with because it's based on your feelings is usually best: "Thank you for the nice evening out. I enjoyed meeting you, but the chemistry just didn't feel right on my end for us to have a second date. I wish you all the best in your search."

Just as you won't like everyone you meet, everyone isn't going to like you— and it's going to say more about him than about you. Maybe you remind him of his high school girlfriend who broke his heart, or your voice sounds like his ex-wife's, or maybe he's dating but he's in love with another woman. Rather than getting hung up on why he isn't interested, realize that it doesn't matter. There will be plenty of men who may dismiss you for the same meaningless reasons you might dismiss someone. Jill refused a second date with an attractive man because he wore a phone clip. Suzanne never met with a man she spoke with on the phone because he complained the whole time. Denise's big turn-off is a man who's too eager. Everyone is entitled to his or her own opinion. If you don't hear back from someone, QTIP: Quit Taking It Personally!

And always remember to trust your gut. If you aren't interested, even if you don't have a good reason, you don't have to agree to another date just to be nice.

To remain optimistic during the dating process, believe that in time you will find the lid to your pot. Denise has had numerous relationships during the five years since her divorce. Though she hasn't met her true love

> "As unpleasant as a few bad dates can be, they don't matter much when you go out with someone you feel a spark with and you both have a great time."
> —Denise

yet, she remains optimistic that she will. "I've had my ups and downs dating, but I continue to date and to believe that it will work out," Denise says. "My positive outlook helps me stay hopeful on those days that a guy I like doesn't call."

YOUR NEXT RELATIONSHIP

You've learned a lot about yourself, your patterns, and what you're looking for. Now it's time to take this awareness into your next relationship. Getting involved with a new man after your separation can be both exciting because it feels hopeful and scary because it involves allowing yourself to open your heart and be vulnerable again. Review your personal dating *man*tra (the five must-have qualities you will look for in a new man) to evaluate your new love interest.

Denise loved the fact that her new guy had a library card and made her pulse race (articulate and passionate were on her dating *man*tra). She let those two check marks eclipse negatives that wound up being relationship poison: He couldn't support himself, had a contentious relationship with his ex, and was emotionally unavailable due to the turmoil of his ongoing divorce. Are you dating the hot guy who can never show up when he says he will? Is he stable but lackluster? Is he fun but doesn't have a kitchen table? Your *man*tra will help keep you honest and on track, which is important because so many of us are still paying the high price of a failed relationship. Be ready to break up with the new guy if you find yourself falling back into unhealthy patterns. Here are the five key tenets that we discovered in our quests for healthy new relationships against the backdrops of our divorces:

1. Pay attention to red flags

It's important to take off the rose-colored glasses when you're falling in love to get some perspective on whether the relationship is bringing out the best in you. Is he adding a new layer of enjoyment to your life, or is he adding more stress and anxiety? He may have the most beautiful eyes and make you feel special, but it's important to see things as they truly are.

Suzanne often overlooked red flags because she liked to be in a relationship. She would fall head over heels for a man and ignore the little voice in her head that told her *something isn't right*. You may enjoy your time together, but if there's something fundamentally amiss in your new relationship—for example, he's angry and controlling, he isn't thinking long term but you are, he's thinking long term but you aren't, or your kids can't stand his kids—then the relationship likely won't work. Some women find themselves dating men who are works in progress, thinking they can fix them. We have yet to meet a single woman who is able to "fix" anyone but herself.

2. Speak your truth

Once you figure out what you want, be brave enough to ask for it, even if it means risking rejection. If he likes to be spontaneous and that's not possible for your schedule, it's important to talk to him rather than to feel stress or complain to your friends. When Jill couldn't ignore her warm and fuzzy feelings for Yoga Guy, she let him know that she would like to date only him. She opened her heart and admitted that she was falling in love with him. She also let him know that she wouldn't be able to continue to date him if they weren't going to be exclusive. Jill knew that she was taking a risk, but she wanted to express herself, regardless of the outcome. They ended up having a conversation that lasted for hours. For the first time, Yoga Guy told Jill he loved her, and they decided to date exclusively.

If you express your wants and needs, and a man isn't ready, willing, or able to meet them, your choices are to accept what he's offering you or to walk away. Be wary of clinging to him as a safety net because you feel you can't go through a breakup on top of going through your divorce. If it's not working and he's not right for you, let him go.

3. Listen to his truth

When you're falling for a man, assume nothing. If you want to know if he's still dating other women or sleeping with other women, or how he views your relationship, ask him, and then hear what he says . . . without glossing over the bits and pieces that don't appeal to you. Then watch his actions. They should reinforce what he has told you. He may say he isn't dating anyone else, but if he's rarely available on Friday and Saturday nights, that's probably not the case.

Who hasn't heard a man say, "I don't want a serious relationship," only to dismiss this, thinking you will change his mind. Going back to a man who doesn't want what we want is what some call "watering dead flowers." Suzanne and Jill now know with certainty that when a man clearly states how he sees your future together, or lack of a future, using sheer force of will to make him change his mind doesn't work. We have learned to believe him. Period.

If a man rejects us, it doesn't mean we're not lovable and worthwhile. It just means that he knows what he wants and what he can offer. Gina straightening her hair and buying maternity lingerie wasn't going to change the fact that her husband wanted to be with a man. That wasn't a reflection of Gina but of her husband's truth.

4. Leave your ex out of it

We found it important to allow a new man to be seen as himself and not in comparison to our exes. Don't use him as your therapist to help you deal with stresses with your ex. You have family, girlfriends, and a shrink for that. It's not only a romance killer but it also places a heavy burden on your budding romance. We've also found that flaunting your new love interest in front of your ex can result in fisticuffs.

Some couples agree not to talk about ex-spouses or ex-lovers. Suzanne, Jill, and many of their girlfriends don't enjoy hearing about a boyfriend's past relationships. "Sharing a lesson that he thinks will help us get along better, such as, he never felt appreciated by his wife and this is important to him, is one thing," says Suzanne. "Hearing the nitty-gritty of what went right or wrong doesn't interest me." For Jill, hearing about her boyfriend's exes makes her feel like he is living in the past instead of the present. At this point, everyone has baggage. You just don't need to take it out to dinner with you. It can get very crowded at the table with you, the new guy, and the ghosts of your exes.

5. Put yourself first

Iris

As you're carving out time in your busy schedule for your new boyfriend, be careful not to lose yourself in the throes of an exciting romance. We have seen many girlfriends so eager to hold on to this new person that they allow the rest of their lives to take a backseat. "I wanted the refuge and escape from all the challenges in my life," says Iris, about the anesthesiologist from work whom she discovered was a player. "For a while, he made me feel great. I changed my work schedule and my child care days to see him more. I stopped going to the gym. It was all about him."

Iris turned her life upside down for her coworker, and the effects were far-reaching. She forgot to pay bills. She spent less time with her kids. She neglected her own health. Her parents told her she was behaving irresponsibly. "All I wanted to do was spend time with him," she says. "I wasn't seeing the whole picture and the impact on other areas of my life."

Now Iris is dating a doctor from work. She has a checklist of priorities to keep her life in balance, including dinner with her kids four times a week, going to the gym three times a week, and seeing her own friends on alternate weeks. Since the new man in her life is also a single parent, he understands Iris's busy schedule—and her priorities. "I feel centered and more secure this time," she says. "Throwing my life into a tizzy like I did before isn't good for me or my kids and isn't sustainable."

What I Wish I'd Known

"Online dating can be an emotional roller coaster. Once I'd done it a number of times, I started to adjust my expectations. I held back from investing myself emotionally until I really got to know someone, because I knew how easy it was for things to fizzle out." —Meghan

Chapter 17

CREATE YOUR OWN COMMUNITY

*"The secret of change is to focus all of your energy
not on fighting the old but on building the new."*
—Dan Millman, *Way of the Peaceful Warrior*

Jamie used to dread those Saturday nights when she didn't have her kids, a date lined up, or other social plans. Many of her married friends were content to spend time at home with their husbands after a busy week, even if they were simply organizing the pantry or doing laundry before watching a movie. "There's a different kind of pressure to have an exciting Saturday night when you're single," Jamie says. "It was hard to enjoy a Saturday at home alone. I felt really isolated initially." When she stayed in reading a book or watching TV, she felt like she was missing out on all the fun that everyone else seemed to be having. That began to change when she attended her first meeting of the Maplewood Divorce Club. "These amazing women were getting through it, and it made me feel like I would, too," she says. In addition to having monthly support meetings, the members of the group would often meet for drinks, movie dates, casual dinners, and more. "I now had all these new friends to go out with on Saturday nights," Jamie says.

Jill and Suzanne launched the Maplewood Divorce Club to be able to offer to other women the experience of being heard and supported that had been such a big help to them. "There's nothing like someone who knows what you're going through at a time that most other people in your life can't relate to your struggles," says Suzanne. "Jill and I had given each other that support and wanted to replicate it in our divorce club, which became a place where you could let your guard down and talk about how you're really feeling."

Knowing we had people we could turn to in our time of need went a long way toward lessening stress and loneliness during challenging times. Numerous studies find that social support is essential for your physical and mental health. Having a support system can increase your sense of belonging, boost your feeling of self-worth, and help you feel more secure, because you have people you trust sharing their advice, guidance, and information.

As news of the divorce club got around, women as well as men in neighboring communities asked for our playbook to start their own groups. We share this information here so that people everywhere can learn how to launch their own group and benefit from the loving support of friends who know your deepest struggles, are there for you in a pinch, and help make the journey more fun.

LAUNCHING A DIVORCE CLUB

We had our first Maplewood Divorce Club meeting in the spring of 2013 at a local bar. We spread the word about the new group via word of mouth, local websites, and Facebook. To our surprise, more than fifty women attended our first meeting. You may only know a few other women who are going through a divorce right now, but once you post information about the group and tell friends about it, you will likely discover that there are plenty of women interested in joining.

Women opened up about challenges they hadn't been able to share with anyone else. They talked about disappointment, financial worries and fear. Tears were shed. Hugs were

"The divorce club meetings have given me a place where I can talk about what's *really* going on in my life. They have been a lifeline." —Denise

exchanged. At the end of the meeting, many of the women stuck around for an additional half hour, mingling and chatting. Several of the members told us how much being there meant to them. Here's an overview of what you need to know to start a divorce club in your community.

STEP 1: Find a meeting spot. Consider a local bar or restaurant on an "off" night, as we did for our first meeting. We were able to use the space to gather at no charge because they knew we would order drinks. A public venue can be an ideal setting for a first meeting since it's less intimidating than going to a stranger's home. Make sure to call an establishment in advance and speak to a manager to "book" the space, confirm a few days before the first meeting, and find out if any small financial contribution is needed.

After our first meeting, we moved to the homes of our members so that we could have more privacy. We asked each club member to contribute $5 per meeting to cover the cost of beverages and light snacks that the host provides. At the end of each meeting, we ask someone to volunteer to host the next meeting at their home. This is not something you want to decide via an endless stream of emails after the meeting.

STEP 2: Choose a name and a regular date and time for your meetings. Choose a time when you think the majority of people could come—we chose the evening of the third Tuesday of every month.

To pick a name, consider including your location (city and state) as well as something you would like to emphasize. For example, our club is named: *Maplewood Divorce Club—Power of One.*

STEP 3: Register your group with us. You will need a group name and contact. Registering with us via email (optimistsguidetodivorce@gmail.com) allows new members to have access to content on our website that is private, and most important, to have direct access to us.

STEP 4: Promote your first meeting. Post information about your meeting on local websites, the town calendar, or other visible locations, such as coffee shops, bookstores, the library, etc.

Here's some sample copy you can use:

Join Our Divorce Club

*The newly formed **[name of your club here]** Divorce Club,
founded on the principles of* The Optimist's Guide to Divorce,
*will have a first meeting on **[insert date, time, and location]**.
All separated or divorced women **[or men]** are welcome to
join us for fellowship, friendship, and support. Please RSVP to
[your or the club's email address].*

STEP 5: Create a secret group on Facebook. Log in to your Facebook account. At the top right corner, click on the arrow for the drop-down menu; click "Create Group." Fill in your group name. Click "secret" group, click "create." Now, invite the people who RSVP to your community post as well as others you think would be interested in joining!

STEP 6: Prepare your supplies. Bring printouts of your guiding principles, sign-in sheets, new member welcome and info sheets, an agenda, pens, name tags, and a timer to your first meeting.

STEP 7: Ask for a volunteer to host the next meeting. Leading a meeting is a small time commitment that boils down to hosting at your home and buying light refreshments.

STEP 8: Keep your group growing. The ongoing success of our once-a-month meetings has stemmed from our willingness to adapt based on what's working. "Take the pulse of your group so that you can evolve and make changes when needed," Jill says. "We considered a meeting a success when women told us they felt unburdened, uplifted, or that they had made a new connection."

STEP 9: If necessary, create subgroups. We found it important to limit the size of each meeting so that everyone had a chance to talk and could fit comfortably in someone's living room. As your town group grows, you will likely need to help other women form subgroups. When planning group activities that can accommodate large numbers, such as a picnic in the park or holiday cocktails at a bar, try to include all the subgroups in your town.

RUNNING A MEETING

To kick off each meeting, we introduce ourselves and remind everyone that everything that's said is confidential so that members feel free to share. We also read our welcome message at the start of each meeting.

Welcome to the Maplewood Divorce Club. We're glad you're here and hope you will find fellowship and support during this challenging time. The purpose of this club is to provide a place where women who are going through a divorce can share their experiences, learn from each other, realize that they're not alone, and create lasting friendships.

We share the hosting duties, taking turns opening our homes to one another. We ask that each person contribute $5 per meeting to offset the cost of beverages and light snacks served. So that members can plan ahead, meetings will be held the third Tuesday of the month with the exception of holidays and school vacations. We look forward to getting to know you, and hope you will find understanding, support, and friendship.

To ease into the discussion, we ask each member to say her first name and tell us one thing she is grateful for, such as her health, a roof over her head, or sitting in a room with supportive women. This gets everyone thinking in a positive way.

We then circulate a list of our Guiding Principles, asking members to read a principle out loud, say what it means to her, and then pass the paper to a neighbor. This serves as a framework for how to participate to get the most out of the meetings.

Next, we ask each person to briefly share what is happening in her life. Depending on the size of the group and the time allotted, we limit shares to three to five minutes. It's a nice way to meet everyone and either learn their backstory or get a glimpse of what's going on in their life. Most people jump right in, despite the personal nature of their shares, glad to have the attention of a sympathetic group.

GUIDING PRINCIPLES OF THE CLUB

1. What's said in the group stays in the group.

2. We share the floor. Everyone gets a chance to speak.

3. We're not here just to vent. Our focus is on solutions to our challenges.

4. Your ex isn't invited. We keep the focus on ourselves by speaking from the "I."

5. None of us is alone in this. We're here to get and give support.

GUIDELINES FOR GREAT GROUPS

We have a clear structure, with an agenda to help everyone have the same expectations for our time together. A key principle is to keep the focus on ourselves rather than on our exes or anyone else.

Our meetings always start promptly so that there is a predictability that members can count on, especially if they hired a babysitter or made special arrangements to attend. Members who arrive late are encouraged to slip in quietly. Iris tended to arrive twenty minutes late in a mad flurry, full of apologies and explanations. After attending a few meetings, she made the extra effort to show up on time. "I realized that this wasn't like my book club, where I could breeze in late and jump into the discussion," Iris says. "I saw that this was a different kind of meeting."

To get the most of each meeting, in addition to showing up promptly, members are encouraged to turn cell phones off and refrain from texting sexysingledad32 during the meeting. They should be ready to devote their full attention to the group for the next two hours.

One of the most important tips to running a successful meeting is to use a timer and limit shares to just a few minutes, depending on the size of the group. This way, everyone gets a chance to speak and no single person monopolizes the meeting. Each meeting, someone volunteers to be the timekeeper, using the timer on their cell phone or an actual egg timer, and signaling when the time is up.

NEW MEMBER SHEET

Name:

Birthday (day, month):

Address:

Cell: Email:

Kids (name, grade, school):

Occupation:

Date of divorce/separation:

Reason(s) you joined our club:

❑ Emotional support from women going through what I'm going through

❑ To meet families similar to mine for playdates and activities with our kids

❑ To socialize with single women, find an exercise partner, make friends

❑ To find a divorcée mentor/role model

❑ Other _____

Skill you could contribute to the group (social media, graphic design, etc.): _____

Would you be willing to host a divorce club meeting at your home?

_____

We ask the group not to interrupt while someone is sharing. If anyone ignores the no-complaining guideline and spends her share time kvetching, we let it go. Those who attend meetings consistently serve as an example of sharing from the "I," meaning keeping the focus on themselves rather than on their exes, as well as talking about strategies that worked for them and sharing inspiring stories. Sometimes members want to vent and no matter how many reminders they get about speaking from the "I," they want to complain about the "he" in their life. With practice, most members do make the shift away from obsessing about their ex's latest transgression.

It's important to be clear about how to react to individual shares in a way that is helpful. Offering understanding and empathy is welcome. What's not recommended is offering specific advice such as, "You should really fire that person." We encourage everyone to share what worked for them rather than tell someone else what to do. It's more helpful to say, "I did," than "you should."

A popular feature is our secret Facebook group, where members can easily stay in touch even if they're too busy to attend a meeting. The Facebook group continues to grow, since it's easier for many women to connect online rather than to make it to a meeting. They can also post to reach out for advice, share book recommendations, or make plans for an empty Tuesday or Saturday night without anyone but club members seeing their update. The privacy of the secret Facebook group is important to group members. Just as everything shared at the meetings is confidential, the Facebook posts are meant to be kept within the circle, too.

> "We ask that everyone share something that could be helpful to others, rather than to simply vent."
> —Suzanne

One of the beauties of the club is that a diverse group of women join— they range in age, ethnicity, profession, and more. Each member has her own culture, history, special skill set, and talents. Take stock of the richness in your club and see how you can leverage it for the benefit of the group. Our next goal is to set up a referral network so members could support one another's businesses. To help members of our club who were dusting off their résumés and going back to work, we asked an HR consultant in our club to present a résumé workshop. Group members exchanged services and bartered for babysitting, home-cooked meals, dog walking, or a custom knitted scarf and mittens.

MEETING TOPICS/GUEST SPEAKERS

We chose topics that would lend themselves to discussions offering a positive and hopeful outlook, such as: *What helps you feel better when you're anxious or angry? What have you done this past week to take care of yourself? What do you do when you want to contact your ex and know nothing good will come of it?* Sharing the specifics of strategies we were coming up with helped us learn from one another. Our goal was for us all to focus on solutions rather than simply dwell on challenges.

SAMPLE AGENDA

MAPLEWOOD DIVORCE CLUB

7:00–7:15 p.m. WELCOME. Sign-in and get a name tag.

7:15–7:30 p.m. INTRODUCTIONS. Meeting leader passes around guiding principles; members introduce themselves and say what they're grateful for.

7:30–8:30 p.m. GROUP SHARES. Members share what's on their minds, either general thoughts or related to the meeting's theme.

8:45–9:00 p.m. CLOSING THOUGHTS. Determine who will host the next meeting.

Meeting topics can be as varied as you want. They can be practical, such as how to make a budget, or frivolous, such as a Sip and Swap, where you drink wine and bring in clothes that you no longer wear to trade. Inviting guest speakers can energize some groups. When club members mentioned they wanted to learn more about managing their money, we brought in a financial adviser to give the basics. Other guest speakers have included a self-defense instructor, a personal stylist, an insurance planner, and a decorator who specializes in living stylishly on a budget.

Interested in how divorced dads view online dating, we invited a group of men, ages thirty to sixty, to participate in what we called "Hot Men in the Hot Seat: Divorced Dads on Dating." They spoke openly about their online dating experiences and were game enough to answer all our questions. When women wanted to know whether they preferred to reach out or have women contact them on the dating sites, the men were resoundingly positive about women contacting them first, noting that they get tired of being rejected and welcome messages in their in-boxes.

Eleanor's favorite meeting was Hot Men in the Hot Seat because one of the men approached her after the talk. "You mentioned that you're not on any of the dating sites. I was curious about why," asked Eugene, a retired jeweler. "I'm getting up my courage," Eleanor said. "I'm out of practice dating." Smiling, he said, "I might be able to help you out with that. I have an extra ticket to a jazz concert this weekend, if you're available." Eleanor was speechless. She hadn't been asked out in thirty years. Regaining her composure, she had a million thoughts in her head but simply replied, "I'd love to." At the next meeting, we asked Eleanor about her date with Eugene. Blushing like a schoolgirl, she gushed, "All those years of being married to Harold, somehow I forgot how much I liked to be kissed."

PITFALLS TO AVOID IN YOUR GROUP

Just as good fences make good neighbors, time limits, guidelines for behavior, and clear expectations are necessary for good meetings. Some of the biggest spoilers we have found are detailed below so that you can be on the lookout for these situations in your group and correct course when necessary.

Inconsistent meeting times

It's a giant waste of precious energy to attempt to find a date and time that work for everyone, always. An email query of "Who can meet in July?" will cause untold email pollution and likely so many responses, it will make your head spin and cause most women to lose interest. Many of your group members will be busy single moms managing complicated schedules. Having predictable meetings will help them plan their lives and likely improve attendance.

We found that having meetings on the same day and at the same time each month is ideal. For example, if Tuesdays 7 to 9 p.m. are generally good for the group, book it. Make the meetings the third Tuesday of every month with the exception of holidays and school breaks. Let all your group members know how you will communicate with them so there is consistency. Whether you email, post to the Facebook group page, or post notices on your town website, be consistent.

Too much responsibility on one person

When Jill and Suzanne began writing this book, on top of their respective jobs and family duties, one of the results was that they had less time to devote to the club. When you rely only on one or two women to keep a group going, anytime those women have extra responsibilities or activities going on in their own lives, the group will

I SEE YOUR "MISTRESS" AND RAISE YOU A "PROSTITUTE"

There have been moments when the ex-husband confessions seemed more like a competition for the worst ex than a share. Some women are so attached to their pain and their story that they seek to prove they have the most strife, the worst ex, and the hardest life. "At least your husband only slept with your neighbor. My husband spent all our savings on hookers, drugs, and Jets games." It's a meeting to benefit all, not a pity party for one. Remind members to share, not to compare.

suffer. The way to circumvent this is to make sure all the work doesn't fall solely on the shoulders of whoever started the group. Try to find ways for every woman who participates to share in keeping the group going and to feel invested and engaged. How? Invite members to volunteer for annual or ongoing positions, such as greeter, new member liaison, treasurer, secretary, etc. In this way, it will be up to the collective group to keep the club going. When everyone in the group benefits, and contributes—either by hosting or by taking on a leadership position—the club thrives.

Constant complainers

Nothing brings everyone down more than a person complaining about her ex without including how she's handling it better or learning how she can still be happy no matter what he's doing. You will likely find that regardless of the limits you set, Complaining Colleens will pop up. They will appreciate having an audience and will work the crowd to get validation and sympathy.

Carlotta

Carlotta initially used her time to talk about how her husband abandoned her for "the whore." A typical share: "He never appreciated all I did for our marriage," she would begin. "He always thought about himself first. He hasn't even called to see how I'm doing. Can you believe how he treats the mother of his child?" Not surprisingly, the energy in the room would sink each time Carlotta spoke. Eventually, as she emerged from her depression and noticed others talk about what they were learning or enjoying, her perspective changed and her shares became more about her and what she was doing to move forward.

Meeting monopolizers

Suzanne

Suzanne will never forget Jed, the insurance agent who repeatedly ignored our hints to wrap it up. An audience full of potential clients was simply too tempting. It was a rainy night, and his pitch never ended. "When I noticed myself jamming my pen into my thigh a few times to stay awake and several club members yawning or texting on their phones, I realized I had to do some heavy lifting and push this man out the door," Suzanne says. "I let him know it was time for group shares. He said, 'I know I'm not in the group, or divorced, but mind if I stay?' We did mind." If group members feel like unwilling captives in an endless sales pitch, be sure to rescue them.

Gracefully let any guest speakers know how much time they will be allotted before the meeting and keep them to it. Make sure that your timekeeper monitors their presentation, gives a five-minute warning, and when the time is up, issues a polite, "This has been great, but we're out of time" to keep your meeting on track.

New-member conflicts

Whoever starts the group will be contacted when a new member wants to join. Our policy has been that anyone who wants to participate in the group can. However, this leaves the group open to potential conflicts among members who may have been romantically involved with one another's former spouse. Of course, you will not know the romantic histories of all the women who want to join the group.

Iris

Jill recalls an incident when she approved a new member, Hannah, only to realize that Iris, a longtime member, had dated Hannah's ex (the anesthesiologist) for a while. Unsure if Hannah was aware of this, Jill told her that a woman who dated her ex was already a member. That way Hannah could decide if she wanted to become a member before she attended her first meeting. Jill was surprised by the strongly worded email Hannah sent back. She said it was "unfair" that the other woman was able to stay in the group instead of her. Still bitter, she concluded: "This tramp doesn't deserve to be in the club. Hasn't she taken enough?" And if you're wondering, no, Hannah didn't join the group. Jill didn't like placing herself in the middle of potential conflict she but she knew it was her job to protect the harmony of the group.

Emotions also ran high when Denise's hot date turned out to be the ex-husband of our newest member, Liz. Denise was upset to learn her date had been married to Liz; he had a different last name and lived in another town, and she had no idea. Denise realized she would have to make a choice and decided not to continue dating Liz's ex for the sake of the group. We now have a rule that if you learn that you're dating the ex of another member, your choices are to excuse yourself from the club (and start another chapter if you like) or stop dating him.

Overscheduling group events

Trying to accomplish too many things in a month can fracture your group and negatively impact the attendance at your meetings. Planning social events, a self-defense class, mom & me outings, and holiday parties has to take a backseat to giving women a chance to talk about what they're going through.

When two members volunteered to plan a movie night, they took on organizing it, and the event was in addition to our regular meeting, not instead of it. We got together to celebrate birthdays, to check out a new restaurant, and to enjoy cookouts in the park with our kids. However, we found that all these events, which developed because of the growing friendships among our group members, worked best when they supplemented regular club meetings.

New members feeling excluded

We wanted to create a safe, nurturing environment that was free of drama. This proved challenging at times in a small community where gossip is a pastime and cliques form just as quickly in adult groups as they do in middle school.

As the core group that met regularly got closer because they had a lot in common, including children the same age, similar interests, and homes near one another, a key challenge became keeping the meetings clique-free so that everyone felt welcomed and at home. Amali, who was close with Iris, Pilar, and Gina, confessed that she sometimes felt left out when other members were rehashing a recent night out, the fun they had at school-related events, and kids' parties. Amali worked long hours, didn't have children, and wasn't always able to participate in the extracurricular activities some of the other women enjoyed.

Be mindful of inadvertently excluding anyone or wearing your thick-as-

WHO'S INVITED?

Our club is for women only. Here's why: Women felt they could be more honest and relaxed in the company of other women going through the same experiences. Members were concerned that adding men to the mix would change the dynamic and shift the focus from women attending to get support and express themselves to women attending to meet men. If there is a divorced men's group in your town, why not suggest a quarterly social with them as an additional activity to complement your meetings.

thieves status as a badge of honor; that may come across to new members as a "Keep Out" sign. Table your side talk at the meetings and make efforts to switch up seating arrangements, strike up conversations with women you don't know well, and go the extra mile so new members feel included, welcomed, and valued.

SHINE ON

The community of women you create and rely on during your divorce can become the foundation on which you build your post-divorce life. These women can be the people you turn to when you're in a pinch or looking for someone to have dinner with, especially if you don't have family close by. Iris's girls took to calling Amali "auntie." Eleanor and Carlotta have a matinee movie date most Wednesdays. Jill's and Suzanne's kids play together regularly. Impromptu get-togethers among women in the group became a new normal we could count on and look forward to.

When your divorce is behind you, your life will get easier in many ways. One of the major stresses—the divorce itself—will be over. Soon there will be benchmarks where you catch yourself thinking, "This must mean I am really moving on," whether it's a first kiss with a new man, buying a home on your own, or even something mundane like putting up a shelf on your own in your office. With each victory big or small, you believe in yourself that much more.

For us, the friendships formed during our divorces have long outlived the divorce process itself. The women who helped us through it are still the ones we turn to. And as we face new challenges, whether it's juggling being a single

STAY CONNECTED TO US

If you form or join a group like the Maplewood Divorce Club, consider it a continuation of the journey you have started on these pages with us. Find stories, virtual support, and sharing opportunities on our website optimistsguidetodivorce.com. You can also download PDFs of all the material you need to launch a divorce club and host your own meeting. We'd love to hear about your challenges and triumphs. Feel free to contact Jill and Suzanne directly at optimistsguidetodivorce@gmail.com.

mom with a new job promotion, a health scare, or a lover who breaks our heart, we know with certainty that an optimistic attitude and a supportive circle of friends will make all the difference.

The journey you started with us won't end the day you're pronounced divorced by a judge. It will continue as you grow in each new relationship; take on everything from managing your financial portfolio to tightening a loose toilet handle; and look for the good in people, places, and experiences. And as you move on and meet women who are struggling during the early stages of their divorces, we encourage you to open your arms and welcome them into your circle, because we are all stronger together.

What We Wish We'd Known

When we wondered whether we had the time to launch a divorce club, we wish we'd known that the benefits would far outweigh the effort and that the friendships formed would be the foundation for our new lives.

—Jill and Suzanne

Afterword
IT GOT BETTER

  JILL AND SUZANNE Creating the Maplewood Divorce Club has been a continuing source of pride. They are happy to be turning the notion that divorce has to be lonely and isolating on its head.

 GINA invested in her salon, hiring several new stylists and a manager. She and Valentina now live with Bobby. Clayton continues to play an active role in their daughter's life.

 ELEANOR took a part-time job at the library and is working on expanding her identity beyond the roles of wife and mother. She launched a popular book club "for bibliophiles only."

 CARLOTTA has planned a trip to the British Virgin Islands with Bailey, and though she broke up with the FedEx guy, she continues to date, and gains something from each person she meets.

 DENISE launched a popular podcast chronicling her dating journey. She continues to live optimistically, care for her son, build her career, and learn about herself.

 IRIS moved into her own two-family house and renovated it. She joined a writers' circle to explore her creative side, and is happily dating a pediatrician from work.

 JAMIE and her boys moved to the second floor of Iris's two-family home. They love their new backyard almost as much as their new Scottish terrier does.

PILAR plans fun date nights with Justin and recently booked a family vacation to go snowboarding with the boys in Sun Valley, Idaho, over winter break.

AMALI continues to expand her IT business. She has become a certified Vinyasa yoga instructor and teaches a free class every Saturday at the YMCA.

MEGHAN was inspired by her success with the Rub 'n' Grub nights. She saved up to open her own wellness office that is so popular it often has a two-week waiting list.

RENÉE became more involved in her community food bank and is planning to travel to Haiti with Larry in the spring to help feed hungry children—and to enjoy an adventure together.

ACKNOWLEDGMENTS

To the amazing divorced women we have met in the Maplewood Divorce Club and outside of it, thank you for sharing your stories so that they might inspire others.

Thank you to my sister, Wendy, and brother, Arthur—you're always with me and a source of inspiration; Abi Maryann and Nancy Kover, the best friends a person could wish for; Lillian Schroth for Tassajara; Jean Grossman for your expansive ideas; Robert Smith for reminding me it's an inside job; Byron Speight for his friendship; Mike for our partnership raising our son; and my parents, Miriam and Eric, for encouraging me to do what I love.   —Suzanne

A big thanks to Judy Evans for wearing purple pants; Shime for helping me find my voice and believing in me; Charlie Pauch for being a shining example of an amazing family man and a great big brother; my parents, Rick and Cheryl Pauch, for the nest, the unconditional love, and for teaching me how to tell a great story; and all the friends and family who have been along for the ride and offered continuous support and encouragement.   —Jill

Heaps of gratitude to our agent Lauren Galit for her invaluable guidance; Jill Billante, a great friend, for introducing us to Lauren; Suzanne Vickberg for introducing us. Thanks also to everyone at Workman Publishing, including our editor, Margot Herrera, for her thoughtful insights and ideas, Becky Terhune for the wonderful design, Barbara Peragine for her creative typesetting, Amanda Hong for keeping us on track, and Selina Meere, Rebecca Carlisle, Thea James, and Moira Kerrigan for getting the word out.   —Suzanne and Jill